THE ACTS OF THE TRINITY

Frederick Sontag

University Press of America, Inc.
Lanham • New York • London

BT
111.2
.S63
1996

**Copyright © 1996 by
University Press of America,® Inc.**
4720 Boston Way
Lanham, Maryland 20706

3 Henrietta Street
London, WC2E 8LU England

Library of Congress Cataloging-in-Publication Data

Sontag, Frederick.
The acts of the Trinity / Frederick Sontag.
    p.   cm.
Includes index.
1. Trinity. I. Title.
BT111.2.lS63   1996   231'.044--dc20   96-15018   CIP

ISBN 0-7618-0363-7 (cloth: alk. ppr.)
ISBN 0-7618-0364-5 (pbk: alk. ppr.)

Mary Jane, Peter and Laura

who represent the past, present and future alumni,

students, faculty and staff of Pomona College

"They only are loyal to this college

who, in departing, bear then added

riches in trust for mankind."

James A. Blaisdell

Table of Contents

Laud and honor to the Father,
Laud and honor to the Son,
Laud and honor to the Spirit,
Ever Three and ever One;
One in might, and One in glory,
While unending ages run.

Hymn: "Christ is made a sure foundation"

PART I. THE ACTS OF GOD[*]

INTRODUCTION

Followers of a religion, any religion, should be evaluated first and foremost by their acts, not by their words. Just as the Trinity can be recognized and made real for Christians by its known Acts, so any follower is recognized, not by what he or she professes by word, but by how he or she acts toward all peoples. We ask: What is distinctive about the action of any religion's claimed disciple? That is, what marks off the person of one religion from another? Jesus did not live the Buddha's life or act as Confucius did. True, all religious leaders and all followers utter words of information or of instruction, but these verbalizations are often subject to misunderstandings, or are even subsequently distorted in their meaning. Watch what the follower/founder does; that is the standard for our understanding. Actions can make the religious view stable, words never.

Of course, actions need appraisal too, since all actions connected to any religious group are not necessarily thereby to be accepted, let alone admired. False or deceptive action and reprehensible behavior are

---

[*] Adapted from an earlier book, <u>What Can God Do?</u> Abingdon, Nashville, 1979.

often supported by fine words. Religious wars and hatreds have killed millions and caused incalculable suffering, all the while the rhetoric in support of the violence may have an emotional/religious high tone. What actions do we admire and consider as a boon to humanity? -- that is our question. By the answers they give religions will be understood and their followers evaluated. By their fruits they shall be known, not by lofty phrases, impressive monuments, or even the accumulation of vast powers, whether economic or political or ecclesiastical.

Christianity was spread world-wide by the Acts of the Apostles. Only a few intellectuals can ever be converted by presenting church doctrine to them. We may need such formulas, and we should define them as clearly as we can state them. Yet these verbalizations do not bear in themselves the power of a life-transforming religion. We know that the Holy Spirit has acted powerfully, both on individuals and within groups; in the case of Christianity, most notably in the Pentecost. Thus, it is important to note that the church which emerged after Jesus was formed neither by a committee nor a council, not even by a charismatic preacher, but rather by the forceful intervention of a divine Spirit.

Thus, today we should pray and wait for similar inspiring, transforming acts. Quakers set the norm for us by waiting in human silence for the movement of a divine spirit, which alone should move them to speech. Even in Jesus' case where we have established canonical scriptures, it is misleading to concentrate on his "words" or to expect these in themselves to tell us much, unless their repetition leads us to feel the power of Jesus' actions moving in our own lives. We are affected primarily not by what he said but only insofar as we feel moved by what he did for us, e.g., he came, he ministered, he healed, he died, he rose. Why should we expect to understand God in any other way than by trying to discern, to witness, the divine acts of power, both historically and now?.

Let us, then, actually begin with God, since in fact neither the significance of Jesus nor the power of the Holy Spirit can be realized in any other way than by discerning God's actions; otherwise the meaning of Jesus' life drifts and the Spirit flounders. It cannot be the other way around except that, by studying scriptures, sermons, religious acts or rituals, we might be brought to some awareness of the presence of the power of God. Nothing but God can be the focal point of the Judeo/Christian quest, however the religious pilgrimage may begin or proceed. Accidents of time and place -- and sometimes, in strange circumstances, intellectual inquiry -- may bring us to the starting point. But this alone can never lead us to the divine activity itself.

Thus, we start with the acts of God. But we move to parallel these with the acts of Jesus and those of the Holy Spirit. The concept of a trinity of divine persons is important, not for its intellectual subtlety, although it involves puzzles enough, but because it is peculiarly Christian to experience God's actions in three ways, that is, from three distinct sources and directions. As we understand how the various actions parallel the three persons, we can understand the unique nature of the Christian experience. In like manner, we can understand the distinctness of any world religion by realizing how its divine center acts in relation to us and to its followers.

Doctrines, institutions, rituals, religious art and music and literature, historical persons -- all these have been and are important for any religious practice. But those who are the skeptics about religion tend to focus on the negative aspects of these powers, their bigotry, their hostility and even their destructive wars. Detractors concentrate on form vs. spirit, treating religious belief as mysterious verbalisms and as philosophical puzzles. Thus, in order to see the value, the good, which has and which can come from doctrines and institutions, we need to move back to the founding acts of God which first gave the institution or group the power to transform lives for the better, as well as to destroy or to frustrate us. To settle merely on form, or on historical phenomena or on intellectual doctrine, is to reduce the religious quest to superficiality.

How then are God's powers and the divine acts to be discovered? Contradictory as it may seem, we must first form words which are adequate to the acts that are to be described. We begin with words, signs; but we look next for the things (the actions) for which they stand, as Augustine noted in Concerning The Teacher. ("I wish you would show me the things of which these are the signs.") We are, then, only taught about God or discover any divine center, as words lead us to experience acts. And words can do that -- at least sometimes, cynical as we often are after being disappointed or misled by false verbiage. In stories, in the world's literature, in religious scriptures of all kinds, we can (not must) be led to re-experience various divine acts, although this does not happen universally or necessarily. That cannot be. All divine spirits are ultimate individualists, as Kierkegaard suspected.

Yet, ultimately, we should realize that it is the Acts of God which we seek to encounter. To this end words are secondary; at worst they become blocks; at best they are mediators to the experience of (in the Christian case) The Acts of the Trinity.

PREFACE

We come to know ourselves, and others, when we learn what we and they can and cannot do. There is no reason why our way of knowing God should be any different. If anyone denies God's existence, he or she is actually denying that we have any knowledge of what God can and cannot do. By the same reasoning, to learn about God is to discover both the divine powers and their limitations. We begin to form our picture of how God can be present, and also absent from us, when we realize what he or she can and cannot do. It does not matter whether these limitations are inherent in the divine nature "from the beginning" or were freely self-imposed later.

Of course, to come to know God is a more difficult task than to understand either yourself or another person. At the very least, we human beings can see each other. Yet neither our visual nor our physical aspects puzzle us the most. We want to learn about those qualities and limitations which we cannot see directly and which become evident only indirectly. God is notorious for a lack of visibility and a preference for disclosing the divine life only in symbolic act or word. This divine habit is not as strange as it might at first appear. The major difficulty in understanding either God or ourselves lies in the problem of learning how to discover what we cannot immediately see. God sets that task for us, else religious consciousness reduces itself to triviality. "No pain, no gain" -- applies to divinity and to weight lifting.

In any age God can easily be overlooked by those who will not put out the effort to discern the divine presence. In just the same way we remain unknown to ourselves and ignorant of our friends just to the extent that we will not move beyond a simple visual and tactile apprehension. But we must look for God's qualities in the way divinity chooses to evidence them in our own age. And we uncover these in the same way that we come to understand the inner life of a friend -- if we care enough to search. We must first look for and discover which events around us might disclose God. But we also need to know where it is useless to look, because she has chosen not to appear in that place or in that way or in that time. If we can first establish a sense of direction, it is possible to build a new knowledge of divinity in any day.

Each searcher after God must discover his or her own way. God insists on acting as an individual, and thus can only be known in an individual way. How each of us will discover the divine cannot be predicted or settled in advance. On these pages I offer one set of suggestions for your search. My hope is that these ideas can become effective to speed God's discovery in our day. Tomorrow I cannot predict. But it is enough if we learn to find God in our own time.

Whenever God is our concern, what has moved men and women to know him in one age can be successful to reveal her in any other. Of course one route may be more appealing in one time rather than in another. Developing a sense of timing is all-important if God is not to be missed. God is neither equally available in every aspect of every day, nor is the divine absent in the same way in each time. Whoever loses a sensitivity to the peculiar qualities of the hour in which he or she lives will cut himself or herself off from God. Or at least, access to God will be made more difficult than it need be if we assume that a once successful approach will automatically be effective in a later day.

Each of us who is interested in God, I propose, should examine those experiences we have all heard reported and which, when properly approached, might open an entry way for us to God. Wherever we encounter these situations, we may meet God. That is, we _may_ if we succeed in building a picture of the divine powers. Our sketch will be incomplete and insubstantial, however, if we do not at the same time become aware of God's limitations. What are the situations in which God is not able to take part or to appear? Or rather, where has he set a limit on the divine powers when she might act but has agreed not to?.

Even if the steps outlined below are changed slightly by each individual reader, they still offer this hope: God can be found in a process of exploration, and a picture of God constructed by the path I am suggesting that you follow here. But we must always remember a major assumption: God appears to each individual as full and real only if we discover both his limitations and her powers. The divine cannot be approached by one idea alone but only by a succession of positive and negative steps.

It would be simpler if only one path or concept led us to or away from God, no matter when we took up the search. Unfortunately, there is little evidence that God designed either himself or her world or us on the simplest principle possible, Rationalist dreams not withstanding. Thus, the task we face is complex, and a success in discovering God at one time in the past does not guarantee a repeat of a divine discovery at another time for anyone else. However, we can be encouraged by a past report of finding God. The divine task set for us is obviously difficult but, judging by the history of all religions, evidently it is not totally impossible.

A. THE ACTS OF GOD

1. GOD CAN SUFFER

We men and women are all too often destroyed by suffering. Thus we fear it. No one in a healthy state of mind enjoys pain. It cripples our powers and limits our action. In spite of this, we also know that it is not possible to understand ourselves fully until suffering strips us of our self-delusions. The pain we dislike also tests both our powers of endurance and our responses in a way that happiness never can. As long as we are in a healthy state of mind, we do not want suffering; we avoid it when we can. Still, to share in another person's suffering, or to have him or her share ours, strengthens friendship. In distress, more intimate knowledge becomes possible than in easy daily intercourse.

Many theologians have denied that God can suffer. To assert God's involvement with pain affronts an exalted notion of divine majesty. God should be protected and prohibited from pain just because it would tarnish the divine dignity, some argue. Since we know that suffering changes us, it might change God's nature too if a divine person were able to suffer. However, all suffering is not due to a lack of strength, and God may be like us in this respect. Whoever voluntarily enters into our suffering gives evidence of his or her power, because they offer themselves to us when they do not have to. Thus, if we discover God in suffering, or at least acknowledge that the divine can act by suffering, we affirm that the divine is able to give itself to others voluntarily. Sometimes we human beings want to offer ourselves to others in this way but cannot. Thus, if God can enter suffering voluntarily, the divine action proves to be more powerful than ours by the very act of suffering.

When we witness suffering, we are never seeing God directly. Even if we accept the Christian claim that God suffered in Jesus' crucifixion, it was an action, true. But only a man was seen on the cross, not God. God's ability to give the divine self freely in time of need can never be manifest directly, as the jeering crowd around the base of Jesus' cross testifies. However, whenever some human being acts so to enter into suffering voluntarily in order to relieve our pain or to support our weakness, in that action we see what God is like.

We may not immediately recognize God in this act, but spiritual insight often comes to us after the fact, seldom at the time. The disciples did not understand Jesus, in spite of being in his presence. First, we must decide that God is able to suffer. Then, in a human act of sharing suffering, we may finally understand something of what God is like. Whatever God's capabilities are, what is divine does not suddenly acquire new ones. We may miss discovering God in these self-giving acts if we do not understand what divinity is able to do. Of course, suffering often changes our nature. When it does, in that act our eyes may be opened to see what could not be disclosed to us before. Jesus, for example, manifested himself by his acts after his resurrection.

Certainly there is nothing automatic, either about God's presence in suffering or about the divine decision to enter into it. It would be too easy if we knew that God would always share in our suffering, that divinity must always be present to us in our troubles and would act to assist us. But if our friends cannot be counted on for assistance and participation, why should we expect God to come to our rescue automatically? All we learn about God is that she is able to share in suffering, not that he must. Perhaps we often miss finding God just because we want to control and to prescribe divine behavior. But isn't it a greater evidence of power if one can intervene and decides to do so but is not required to in every instance? We understand that God may, not must, share in suffering and give divine assistance to others. Thus, when God's presence comes to us in this way, it has the aspect of a surprise, of a revelation.

Observe the events involved in the passion story as the New Testament records them. What Jesus' disciples understood least of all was the aspect of suffering involved, and this blocked their ability to visualize God in Christ. As long as Jesus evidenced his power by miracles, it was easy for his followers to accept him as a divine figure, as a Messiah. But when the tables were turned and Jesus stood meekly before Pilate, his once devoted friends became confused and divided. They could not understand either how divinity could allow suffering or how Jesus could fail to use his divine power to overcome it immediately. They did not understand God's acts.

Seeing Jesus suffer, they felt sorry. Yet it is hard to say whether they were more sorry for him or for the disappointment of their own hopes. The recovery of their hope, and the beginning of Christianity, came with the resurrection Act. 'Christianity' means the realization that God can enter into suffering, and that one who is divine does so freely, not out of necessity. God's power is seldom immediately visible. At times of withdrawal, our divinities can appear to be just as powerless as any human being. Jesus submits, but still he overcomes that death toward which all suffering leads us -- or so those who become Christians believe.

2. GOD CAN ACT OUT OF LOVE

The waiting rooms in psychiatrists offices are filled with people who cannot love, or at least who only demand it but cannot give love freely. Some no longer even feel the desire to love. Among those whose desire is still strong, many are frustrated by their inability to love fully and freely. Except for one whose emotions are blocked, all of us can give love sometimes and to some degree. Yet pain comes to us because our love is often expressed "too little and too late." What we would like to be able to do is to express affection when it is needed and in the way we would like to offer it. Rare, and also happy, is the person who can convey love whenever he or she wishes, to the persons one cares for, to the degree intended, and in a way which can be understood.

We have all found ourselves singled out as objects of attention simply because someone wants something from us. However, to try to achieve a mutual satisfaction of desire is not a bad human trait. On this ground some of our closest relationships are built. The situation of satisfying a double need only turns sour when someone wants affection from us solely to satisfy his or her own desire. This happens when one gives nothing in return or else offers a false affection, one which is not genuine but simply a mask for emotional greed. We are not satisfied for long if we receive merely an artificial pretense of genuine concern. But beyond the joy of mutual sharing, we yearn to achieve a level of existence which enables us to commit ourselves without becoming entangled in self-centered desire. We would like to be able to give affection simply because someone else needs love. And we wish for the ability to love, and the power to do this in a way that does not bind the recipient to a forced expression of gratitude.

Sometimes we find that we are able to convey affection freely and fully, all the while still retaining control of our emotions. Whenever love frees us and does not drain us dry, we encounter the way God acts. More than that, whenever we receive affection without an accompanying obligation being imposed upon us, we witness God's power in action at its fullest and at its best. But it is seldom that we escape our own needs and succeed in acting generously without creating a reciprocal demand.

Whatever God's needs are -- and the divine ability to act out of love would indicate that God has some -- these actions are never totally dominated by divine desires in the way that base human emotions are. God can and does move independently of the divine needs. Divinity can convey love without attracting attention to itself. We often would like to do this but are only sometimes able to. God may be the only really disinterested lover in the world. That is proof enough of divinity. This is especially true if divine disinterest reflects, not listlessness and coldness, but the power of emotional self-control and outer-directed compassion.

All love affairs are complex relationships, even when they are satisfying. This is because our own needs inevitably become entangled with those of the persons we love. Even when our impulse to love carries us so far out that we begin to consider the needs of the one we love ahead of ourselves, the success of such a relationship depends on our ability to match and to coordinate two sets of needs and desires. We experience the divine life, then, whenever we discover that God is able to act from love without involving us in divinity's own internal desires. Where God is present, our relationship need not become tangled in explosive emotions, as so often happens between human beings. To feel love freely and to express it fully -- a love which seeks the other's and not its own fulfillment -- this is to meet God in action. God is found in the form of love which we seek but rarely find.

At the end of a Zazen session in Kyoto, an American girl reported to the assembled Zen students that she had trouble offering her love. The Zen roshi snapped back: "That is the trouble with you Christians. You always think you have to love someone." The point he wanted to make was that the aim of Zen is to train you to rise above, to empty yourself of, the tangled emotions of love. The 'disinterest' which Meister Eckhart discovers to be at the center of God is more like the state which Zen seeks than is passion.

However, the basic issue is whether disinterest and love can ever be compatible. Our ordinary love, one which one human being offers to another, is far from disinterested. It wants what it wants when it wants it. By contrast, we discover God whenever we meet an act of disinterested love, that is, love communicated freely and without self-attachment. To experience that is to encounter God in act. The question is: Can human love be reformed if we work toward that model? Or, is it only by a relationship to God that we can achieve that state and base our acts solely on love, as divinity does?

3. GOD CAN ACT FREELY

Those whose education has encouraged their self-liberation respond by seeking new areas in which to exercise their abilities to act. Not all people learn to extend their freedom in this way. They understand neither themselves nor the world well enough to discover what avenues of expression are and are not open to them. Change becomes possible only when one knows that he or she can and wants to live other than in a present state of inferior self development. Thus, it takes strength and intelligence to achieve liberation.

One is not born free. Usually, one lives in the condition one is born to, and often one does not become self-conscious about freedom until maturity is achieved. In fact, maturity can be defined as gaining the knowledge of both one's potential and one's limitations. To become adult is to accept the task of achieving liberation and of releasing your powers from artificial restraint. God enters into this struggle too and must do so in order to act freely.

God has both the intelligence and the power necessary to sustain the freedom to act. And divinity also differs from us in always having possessed full self-awareness, rather than acquiring it gradually as we do. Still, where relations with the human race are concerned, God must also strive to achieve full freedom. One who is divine cannot relate freely to one who is not free. A free person cannot be comrade to a slave. To share the human condition is to share limited freedom, or at least the limited degree to which most men have developed their inborn powers. A fully free being, whether a God or a human being, desires that others be free in the same way. Only those who are partially free and partially bound envy freedom and conspire to inhibit the potential of others. The power of genuine freedom is the ability to free others in their relationship to you.

In this sense, God's full freedom would be empty if it were simply an expression of unrestrained power. For example, by divine power God could determine every event in advance, but freedom also allows one who is divine not to do so. To be meaningful, our freedom must be involved in the life of someone else. God committed the divine power to our struggle for liberation, from the moment the divine act gave the signal "go" for the evolutionary creation of our world. When we meet God, we do not encounter simply another blind power struggle. We discover someone who possesses both the power to be free and to control us, but one who nevertheless accepts our weak human freedom in relation to the divine total freedom.

Others, those whose freedom is threatened and so is precarious, are afraid of every action they do not control. A weak person is comfortable only when he or she can hold other persons within the boundaries of an imposed code. Some of us would turn God into a source of comfort by convincing ourselves that the divine nature is characterized by necessary boundaries in its action and that that is the way God should be. To face a free God is an overwhelming experience, at least for anyone not confident of his or her own power to sustain free action. Even theologians -- whose business it is to talk about and to God -- often flee from this unsettling confrontation with an open-ended divine freedom. They plead instead for a necessary God, one whose actions are not so unlimited.

Whenever we meet someone who is able to let others relate freely to them, we know he or she does not feel threatened but instead encourages others to be free in their own expressions. We also experience an important aspect of God's nature. Such freedom does not mean capricious or irrational behavior. It includes the ability to act on the basis of what one thinks and plans, as well as the capacity to develop our own human potential into an effective instrument. It is necessary to achieve such control if we want to create anything novel or new.

One who is fully free can explore what might be as well as what is. There can only be one God, but many beings may share freedom. To meet God is to realize that we are encouraged to work for freedom by one who is not jealous simply to preserve divinity's own uniqueness. God can and will share with us what is characteristically divinity's own. That is, we can achieve equality with the divine if we are ready to follow God's lead and shape our own course of action decisively, thus reflecting how we have come to understand God's mode of action. The present struggle of minorities and "Third World" peoples represent perhaps the greatest press for freedom in human history, at least since last century's push against monarchies and empires. The Black experience in America illustrates the power which religion offers in order to survive slavery, and also the strength it can add to the drive for liberation. In spite of oppression, many Black Christians stayed close to traditional Christianity and did not suffer "the death of God" with liberal Protestants.

Prison literature established a powerful tradition beginning with Paul. Nevertheless, the depth of spiritual literature which prisons can produce cannot be used as an argument for perpetuating slave conditions. A life of ease actually subdues our press for freedom, while the struggling search for liberation sustains religion, due to its stress on Act. In this battle, and not in rest, God can be located. However, the divine nature allows neither God nor us an easy freedom. Freedom involves a constant pressure to remain open and to control the powers that would enslave us all, God included. God succeeds in this drive to remain free to act. We men and women walk along God's path when we succeed in sustaining our openness too. We follow the divine pattern of action as it has -- or has not -- come to affect us.

4. GOD CAN ACT TO SUSTAIN CONTROL

There are moments when all human beings go out of control. And there are times when situations no longer seem to respond to anyone's guidance. There are also occasions when some remarkable people, in public and in private life, are able to keep themselves in check and thereby direct events. We admire this ability to exercise definitive control, whether it is exhibited physically in athletics, exemplified religiously in high spirituality, or manifested politically in public affairs.

Whenever we encounter a power of control that is capable of giving life to human or to natural potentialities, we learn about God by virtue of how God is able to act. As men and women, we fight constantly to sustain our control over events, because any previously successful formula for control seldom works as well in a new situation. Our power tends to ebb if not continually reinforced by our will. God is exceptional (i.e., divine), because divinity acts to control without being forced to renew this effort constantly.

God is able not only to enforce control in order to sustain present action but also to extend its hold into the future to assure that the divine aim is accomplished. What is past appears as if it were the live present now going on. If as human beings we look at the past as it extends forward, we can recognize what God's power of control means. Divinity can hold itself to any elected path. God does not reject divinity's own past, as we often do if ours is full of mistakes. God accepts what the divine actions have produced, whereas we men and women often spend our time running away from our past decisions. Accepting past mistakes insures the future, but only if our control is sufficient to make the needed changes. We witness this important fact in God's mode of action, insofar as we experience it and come to understand it.

However, for now we encounter God's ability to control the future only in the form of a promise. If we accept the divine promise, this means that we sustain our confidence in the divine future and acknowledge its ability to reconstitute our world from the way it is now, and as it was meant to be, by some future act. It also means that we recognize how the divine sustains its own past. God's capacity to control the present is the same thing as his power to refrain from total dominance. This is God's offer to share control. All direction that deserves the name 'divine' is not offered on an all-or-nothing basis. God has the power to "stay loose".

Those who are uncertain of their ability offer the greatest resistance to any request we make that they share control. Such men and women prefer to coerce the future by attempting to determine everything open to their influence. When we meet someone who allows the future to remain open, we uncover an image of God's mode of action. God is able to impose necessity but allows contingency or uncertainty. What is divine is able to overpower everything that lies in its way, but it restrains this ability of total control in order to permit others to exercise their directional energies.

God could make the future into a mirror image of the past, but he restricts this power and accepts uncertainty with its resulting incompleteness of knowledge. Only those who are trying to be God picture God as eternally possessing certain knowledge of all events. But God's control is so powerful that it does not need to coerce everything and everyone in order to prove its ability to act. God can afford the luxury of being underestimated and misunderstood.

God's willingness to restrict divinity's power in order to share control with us evidences the divine ability to assume command at a time of her own choosing. Considered abstractly, we do not know when, or even whether, God may want to exercise this ability to intervene. Nevertheless, this capacity for control extends to the total reconstruction of events and peoples and worlds. What God concedes to other sources of control for an indefinite time, that divine action can also reclaim and reconstitute. When we discover a power so self-confident that it need not press to determine every event, we have met a God of relaxed command. This divinity is one who can release control and leave options open to us, just because what it divine is secure in its abilities and sure of its acts of power.

Aristotle, Augustine, Calvin, and a host of traditionalists have all wanted God to determine the future with an absolute fixity in order to stem the panic we humans feel when we face constant uncertainty. Due to our uneven ability to hold things steady, God understands why we might want a divinity to determine events once and for all, but what is divine refuses to be stampeded by human anxiety. God can open the valve on human contingency and allow us freedom just as far as we like. He even allows a certain leeway into the processes of nature, an element of chaos. Still, what is divine does not have to worry about its ability either to maintain or to regain control once an act is endorsed.

Human beings are certainly unlike God when they scurry about constantly protecting their possessions. God laughs a little upon hearing Jesus tell us to "Consider the lilies of the field; they toil not neither do they spin." God knows that this is a God-like attitude and that few men or women will be able to calm themselves down far enough to follow Jesus' advice. To rest like a lily, to grow like a lily without concern, is an image that reveals God's approach and mode of action, but it is one that is not very often ours. Then Jesus' actions tell us as much or more about God than they do about ourselves. Our own insecurities we know all too well. It is God's life that we must try to relate to. It is the divine action that arouses our real curiosity.

5. GOD CAN ACT SO AS TO
BE PRESENT WITH US

Quite often people complain that God is either distant or withdrawn or hidden. (Of course, there are also those who claim to find the divine activity obvious.) Probably on most occasions God does not intrude but stays patiently out of sight. Upon reflection, we may agree that this is not such a bad characteristic. However, it would be more comfortable for religious men and women if they could always be sure of God's presence whenever we witness suspected divine acts. But if we put aside our selfish desire to have God available to us on demand, we come to realize that the one important divine ability is this very power to be present only when God wants to be. Most of us lack this quality. At crucial moments we are sometimes unable to make ourselves available to others just when we most want to.

More than physical presence -- which is a relatively simple matter -- we human beings find it hard to act so as to reveal our attitudes, our emotions and our wishes, with the clarity we would like. When we try to act, to speak, to make ourselves known to someone, we often do not succeed. To open ourselves fully to another human being requires us to empty ourselves of our concerns and our preoccupations in order to become at one with another in his or her life.

To become the other *qua* other is our most difficult task, in spite of Aristotle's belief that we acquire knowledge in this way. But whenever we see this accomplished, we recognize a divine power that works a life-changing act. Divinity is sometimes pictured as being so powerful that God's immediate presence would either destroy or overwhelm us. The truth is that the divine is able to set power aside and to become one with us without threatening our independence. Jesus' phrase, "blessed are the humble in spirit," is amazingly applicable to God.

Humility is a mode of action, if properly understood, which is a subtlety Spinoza did not understand. Even when we are able to place ourselves fully beside another human being, the resulting effect is often coercive. The person still feels under pressure to be like us, although we may deny that that is our intention. Yet, even if we do not intend it, any exercise of superior power naturally creates, not a situation of equality, but one of condescension on our part. God's unique activity lies in being able to become present to us without imposing coercion. For just this reason, ironically, many of us remain unaware of the divine availability and its latent power.

If we consider God's presence in Jesus, we know that it must have been non-coercive, because we are still divided over how to respond to Jesus. This uncertainty began during his life and continues still. If God exuded unlimited power, the divine presence would always force a consistent response from us. Instead, Jesus' appearance among us was so non-coercive that we are still mystified over how God could have been present to act in Jesus and yet not control our reaction to Jesus' appearance. Evidently, divinity does not need the uniformity of response that we human prima donnas often demand. God's active power takes subtle, not always bold, forms.

Instead of destroying us or even coercing our response, to feel God's activity has the unusual effect of setting us free. Thus, when we feel free, it must be because God is able to make divine action available to us on our terms rather than on a divine plane. This is an amazing ability, since divine power would allow God to dictate any stipulated conditions. Our presence with another human being, however pleasant and comforting, too often has the effect of constraint. It simply forces him or her to bend toward us and our ways, no matter how innocent our intent. It is the essence of divinity to be available to us, to act upon us, and yet at the same time to increase our freedom. God adds to our sense of release as few persons do, because we realize that what is divine seeks only to control itself and not others. To meet a non-coercive presence whose effect is to stimulate us to seek our own independence, that is to discover God in an unforgettable moment of active encounter. No human being could have quite the same effect on us.

"Let it be, let it be" advises the verse of the Beatles' song. And we like to listen to words like that. In fact, ours is an age caught up and absorbed in a world of strong sound not quite of human dimension. However, we often cannot let it be; only God can. We create and we want to control our creations. It takes power and an infinite self-assurance to be able to release to itself what we have made or once enjoyed. This is what prayer is all about, or what it should aim to achieve. In our natural state, we leave neither ourselves nor others nor nature nor God alone. We will need to pray a lot if we want to be strengthened enough to "let it be".

Our human powers are often considerable, but we know that they still fall short of absolute control. To have our prayers answered means to make ourselves able to act but to do this so as to release our control, to trust rather than to despair over others. To feel the presence of such a power of self-control is to find ourselves in God's hands, i.e., affected by divine action. God can let us be, whereas we constantly beseech and besiege both divinity and others to yield to our demands. "He's got the whole world in his hands," says the Negro spiritual. That is neither an obvious fact nor is it easy for frail humans to accept. Yet whenever we do manage to accept and to relax, we know that God's power has come up behind us to support our accepting action by a divine undergirding activity.

6. GOD CAN ACT SO AS TO USE FORCE

If we paint God only as docile, then we have not met divinity as an individual. We might be more comfortable with a tame God, but the violence of the world stands unexplained unless God commands and acts with at least as much force as we observe around us. Actually, a divinity must have enough power at its disposal to exceed the terror and the coercion we witness in the action all around us. It takes force to control force, action to offset action. The powers at loose in nature and in us are subject to no final restraint, unless God can match and control these with his active legions, i.e., 'angels'. We need not always see or feel God's force, but it must be such as to be able to unleash action at will. If not, we will all finally be crushed between the world's contesting powers.

Any use of force always involves some destruction. Therefore, divinity must be able to absorb into its nature such loss as the possession and the use of power to act entails. Divinity is not so timid as to refrain from using the force at its disposal simply because some destruction is involved. However, if active power is constructive as well as destructive, God must be able to turn force loose to destroy in such a way that nature and humanity will still survive, in general if not in particular. If force can annihilate, it can also revive life. To use power amateurishly means to be unable to reverse its destructive side effects. Perhaps we see God's divinity whenever force acts with destructive power and yet life survives or is even revived in the process.

Perhaps men and women cannot remain creative very long unless they feel force applied to them from time to time. Our human tendency is to close ourselves off, to shut ourselves up, in much the same way that business corporations and political societies turn rigid and then stagnant in due time. In this case, only force can act to blast open what has become closed, although such energy cannot be unleashed without effecting some destruction as a side effect. However, if force is unleashed with an accompanying control, the loss of present structures, which at the time may seem like death to societies and to peoples, may become a prelude to new life. Active force can create new forms of life as well as destroy, provided its use is divine in its control and is not held in fumbling hands. To feel the impact of force, to be undone by its action, to survive, and yet to find greater vitality released -- this surely is to experience God's ability to use power creatively.

If we face a violent force rampaging blindly or without regard, we speak of the destruction that comes in its wake as "tragic", as a loss which is to no avail, as "the work of the Devil." All applied force comes so close to demonic destruction that many want to paint God as a pacifist in order to keep divinity clear of such involvement. Just because power is often destructive and viciously applied, we associate force and action with loss. Nevertheless, hard pressure is needed before we can create anything new. The person who has not been bent by the action of force cannot have learned God's depths which comes out of the struggle to survive. God is present whenever power is used, but only if both control and survival are the aim of the pressure that is unleashed in the action we experience.

In The Saviors of God, Kazantzakis depicts God as needing help from us. God struggles constantly, as Kazantzakis portrays it. The force involved in this clash is often painful and bloody, although it can sometimes be ecstatic and rewarding. And God may demand assistance from us as divinity struggles with itself. But the issue is: Does God do this because it has to or because it wants to? In Zorba the Greek, we sense that God loves the earth and its human pleasures. In Saint Francis, Kazantzakis depicts the struggle that is necessary if we are to be converted away from our attachment to sensuality and then move to achieve spirituality.

All this toil and agony is a part of God's life, the divine pattern of action. It also opens us to the only avenue for human insight. God is sometimes gentle with us, but not very often. Ironically, a kindly priest or a gentle mother reveals very little about God's active use of force, comforting as both figures may be. God created power; the divine life is based on force; God uses and controls it. To discover the divine activity, however, is to read Kazantzakis' portrayal of the struggle to subdue destruction and then the acceptance of its savage consequences, only to find that the earth is still alive and life has been preserved after the storm has passed. "And the bush was not consumed."

7. GOD CAN TURN ACTION INTO UNDERSTANDING

We all want to increase our human understanding. The problem we face is not so much that the world is either opaque or that it exceeds our grasp. The difficulty is that we often lose our power of self-control; our actions get out of hand. And increasing understanding depends on keeping a steady grasp. Whenever we are able to comprehend with ease and without interference, we intersect the same line which God's action observes, and a resultant increase in knowledge should follow. The difference between God and us is not that God is omniscient, as divinity is so often pictured. In order to be God, divinity does not need to hold every fact about the world continually in sight. Yet God does need to be able to marshal the divine understanding to act with ease and in such a manner that an intellectual grasp never slips away from control. God can afford to be patient about the future. Whoever is divine does not need to demand the final resolution of all events in advance. However, this ability to fathom events fully as they arrive, and never to lose control, marks the quality of God's understanding as divine and differentiates it from ours.

Few, if any, of us claim complete self-understanding. Self-clarity of such depth may lie beyond human grasp, Freud's Rationalism not withstanding. Or, if moments of full disclosure do come to us, we do not seem able to sustain them for very long. Rather, the rare moments of lucidity we do achieve must be held over in memory in order to be enjoyed. God is unique in being able continuously to sustain full self-understanding, even though this super-awareness needs constantly to be adjusted to the changing course of events instituted by free, and very often violent, human beings. God's mind meets each novelty with instantaneous realignment. Whenever you find clear, sustained self-understanding held in firm relation to the actions of others, you have met God--whether you realize it or not.

Of course, God also perfectly understands the events of the physical world and their evolutions. Freedom and decision are not involved in following the course of the stars, once they are fixed in orbit and the laws governing them set. Thus, God's understanding of the natural order is neither as difficult as self-understanding nor as the divinity's constant endeavor to understand why men and women act as they do. Both divine and human nature involve a freedom that is difficult to control. Men and women try to act freely; God achieves this through self-understanding and control and also by interruptive action.

If we have trouble understanding ourselves, comprehending others is even more difficult. In the first place, if full self-comprehension is required as a condition for the clear understanding of others, our vision will remain clouded, or at very least it will be incomplete. Beyond that, however, lies another difficulty: we often interpret others from our perspective rather than from theirs. Therefore, our goal should be to set aside our own categories and experiences in order to understand others just as they are, on terms appropriate to them rather than to us. We often settle for interpretations of the actions of others which mirror our self-interpretations. We need first to put forth our actions and then let our understanding follow that. We discover how God understands on any occasion when we are able to set interpretive schemes aside and fully understand someone just as he or she is evidenced in their actions. Zen's goal and our attempt is God's achievement.

Such power and clarity of understanding, one so calmly disciplined that self-images are set aside and another person is known simply as he or she is -- this is a divine prerogative. In our own lives we may find that we understand ourselves in the midst of a struggle to understand someone else. And in a sense, God understands the divine activity more fully when it comes to know us as our human lives develop freely. But for God this is not a disclosure of hidden parts. That is, divinity does not need to struggle with himself before she can understand us, nor does God try to mirror divinity in the life of another as we seem to do. Where the ability to understand can be sustained, and where another is known in and for him or herself without self-involvement, there God can be met in divine act. Human understanding is seldom able to complete this task; God is recognizable by just that ability.

In his Ethics, Spinoza claims that all of our individual minds are, in varying degrees, part of the divine mind. If this were true, we would not have to go very far afield to see ourselves and our world as God sees both the divine life and all others, that is, fully and completely. The problem with Spinoza's theory is that our minds simply do not feel in communion with divine insight or up to the level of divine action, even allowing for Spinoza's admission that our minds need improvement before we can expect to exercise such divine understanding. Of course, we sometimes sense a divine power of insight when we are in the presence of "a few good men and women.".

However, even if we could succeed in achieving our goal of universal education, we have largely abandoned the hope that very many can be sustained for very long at such a high level of insight. Besides, to do the good does not always result from learning the good. Therefore, destructive minds also achieve a powerful level of insight. We have just lived through a human holocaust which came on us even after we had brought a portion of humanity to enlightenment in the Modern Age. Thus, we stand amazed before God's depth of understanding, and are even more startled by the divine ability both to sustain it and to employ it constructively in order to act. We human beings seem to do this only rarely. By contrast, insight often paralyzes us. We can raise a few to this level of insight and action, but not enough of us, or for long enough, to overcome our limitations as a people.

8. GOD CAN USE POWER TO CREATE

We celebrate our talent to create, whether in art or in science, and we enjoy the visible results of such power. But those who find themselves able to create are also often plagued by self doubt and pain. This agony blocks out the joy they could feel over what they are able to bring to birth. We are proud of all that humankind has learned to do. But the unpublished human story is one of vast talent wasted by impotency and failure to act. The sad tale, one which we tend to suppress, is that of human creative powers stopped in midcourse and thus denied fruition, whether by internal or by external opposition. Thus, in surveying humanity as a whole, we are more aware of our inability to create than we are of our power to give life to new forms. The few magnificent exceptions, which are dramatically publicized do not paint either a realistic or a balanced picture of the waste involved in our human struggle. We prefer to celebrate the accomplishments of human culture. Therefore, when we see in God the power to create new forms of life, this is an activity more rare in human affairs than we like to admit. Our actions seldom match our potential. God's may not but they can.

Human creative ability flowers magnificently at times. When it pours forth, it seems almost inexhaustible. And this is one reason its unknown depths terrify those who would like to but cannot move to create novel art forms or new theories. A genius is haunted because he or she is not sure that his or her creative capacity can be sustained for very long. It is better to be born without the ability to create than to possess a talent and to be unable to carry out its promise. Men and women are often tortured more by what they might do but do not than by what they actually accomplish.

Thus, if we discover that God encounters no internal impediment in exercising the divine creative expressions, we locate in God such self-fulfilling power as we only dream of. We establish a model for God's uninhibited life if we outline those conditions which set the active, creative person apart from others. First, all self-concern must be set aside. If a person's attention constantly swings back to his or her own personality, the risk is that talent will simply spin around in self-absorption instead of being given a definite form outside the person. Somehow we need to lose the fear we have of experiencing our creative powers. Rather than cringing in anticipation of adverse judgment on our attempts at new expressions, we should work for what we want to express and center our attention beyond our own ego. We need to concentrate on what might be and not paralyze ourselves by fear of failure and our inability to act.

'God', then, means the one who is able to externalize creative powers freely. Thus, whenever we encounter such spontaneous action, we may understand God better. We can use this experience to form our image of God's ability to create, but we can also use it as our own model of action. Nothing blocks God's self-expression, except the divine concern not to destroy what already has existence. Of course, this principle of non-destruction is not perfectly embodied in the world, since many of the forms we create compete and so destroy each other.

The constant presence of conflict in the world testifies to the depths of God's limitless creative capacities and to the conflict God faces when divinity makes any decision. But evidently God decided to allow destructive competition into the evolving elected world order. To know God is to understand this unopposed ability to create new forms of life outside the divine sphere in any way it chooses. That is, God creates without the conflict of internal inhibitions. On the other hand, fighting ourselves is a primary human occupation. In a poem entitled "An Island in the Moon," William Blake laments the agony of anyone who is talented enough to create but who cannot bring forth.

To be or not to be.
Of great capacity.

Of course, we often romanticize our human powers. We talk lightly as if creation were an easy matter. In point of fact, our unused talent often destroys us from inside just because we are painfully aware of what we could have done but have not worked to accomplish. We feel that all the world will be our judge if we fail, and we know that we can lose when we try to create something new. Acting in fear, we attempt to conserve our power by burying our allotted talent in the ground, just as Jesus depicts this in one of his parables. Yet once an artist or writer or craftsman hits his or her pace and finds a mold into which latent talents can be released, new productions pour forth, and any adverse judgment seems insignificant. But few of us make it to that near-divine status. The majority of us cringe in fear, uncertain over our abilities and our powers, or else we bemoan our lack of it and so fail to act. We come near divinity when we know God in the unrestrained ability to act to create.

9. GOD CAN BEND ACTION TO WORSHIP

Worship is a special function, and many are neither suited for it nor should they expect to be able to enter into it. Yet, if we pay attention only to our base human abilities, we will either never find God or else uncover only a rather bland image. We are much more likely to discover God in unusual and difficult human activities and capacities, although this is true only if we are willing to go beyond our inhibitions in order to explore eccentricity. "To worship" means to admit that we are inferior to a greater power, even if we think we possess magnificent abilities. In order to enter into worship, we must humble ourselves and draw strength from giving thanks. To evidence appreciation genuinely in prayer means to admit that we depend on another for the power and the assistance we receive in order to be able to act.

Not all of us can accept such a posture, and so the ability to worship freely remains rare. All who go to churches are not worshipping. Whenever we are able to place ourselves in such an attitude, the resulting experience is decisive in our quest for the divine. If we fail to worship, we will miss at least one important face of God. Anyone who cannot learn what worship means, who cannot feel the human need it serves, is blocked from realizing God's active presence.

However, difficult as it is to achieve a state of worship, what is strange to discover is that God is able to worship too. To say this only seems odd because God is usually thought of as the object of all worship. Thus, we seem to be forced to say that divinity worships itself. In a certain sense this is true, in that God draws strength from giving thanks; yet all the while divinity is the source of strength. Divinity's thankfulness is for its own nature and its creative powers. However, occasionally God gives thanks for the assistance rendered by men and women toward completing the divine projects.

We find God through worship only if we discover divinity as it worships beside us. Many of us miss God in services of formal worship, in music, in the recital of liturgies, or in the performance of rituals. This is because we expect to find God as our main object of attention, the receiver of our thanks. Of course, in a formal sense God is. But we will miss the inner vitality of God if we do not understand that divinity is just as able to give praise and thanks as to receive it.

God can sit beside us and be silent while we are deep in prayer. As human beings we tend to be grudging. We hoard any praise given to us. God has the refreshing freedom and ability to turn praise around and to join us in giving thanks. To be able to unbend, to offer yourself to another freely and without restraint -- that is God's secret source of strength. However, the first time we try this, we may feel only an increased vulnerability rather than strength. God can offer the divine life to us in all genuine humility, because no divinity is as afraid of ridicule as we are. In order to give thanks ungrudgingly, we must be able to surrender every position of superiority. Odd as it may seem, God discovers strength from confessing sins (e.g., the violence allowed into the world) in just the way we do.

Divinity has directed men and women and nature to go down a difficult road, due to the less than optimal decisions made at the moment of starting creation on its evolving path. God needs to say thanks for those who continue, in spite of the questionable divine choice of a fallible world, to follow the divine path in trust. God's sins are not ours, but divinity has on its shoulders the burden for allowing negative -- even widely destructive -- aspects into the world that was chosen for creation. We worship because we need strength to face that fact. God worships in order to pray for our strength in the face of the adversities which divinity freely created and placed in our way. God draws strength from the ability to yield in worship. Thus, we discover God in worship when we understand how and why God wants to join us in prayer, and how prayer is also a divine form of action.

Jesus' use of prayer provides a model for us. He did not retire from the world to pray. He was arrested and then killed while in the midst of praying. Jesus derided long, formal, self-righteous prayers on the grounds that God already knows us better than we know ourselves. In fact, God may know more about us than any divinity cares to know. Jesus did pray and worship on occasion. However, he did so in such a simple way that it should lead us to suspect that we really do not have to go far to reach God, if only we can find the way. The divine modes of action are in fact before us.

The whole meaning of the Christian doctrine of the incarnation, after all, is to assert that God has joined us. If this biblical report is true, God should be able to join us in worship. Too often our churchly forms of worship appear to be a concerted effort to raise ourselves up to God. The truth is that God joins us quietly and often without our recognizing it. We need not spend hours in agonized prayer, if only we could recognize divinity's presence when God is active beside us.

10. GOD CAN BEND ACTION INTO HEALING

The human body often has an ability to restore itself, but such power has certain limitations. The body's resilience gradually decreases over the years, and some attacks upon it are destructive beyond any medical ability to repair. The same is true, of course, of both our psychic and our spiritual lives. People sustain wounds in their daily intercourse from the battles into which they are drawn, and many never can recover. We can repair some damage to our psyche and spirit, even though in certain cases the road to health is long and difficult. If it were not for this self-regenerative power, we would always be cripples both in body and in spirit. However, we know that we cannot ward off permanent destruction forever.

Physicians come to us in all types and sizes. Healing comes to us from without as well as from within, through our natural powers of renewal. When we freely acknowledge that the instrument which heals us comes from beyond ourselves, we are in that special situation in which God can be known. God also heals the wounds within the divine being. And God needs to do so, for divinity keeps itself open to all the wounds we constantly inflict upon ourselves and others. Yet, divinity is not content, as we might be, simply to restore itself. God continually offers healing to others, and a divine person is one who also offers us the ability to restore ourselves. But God does so without regard for the merit or the lack of it in our particular struggle. If healing comes to us through an instrument which makes no demand for reward, this experience of healing is the context within which the recognition of God's action can take place.

The difficulty is that such healing, at least as we experience it now, is at best partial and always subject to repeated loss. Moreover, some of God's promised healing is postponed to that unspecified future time when all destructive forces in the world will be brought to a halt. Our present experience with religion is more one of the realization that healing has been promised to us, rather than that our health is now completely and permanently restored. To heal means to act to control that which destroys and to provide the power to reverse such damage. We experience some divine healing at present simply because of the promise of future restoration. Thus, the accomplishment of future healing depends on our belief that God's control and the divine action are sufficient to subdue all the powers that destroy. 'Faith' means that we who suffer trust the eventual capability of the one who promises to act to heal us and to restore all damage.

To believe in the power of God to heal our psychic and spiritual wounds is to trust in God. And at the same time we discover divinity in this very act. Since a promise of future action is involved, a God who would do this cannot be fully and finally uncovered in any present event or act. Therefore, to believe in God's power to restore what has been damaged is to know divinity as future-oriented and as only partly known to us now. Most of the destruction we witness all around us daily remains unrepaired. Sometimes we are able to effect new life and health through our own efforts. But we will never find God if we look for divinity only in our present experience.

The key to discovering the core of God's being is the realization of the divine power to act to control the future. Yet, the center of God's nature is never fully open for our inspection. Even in the divine life, God lives more in the future than either in the past or in the present, in spite of some theologians' attempts to present divinity as totally eternal. After all, healing is pointless if it is not accomplished with the future in mind. Only the sick in spirit are interested merely in setting past injuries straight. One who is well can forgive another just because his or her own energies move in a different direction from an obsession over the wrongs of the past. To come alive again means to recover a future orientation -- and perhaps to find God, because both the divine and the human are moving in the same direction and acting in consort.

A medical doctor is one who is engaged in a life of healing. This science has advanced in power beyond any dream primitive man had of controlling his health. Yet still today all doctors feel the limitations of their healing powers no less than before. Modern medicine can extend life, but no doctor can either reverse death or guarantee that the life restored will be pleasant. If we survey the array of instruments and the technologies which today's doctors can employ, we realize the immense powers that are at their disposal, but we also discover the limitations beyond which neither God nor we can go.

Ministers of religion and psychological counselors practice healing, but the number of people still locked within themselves or within asylums testifies to our inability to cure all human beings in body and/or in mind all at once. We can neither reverse the past nor escape the present, but doesn't healing really mean to act to open a new future for us? To discover a physician who can do that for us is to find an instrument through whom God stoops down to earth to heal. As a healer, God is the effector of our future.

11. GOD CAN ACT SO AS TO RISK REJECTION

We frail human beings spend a great deal of time trying to prevent being rejected. Ironically, God controls rejection perfectly. Thus, divinity can also control acceptance easily. The course of development in our world, and of every action in it, could have been fully preprogrammed, as Augustine and Calvin claimed. Had God done this, divinity could have insured its own worship and praise. God, however, is a gambler. Since divinity invented the laws of chance, God need not insist on maintaining strict control over us. Because God can stand to experience suffering, what is divine is able to humble itself. But of course, in setting aside the divine power even in its own interest, God risks possible rejection, which granting freedom to another always involves.

God could have decided to remove all chance and human decision in the shaping of events. Then, all events would be based on natural

causes, whether internal or external. Our world would be simply the
fixed result of necessity, a neat arrangement that would please many
naturalists. God and humans often enjoy thinking along those lines,
and in our minds we often construct necessary worlds. In point of fact,
though, God seems to have preferred the chance involved in a constant
contingency. Divinity is pleased to accept the risk of our rejection
which living with uncertainty involves. We recognize this fact about
God only when we first accept the way we naturally respond to the
world. Then we find ourselves funneling our innocent reaction into a
source of new insight into God.

Why would God do this? Why would a divinity accept contingency
when it could impose necessity? Why should God compromise the
divine interests and even endanger its goals? God has the power to
insure control and to guarantee success by clamping down an iron
necessity all around us. If our recognition of God is left clouded and
uncertain, the danger of our rejection also involves a risk for God. A
system which would outlaw contingency and freedom and give us a
clear knowledge about God and the divine mode of action -- this would
constitute a much safer world than the one in which we find ourselves.

Certainty would help us to relate to God and to accept the fact that
divinity's program is still not fully clear and so is subject to change.
Instead, even our vision, if we do not see God properly or with any
steady grasp, may turn us away from him. On the other hand, many
men and women try furiously to reveal themselves fully to others,
hoping thereby to gain acceptance and understanding. Children
naturally and spontaneously turn outward to others, until they become
hurt or sick. As they mature and experience slight or rejection, they
become more guarded. The young turn inward in self-protection only
as age and sophistication creep up on them and dampen their youthful
spontaneity.

When we reflect on it, to humble oneself, even partially to
relinquish control, to risk rejection -- all this can be an act of strength
and not of weakness. Whenever we feel we are forced into a precarious
position, we usually confess our weakness. We would control every
event if we could. But we too easily become confused by the magnitude
of the task, and we can't take that chance. Only the truly strong dare to
risk bending down to others when they do not have to.

To be gentle and passive, when one could control by force, this
actually requires great restraint. God's physical power is enormous;

divinity's past actions testify to this. God's mental ability to control the divine thought, however, is even more phenomenal. Whenever God is gentle, it is not through impotency, as so often is the case with us. Rather it is because of a conscious concern for the effect which the action might have on those who are vulnerable to injury.

What perhaps is most phenomenal about divinity's actions is that God is able to shorten the divine memory. Human recollection is often faulty through our own inadequacy. God can instantaneously recall from the memory bank every item in the world's history to date. However, at times Divinity chooses to blot out such remembrance and to remain piously ignorant. It is fortunate for us that God has this ability to forget selectively and that divinity also chooses to exercise it. Otherwise, it would be hard for God ever to forgive us completely.

We forgive neither ourselves nor others when we refuse to forget. Instead, we constantly pour over the same old issues. As an evidence of our weakness, we insist on tying our memory to the past. God is more future-oriented, both in the divine thought and in action, than we are. Yet at their best human beings can be future-oriented too. God has the power to remember and to hold onto the past. God does so at times but actually prefers a future-orientation and the forgiveness which forgetfulness makes possible. That is, God forgives and forgets when we allow divinity to relate to us in this way. But first, we have to stop nursing a grudge against the world's "unfairness".

In our relation to other human beings, memory is as much a hindrance as a help. We need to recall past experiences; they are the ties that bind us to one another. The child who forgets his or her parents is worse than ungrateful. God promised Israel he would not forget them as his chosen people. Jews live scattered all over the world, but they still have the memory of their past relationship to God. And they wait for the divine promise to be fulfilled. On the other hand, once an unfortunate incident has arisen, we often change from what we once were. Bitter memories block us from easily resuming a former relationship.

To possess a memory is often to remind someone of what we know about his or her past. Sometimes that simply makes that person avoid us in the future. We always fear that some preserved memory will return to evict us from the secure life we have built on top of an early folly. Actually, we can risk a haunting memory if we couple it with forgiveness. When we are successful in doing this, we continue to move out from our newly secure position and to risk rejection, just as the venturesome young do so easily and naturally. Youth is a matter of being able to accept risk and to move on to the future, rather than to let memory stop in the past. In its action to restore, God demonstrates divinity's lack of age by the constant risk of rejection for the sake of the future.

12. GOD CAN LAUGH

When we look back, it is amazing to realize how God's sense of humor has been overlooked by those who have described the divine life, particularly by serious theologians. Of course, God cannot have a careless, an easy, or even a vindictive sense of humor such as ours is at times. However, God has often been described in harsh, cold, and austere images. Even those who see divinity revealed as loving interpret this as a very serious love. God's affection is portrayed melodramatically, with a touch of sadness, rather than as gay or enthusiastic or spontaneous, which so much love is that we find attractive in human beings. True, the world has enough depressing aspects to give any concerned God enough to weep about. Who would care to know a divinity who achieved its humor, as some of us do, by belittling human suffering? We would reject a God who used laughter as a means to shut out the pain, both that around the divine life and within us.

Nevertheless, the ability to laugh is crucial to those who achieve effective insight into others and into themselves. Those who are too intent and too constantly serious are likely to misunderstand both the world and themselves. Such people are distrusted by their fellows, because they press down too hard and thus are depressing to be around. A sense of humor requires a lightness of touch and, above all, a sense of perspective. If we lack a balanced perspective, even an 'enlightened' understanding can become "too heavy" and miss its mark by being ponderous.

All too often we are sanctimonious and self-important buffoons. Surely any God who understands the divine nature must at times laugh at our foolishness. Many aspects of human behavior are genuinely funny, and surely God must respond to rare talent just as we do.

However, like us, God must often be torn between laughter and tears. Divinity is a "Jewish comedian," retaining a touch of humor in spite of a tragic sense of life.

Above all, to find a God who is able to laugh is surely one of our few hopes. Whenever we lose the ability to laugh at ourselves, we know we are close to being trapped in our own mental torture chamber. When this happens, we fall into a psychological pit from which we cannot escape until we learn to laugh again. We often find aid and our release coming from life's humorous side, rather than from the intense accusations of "encounter groups." We gladly pay millions in order to laugh. We seek out that most prized of all human talents, the comic, just because he or she relieves our too-heavy seriousness. Comedy induces a needed self-perspective.

If our relationship to God were always sanctimonious and heavy, joining in religious practices would only indulge our introspective self-intensity. God would then be the most self-defeating being we had ever met, if seeking the divine could not save us from our obsessive seriousness. To be saved means partly to gain release from a too intense self-concentration. A totally serious God would only lock us more deeply inside ourselves. But if one who is divine can also meet us with a sense of humor, that might release us from our self-imposed burdens. To know God is to learn to laugh with God, not always to weep.

As a revelation of God, it is true that the New Testament is not a very humorous book. Yet, it is also true that Jesus evidences more self-detachment and less pomposity than the more formal religious followers around him, particularly most of those who came after him to control his church. There is a brightness in Jesus' promise and an openness in his attitude toward the future which the professional religious often lack. All of this indicates that God is able to smile more than his priests may care to admit.

There is laughter in heaven as well as rage, humor in God's speech as well as moral exhortation. A lightness of touch in self-reflection leads God not to take the divine power as seriously as we do. After all, anyone who is 'divine' does not have to struggle as intently as we do for self-understanding. God can smile at our frantic efforts and laugh at our foibles and mistakes. Given this power, God can afford error and a humor that rests upon realizing that divine power is still ultimately in control. Every comedian seeks to imitate God and envies the rapt attention with which religion's earthly audiences listen.

Woody Allen is sometimes a very funny man, but his humor has a serious touch. In Getting Even one chapter is called "My Philosophy." It is a parody on both ponderous philosophy and too-serious philosophers. "Eternal nothingness is OK if you are dressed for it", he says. He ends with an aphorism which I'm sure God would find funny too: "Not only is there no God, but try getting a plumber on the weekend." What theologians must do is explain the art of the humorist, even if they cannot be one.

Since God had options when the world was ordered, it could have been created dry and humorless. The fact that humor is possible gives us some idea of where the humorist ranks on the divine entertainment scale. God could have kept laughter away and insured religion's totally serious reception. Priests and ministers would be more comfortable if they could only be sure that their seriousness would never be taken lightly. But, if God can indulge in laughter, they are always placed in danger. Shouldn't humor open up one path to divinity for us -- even if its surprise element threatens all of us and drives some away?

13. GOD CAN APPEAR IN THE DETAIL

"God is in the detail" is a famous remark which Mies van der Rohe made about architectural style. Yet this is as illuminating about God and the divine powers as it is about the beauty of a building's structure. We have all seen poorly executed examples of a basically beautiful style, whether in music, in art, or in literature. Evidently, genius lies not so much in the overall concept as in the care and precision with which materials and surfaces are brought together. The real master is the one who is in control of subtle detail, and this is as true of slick modern buildings as it is of a baroque chapel or a medieval cathedral. We all know that radical ideas -- whether in politics or in art -- often come too easily. Few have the skill, the patience, and the subtlety of mind needed in order to carry out new ideas with a precision and an intimacy of detail. It is easy to copy the broad design, difficult to get the master's nuances. God, then, appears more in the detail than in the broad design of the universe.

Thus, we waste our breath -- unless we enjoy cocktail party conversation -- when we argue for the superiority of one historical period, or one style of art or etiquette or religion, over another. Life can be lived in many ways. Men and women can be dressed and combed in many ways. It is possible to design religions along many styles. Everything depends on the care taken with the detail as to whether the result is crude or admirable. We also waste our breath, then, when we argue that we will liberate men or women by changing from one form or style of life or of religion or of politics to another. Why? Because we can turn any way of life against ourselves and use it repressively rather than creatively. Our dilemma is that the care with which a design or a program is executed is a matter of individual style and talent. Thus, it cannot be designed for mass consumption, nor can it be programmed so as to be effective in every individual instance. Neither can God work effectively with all of us at once.

Now, if God is in the detail in architecture and in human affairs, the world has ironically been designed so that it is easier to miss divinity than to find him. A person who either does not care to see, or who will not devote enough patience to an intricate search, he or she either misses God every time or else settles on some crass and unthinking popular idol. A God who lives in the detail of life or art or religion is always hard to find. Few of us hold still long enough to discover what is divine in subtle places. Of course, the reports of coming up against God are many. Successful organized religion is built on an ability to popularize God publicly, to make appealing to the masses what is supra-normal.

Successful priests are gifted with this interpretative ability, a skill in mass-producing an experience of God for the many -- at least momentarily. This is a necessary art, just because God's forms of presence are so subtle that divinity will be overlooked unless professional religion magnifies God's image a thousand fold. Of course, we inevitable encounter some distorted exaggerations in this process. For this reason, some of us eventually become disillusioned by popular religious movements. This is when God still seems to elude us in the long, quiet moments, no matter how dramatic divine appearances are proclaimed to be in any church.

It is only in the care of the detail in certain experiences, e.g., in the visual arts, in the use of words, but finally in distinctive action, that God can really be captured with any lasting result. Learning to do this is an individual affair, and one person's success can never be easily duplicated for another. We can teach others to speak in formulas, but altering their actions is more difficult. As with training in music appreciation, one can be taught to listen and to learn how to be aware of detail, but this only prepares us. It neither provides us with a final grasp nor does it enforce an appropriate response.

A God who cares about detail is both more interesting and more personal than a raging God of war or a thundering moralist. If the general rules of life are not as important as the way they are carried out, this leaves us some latitude in styles of worship. We can carry on our politics or our moral life in a variety of styles (although 'immorality' of any type seldom carries divine sanction). We, of course, prefer to argue for the absolute superiority of one code or form or act. Only in this way can weak human leaders hope to maintain control over the masses. But a God-of-the-detail is an individualist and can only deal with us and evaluate and judge us on a one-to-one basis. Immanuel Kant feels more secure with a God who enforces a universal moral law. But, although the stars run in a relatively fixed order, where men and women are concerned God seems to have elected a more individual approach.

Of course, all this means that we must revise our notions about finding a final proof for God's existence in the natural world. We can argue for God from a general observation of the purposes in nature or from cause-effect relationships. Such an argument may lead us to uniform principles, but it will not get us to God -- primarily because 'knowing' God is principally a "matter of how we act" rather than of how we think. What is divine must be looked for carefully, quietly, observantly in small and in subtle places. Thus, the pursuit of God can neither be generalized nor universalized nor finally concluded. The divine does not appear in our life in a way that makes such conclusiveness possible, since action is individual, even if words can be universalized. The best overall plan of the universe may not show us much of the divine touch, but the intricacy of the design in the subtle detail may do so, particularly if its perception leads us to new, effective action.

God's refusal to appear exclusively in mass celebrations, plus the divine preference for care in the detail, explains much about our recurrent religious disappointments. When some subtle note or word or act suddenly stirs us deeply, we often think our insight has come from the situation we are in, from the ritual we have witnessed, or from the words we have heard. We think that if we join that group or repeat that external setting this will sustain some momentarily powerful insight and make God real for us.

Alas, God is more easily lost than found, and the divine presence is always hard to sustain. Some subtlety of the moment stirred us; some special sensitivity on our part made us receptive. But above all, God refuses to be bound by any formula, particularly since uttering words is neither the divine aim nor its principle means of self-demonstration. Mere repetition, ironically, kills the possibility of God's reappearance. However, if sensitivity to individual detail is the right approach, we can at least learn how to train our eyes and, hopefully, our responses. Mass religious displays, or even the regular routines of ritual, are all right, but only if one finds profit there. However, God will not be found on the surface of anything, since altered action stems only from a depth response. What is divine appears only as our senses become attuned to subtle detail and small facts. Even then, no certainty is promised as the result.

With a good IBM computer any architect could design the general frame of the world. But the world of art and architecture and religion exists just because the possibilities for intricacy in detail are endless. God must have taken infinite care with the nuances of creation, even though divine power could have gotten a world going with much less attention to detail. Evidently the only real link between God and us lies in the subtlety of the detail in our relationship. Thus, we never find God in universal laws or on the surface of the world. Detail of perception and response are the key to altered action, and thus to changed lives.

14. GOD CAN STAY BEHIND THE GOSPELS

The nineteenth century sparked "The Quest for the Historical Jesus." We thought divinity could be located if we understood the record of history properly. The hopes and the assumptions behind this quest outline for us the assumptions of that century. But as the twenty-first century approaches, it is clear that quest did not recover the "pure Jesus" it hoped for. Perhaps the tools of historical scholarship were not as powerful as we thought, or perhaps we sought the wrong person behind the Gospels. We tended to confuse the Acts of God with mere recorded words.

To find the human, historical Jesus of the gospel stories would actually solve few religious problems for us. We need to know who stands behind him; and God hardly appears in the New Testament narratives as such. Jesus speaks about his 'father' in various ways. Yet except for a few words from heaven on the occasion of Jesus' baptism, God stays behind the scenes. Jesus remains just another religious figure -- unless we can locate the-God-behind-the-Gospels, one found not the pages of a text but only in decisive Act.

Our direct evidence is minimal, and even the accounts of Jesus' life are multiple. At the outset we know that we can never find one picture of God such that all who listen to the gospel stories will agree upon it. Still, it is crucial that the quest be undertaken, and perhaps each age will see God somewhat differently. Or to put it in another way, perhaps God turns a different face to each generation. If so, we must relocate and redescribe the face of the divine in each new age. Otherwise, God remains distant and voiceless in our time. We cannot decide who Jesus was or what he did independent from a search for God and the Acts of both. Jesus comes alive for us only as we succeed in filling in the picture of the God who stood behind him and how God acted in relation to him, e.g., with Jesus' miracles, in the inspiring Acts of the Holy Spirit.

As almost everyone agrees, Jesus' references to God are given in explicitly personal terms, e.g., Father, Good Shepherd, etc. Although God does not appear directly, Jesus talks as if he is on familiar terms with the divine power. Jesus finds no difficulty in voicing the message which he feels God wants expressed, which means primarily to work toward a distinctive healing Act. But the details about the words Jesus uses are unimportant, since Jesus does nothing to establish a definitive, precise, canonical text that contains his doctrine securely. The founding documents are in fact his Acts.

Jesus seems to prefer to push the interpretive burden off on to the individual rather than to make every meaning clear for the listener. His use of indirect techniques, storytelling and parables, all this indicates Jesus' lack of concern for simple and direct expression, plus his understanding that Act proceeds word. Obviously Jesus' disciples did not really understand him, nor did they comprehend God's plan fully at the time. Only later, perhaps, could they make clear affirmations about God's intentions, as Paul does. But neither Jesus' presence nor his words about God cleared up the uncertainty at the time. "In the beginning" was not the word but the Act, and so God and the world and Jesus must also be understood first by Act.

God must like retrospective understanding and have little concern for making programs clear in advance. The certainty for which we strive reflects our own uncertainty and our desire to overcome it, not God's concern for security. Nothing in the Gospels leads us to a God who fears to take a risk or who determines the future with absoluteness. Furthermore, we seem to face a God capable of deep feeling and of being affected by human actions. Compassion is a key factor in the divine emotional life, and God does not hesitate to take a difficult path even when loss and bloodshed may be involved. The way is made neither easy nor obvious for any religion's followers. The ethics of divine action, as Jesus represents it, allows for individual variation. God must prize variety above conformity in a people.

As we read the Gospels we do not get a clear impression of God's closeness to either formal religious institutions or to their leaders. Certainly, Jesus worked independently from "the system" of religion in his day. He never left it, but neither did he join it professionally. Ecclesiastical leaders often put too much stress on words. Jesus seems to prefer silent action. The-God-of-the-Gospels appears to be critical of ecclesiastical argument but concerned for the people involved in the religious system, as well as for those outside its official confines. Thus, any God we restrict to church channels cannot be the God standing behind Jesus, even though the divine may be presented as such by some churches.

The-God-behind-the-Gospels seems full of power, although divinity uses this very little to intervene in our lives. Divinity is often simply silent. True, the New Testament is full of miracles, but they are a "special show" and cannot be the way God acts every day. The divine response to insult is seldom thunder. The God of the gospel stories and the Acts of the Apostles does not seem concerned about where one sits at official, state, or church functions. If God is an author of religious doctrine, that divinity is rather silent and modest about it all. "Actions speak louder than words.".

Although full of power, the God who could cause the Gospels to be written was capable of accepting death without responding in violence.

Such passive behavior disoriented those who expected more from God by way of defiant leadership. In particular, his disciples expected more support from God when they agreed to join Jesus' new religious movement. But even when God wants to show his power over death, it was not done so decisively that none could doubt the power exercised. Divine action alone does not determine a response. In fact, even today many remain unconvinced that God is really behind the gospel story.

At the very least we have to admit that millions discover the divine presence elsewhere than in the Gospel accounts. Any God-of-the-Gospels, then, does not give us doubt-proof revelations of the divine intent. Such a divinity is capable of being missed and misunderstood. Evidently God can operate in a variety of contexts, not just one. The divine power and action behind Jesus must be both flexible in its nature and cautious about taking any direct action over the heads of men and women in order to enforce a divine desired behavior.

15. GOD CAN LEAVE US WITH OUR TASK

God appears and acts in many ways. Thus, it is our task to discern the many faces of God in order to find an acceptable picture of God's behavior among the many accounts of the God given to us. Gods do not of themselves do this for us. We have, I suspect, always been aware of the multiplicity of the ways in which God has acted and become known, but today our task is more difficult and also more challenging. For centuries we pursued the holy grail: the notion that soon, eventually, we would discover the Divine itself among the Gods, or validate the one face and the decisive act among the many as truly God's own. It was a modern, a Rationalist hope, but it tends to end in either atheism or in self-destruction.

If we search for certainty and finality where none is possible, we can turn into fanatic zealots who try to create certainty where none exists. We revolt against one God when many Gods are all around us. Determined to find the One with certainty, we overlook the Many. Today our task is no longer the fruitless search for a final elusive unity but the attempt to find God where the divine lives, in the plurality and diversity of act and word. This does not, as we shall see, mean that God is everything that all men or women have ever said or how all divine acts have been described. That suggestion is both repugnant and impossible. Since the divine variety in act and in word indicates that God's reality lies first in plurality, we must accept every face of any God suggested to us before we can hope to find what God is like for ourselves. What we must explain is how God's nature makes it possible for what is divine to be seen as acting in so many ways.

God must be such, then, that it has been left to us to specify the divine nature definitively in concepts. Within the vast range of the divine nature, God cannot be one thing. Thus, we begin always with 'Gods'. In the divine life, God maintains an infinite richness and flexibility. God can appear and be grasped as one thing at one time. The divine can act in a single decisive encounter, but this does not preclude being apprehended and encountered in a slightly different way at another time.

One who fails to understand God's tendency to become many Gods will be left with an empty shell. God moves on while we remain, wondering why a once vital mode of God's appearance now seems so lifeless, why a religiously decisive action does not seem to be repeated often. Saying this does not commit us to accept equally every way in which Gods have been presented, but it does mean that the task is ours to single out "God" from among the many Gods. God is able to leave that job to us, just because divine action is unrestricted, which ours it not.

God has not specified the divine nature for us, and that very fact is the central clue to the divine life, as God knows the divine interior. How can we, then, accept this and not fight against it? How can we proceed to set up the criteria which are necessary to select out the acceptable faces of God from among the many Gods and decide which acts claimed as divine are acceptable and which not? Admittedly, some divinities are hideous and destructive, and against these we must learn to protect ourselves. To begin with, we must elect a focal point, some word linked to an action of God which seems to us to be a central clue that has been given out. Once selected and focused on, we can use this as a stabilizing reference point to sort out all that has been and can be said about the multiple faces and actions of all Gods. But given the original diverse core of divinity, no such sorting or stabilizing process can ever be final.

No one is prevented from claiming that he or she has discovered God in one true face, in one experience, in one setting, or by seeing it emerge from one form of action and practice. Indeed, given the lack of rigid cohesiveness in God's nature, it is necessary for us to claim to have found such a focus. Otherwise one God will never be known to us personally in distinction from all the many faces and behaviors. The meaning of 'faith' is to make just such an affirmation "stand out or die" in the attempt. We call it 'faith' just because obviously no God is ever the sole possible center of all religious attention. No one God stands out obviously from among our experiences of many Gods, including those who are negative, disappointing, and even destructive. Only if we cling tenaciously to one face or action as revelatory does God stand still and appear. Relax your grasp and that face disappears. If we cease to act as God has modeled this for us, God vanishes.

Not all God's appearances are due to human effort. What is divine may appear with power at any time and place of its own choosing, e.g., with Moses in the burning bush, with Jesus, with the Buddha, or even with Sun Myung Moon. But these divine interventions are misinterpreted and will disappear if we think that God remains either at one place or is alive only within one account of certain events and actions. Because God's form is not permanent, it is seldom present for very long in any appearance.

We can say God appeared, that divinity spoke or acted, but one cannot say either that the divine always remains at that place or that all future divine disclosures must take exactly this mode of action. "God is free" -- this is our major proposition, and thus we are free in our response too. God is only bound to be what the divine acts have been, not as to what they may become. God does not deny the divine past, as we sometimes do. What is truly divine remains steadfast to its former word but makes no promise to us not to utter new words or to Act again.

All the recorded visions of God's face must be considered as the result of a joint effort of God and of human effort. Karl Barth is notorious for wanting to free God from human shackles, leaving God free to be the exhaulted divine self. God is free, of course, and can appear as the divine wishes, but this freedom does nothing for God if no one recognizes this presence. Recognition and transformed action are divinity's intent. Without this even the most powerful God seems dead as far as its influence on human life is concerned. Could God force us to recognize the divine existence? Yes, of course. Any God worth the title could. But the basic characteristic of freedom -- one which millions recognize with peculiar forcefulness today -- this keeps what is divine from pressuring and coercing us, just because that which is divine rejects such intimidation.

The most powerful divine appearances or acts can pass away without exerting any human influence, that is, if they go unrecognized and unresponded to. In Jesus' case, most of the people in his time did not recognize the significance of his life and actions. This is often true with divine appearances, that only in looking back does one begin to grasp the significance of the divine presence or recognize the act as divine in its source.

If the God who appears always disclosed exactly the same face by performing exactly the same acts, the role of human response might be less significant. But since our task is to discern one God from among many Gods, this refining and selecting is the chief religious function for all of humanity. The pictures made by the appearances of many Gods are diverse. Yet in comparative religious studies we sometimes try to synthesize them all.

But God smiles. What is divine knows that, if we ever see one God, it will be because we have learned to deal with, and are responding to, what by nature is plural and never fully specified in itself. Such a situation frustrates our plans to domesticate God by putting all religions together, but it offers a more interesting picture of the life of God. Through plurality and diversity the divine achieves a freedom that offering a single face would never allow.

B. THE PASSIVITY OF GOD

1. GOD CANNOT ACT SO AS TO BECOME NOTHING

Children learn about their parents, as well as about themselves, by exerting pressure and then evaluating the responses which are given to them. The young need to learn how far they will be allowed to go in their actions and in their search. Adults reach understanding, too, when they realize the limits beyond which they cannot go, when they understand what it is that they cannot do. God would lack self-understanding if a divinity could not recognize what should be known already, that is, what it is that even a God cannot do. The divine limitations define God's nature for us just as much as knowing how God can and has acted. God could not remain divine if what has a supra-nature did not work in and through these self-imposed limitations on power.

There are good reasons why a divinity finds itself restricted. Not to be able to do some things and to act in certain ways is just as necessary a quality as to be able to exercise certain abilities. Words, of course, are less restricted; they are powerful at times but also less trustworthy. Almost as many forms of power are destructive as are constructive; therefore the exercise of some powers is to be avoided. For instance, the opportunity to build a human society on the basis of freedom would not be possible if God did not set limits on the divine action. Without self-restraint, any divinity would overpower us all.

For our sake as well as for the divine life, God prohibits some acts that could be engaged in. What is divine could indulge itself. But if it did, it would plunge the divine life into chaos and our world into oblivion. Wherever and whenever we resist the devastating forces that lead to destruction, we join God as an ally. In the midst of this resistance movement, we may recognize God as our silent, but powerful, active partner. Both of us seek to set restrictions and limits in order to call a halt to chaos-producing subversion.

God, however, cannot reduce the divine activity to nothing. This is not because divinity could not move to block off its own powers and thus reduce itself to impotence and the world to chaos. God could self-destruct just as we often do. But the divine sets itself against all such dissipation of power. God checks any inclination to drift in this direction in the way that human beings often let themselves race on toward destruction. Given God's powers of calculation, a perfect plan could be designed by which divinity would suppress all its powers at once and so self-destruct.

Instead, God's own natural direction sets divinity toward positive construction. However, every move need not be positive. If it were, the world would not be covered with the vast waste that constantly threatens to spoil it. Still, the directional flow of God's nature makes the divine unable to reduce itself to nothingness, in spite of the fact that not all powers in the divine nature, or in our world, are constructive.

We overlook this inability of God to become nothing just because the divine so often disappears from our view. Yet to experience such absence amounts to the same thing for us as God's becoming nothing. When God evaporates from our lives, particularly if the divine has once been powerfully present, this absence leaves us with the psychological impression that we are lost in a void. However, God's self-limitation on radical behavior always leaves open the possibility of a decisive divine return, a new constituting action appearing at even the places where absence has been most deeply felt. If the divine disappearance is painful, this departure of course causes some to celebrate, because they are glad to be rid of religious restrictions. The Modern Age even hoped to make this absence permanent. However, the accompanying pain or joy is always brief, because God never lets the divine life drift out beyond all recall, as we human beings often do. That which is divine can return when it wants to, and God often does, as powerful revivals in our religious history illustrate.

Science fiction is a phenomenon of the Modern Age and is an unpredicted by-product of our scientific advance. We humans have always had a vivid gift of imagination, but the dawn of modern science opened new horizons for us to indulge our speculative bent. Even God is enchanted with the literature science has inspired. The divine response to this is more enthusiastic than to the weird notion of God's own death.

Even given the fantasies and the inventiveness of the stories written by science-fiction writers, it is not hard to imagine a tendency on God's part to drift toward destruction. We might fantasize this, but at the same time God knows that that which is divine can hold itself in control and continue on in existence. The television special that dramatizes the problems God has with the divine nature is yet to be made. What is divine retains the power to conquer the forces within itself that threaten to destroy both its life and ours. God finds Hollywood-style movie endings, where the best man always wins, not surprising. After all, that is the way what is divine has, or will, write its own script.

2. GOD CANNOT REJECT ANYTHING

All of us spend part of our lives trying to reject responsibilities that are thrust on us. Adam blames Eve; Cain is sure that Abel is at the root of all his difficulties. Both in public and in private, vast amounts of energy go into trying to prove, either to others or to ourselves, that our own error is someone else's fault. But God cannot bring the divine self-focus to do this. The very vastness of the divine creative powers force it to accept responsibility for every existing creature, plus every thought and action, that comes before the divine gaze. And nothing whatever is prevented from coming before the divine apprehension. This situation could have been structured in some other way. God senses this power to do this all too keenly. But for exactly this reason, nothing is rejected. God accepts all. The divine awareness of sin surpasses human understanding.

God is all things. All power in the world, whether it enhances or destroys life, reflects some facet of the divine nature, just because nothing that exists need be as it is had God decided to prevent it from entering the evolutionary world. No matter how attractive or deplorable some aspects of life may be when considered in themselves, nothing could be part of our existence if God were not in part like that. Yet what we see and judge at any given moment can never give us a full picture of God's nature. To assess the divine net worth is more complex, and it may have to include future intentions not yet fully operative. Nevertheless, God rejects nothing as unrepresentative of some part of the divine nature. If we search those depths long enough, we can locate the source of both the best and the worst in existence.

When we understand that God is not allowed to reject anything, that everything under the sun finds its origin in the divine nature, this helps us to comprehend both the vastness and the complexity of the divine being. At the same time, one of the fondest human hopes is taken away from us. Divinity, if it rejects nothing, can never appear as One or as pure Goodness. The divine multiplicity is nonreducible.

If only unity, purity, and simplicity lay at the core of the divine nature, both God and man could rest more easily. If the age-old dream of God's simplicity could be realized, we could resolve so much that is perplexing. Our mind would be able to rest transfixed in simplicity whenever it saw God. Of course, we keep trying to reduce God to some unity (as Einstein hoped to do) so that divinity can be known in an easy way. It is just that God eludes all our attempts to tie the divine down to only one way of being and action.

God's inability to reject anything burdens what is divine to accept all things as having their source in its nature. Unfortunately, even if God either appears to us or acts decisively, no single apprehension can ever be final. Where God is concerned our understanding will always continue to shift . This is not due simply to a lack of mental power on our part. It reflects the fact that God's nature is too complex, its actions too bold and varied, too full for us ever to get our hold on God such that divinity would be incapable of being grasped in any other way.

If we want to apprehend an object simply, we must reject much detail and fix on some single core. We are pleased with ourselves as human beings when we can do this. In God's case, this is not possible. To simplify, to reject too much, is to miss the core of what divinity means, or at least we will lose God later even if we have caught "the divine act" for a minute now. We may grasp some comfortable, substitute divinity, but we have not found the creator God who accepts everything as a representation of what 'divinity' means and does.

Mystics often seek to identify with a unity that lies beyond the plural surface of the world. The attraction of this goal is due to the blissful rest that union with a principle beyond the world produces. Zen Buddhism goes further. It aims to discipline its followers to break through to a nothingness that lies beyond the division between unity and plurality. Although hard to attain, this is a blissful, a releasing state. One who masters Zen meditation is set free from normal restraints. And God often considers joining the Zen monks in their seated meditation. Even what is divine envies both the Zen master and the devotee of John of the Cross. Unfortunately, divinity is too involved with men and women and the universe to indulge itself in the luxury of such a quiet state. God can withdraw; we have experienced that. But in any day action is still the clue to the divine favored location.

God can assume the lotus position and spend an eternity in contemplation. What is divine can at will empty its mind of all thought and see the nature of the world as it is without action or words or any form of mediation on its part. God can also learn any meditative technique you care to name better than any man or woman, but most Gods do not have time for such basically self-centered activity. The demands which creation puts on the divine nature, plus the complexity of the projects that have been undertaken, keep God away from unity and rest.

God cannot escape the task of keeping constant control on complexity. In fact, what is divine rather enjoys this. No matter how diverse or tension-filled it becomes, the world never moves away from the range of God's grasp ("He's got the whole world in his hands"). And what is divine never avoids or shirks its constant burden. God rejects nothing; it accepts all as originating in the divine intent. The results of divine decision and action are never rejected. This is a prime characteristic of 'divinity' vs. 'humanity'.

3. GOD CANNOT CONTROL THOSE WHO REPRESENT DIVINITY

The greatest difficulty we have in discovering what God is like is our tendency to turn first of all to God's self-proclaimed religious representatives. This seems like a natural place to start, for we expect to meet God in a sacred person, in a church or in a temple setting, more than in the secular world. We tend to believe -- or at least to look to -- those who tell us that they are authorized by God to speak and to represent the divine to us, particularly if they evidence some personal credibility. The problem is that all religions attracts their share of crazy spokespersons. Yet it is not so much the nonsense of various religious claims that frustrates us as it is the fact that even good religions and trustworthy prophets are irreducibly multiple. They do not all speak with a unified voice. Can God be heard in dissonance as well as in silence? Watch for the Act that emerges from silence.

Some who profess to be our religious guides are charlatans and fakes from the beginning. Where humanity's concerns are deep and important, con men and women always lie in wait to build fortunes by pandering to those needs. Even what is false in much popular religion can provide temporary relief; it just does not last. The history of all religions is full of shocking conduct and the resulting human destruction, as well as heroic acts and inspiring stories. Like all important endeavors carried on in God's name, in spite of all that is false, there usually is a core of truth and spiritual aid in God's popular religious representatives.

No one can make headway in any important venture if he or she cannot distinguish the genuine from the sham. And if we let our anger over what proves to be false make us mad, we may overlook what is true but lies under the surface, the strong acts that support uncertain words. Organized religions have great difficulty in gaining and in holding on to popular acceptance as God's spokespersons. This is not simply because institutional religion is not always pure. In any organization or profession, we must reject many candidates before we locate a representative who can be trusted. Religion is no worse than any other human enterprise. It is just that we usually think it should be.

God cannot control those who represent the divine, or at least some Gods do not seem to want to. Some religious representatives claim to operate directly under God's authorization. Our problem is that more than one voice announces this, and we can never form a complete unity among all the varied claims. God could control these representatives by ordaining a kind of divinely instituted state church on a worldwide basis, but it would have to control all action as well as audit all words. Such a church would need a fixed ecclesiastical hierarchy with direct contact to heaven at the top, and each function should be affixed with a Good Housekeeping seal of approval. Of course, some claim that God favors one man or woman or a particular church, or that the newest divine personal message resides with some attractive revivalist. Even so, we cannot deny that God allowed the religions of the world to be myriad, multiple, irreducible, and even conflicting.

Impurity in the priestly strain makes it impossible to accept any self-proclaimed representative as our sole model for understanding God. The priestly acts are not always decisive and pure, whereas we know that God's are. It could be that, personally and privately, God favors one brand of religion more than another. Or it may be that what it divine is more fully present in some religious events than in others. Still, we must decide for ourselves where to look for authenticity. And we do not possess the advantage of having a single authorized agent to determine the right direction in which to turn. We are left on our own to explore the choice of how to find an original avenue to God.

If God does not fix an exclusive line of communication with one of the world's religions, no single locus is given to us from which we must search for God. Still, each of us is free to testify that he or she finds God in one place more than in another, in one activity rather than in another. Divinity may be as secular as it is sacred, although surely it is not irreligious. This need not mean that God can be found equally everywhere. That which is divine may elect special places of sensitivity, divine "erogenous zones," where care and stimulation at that point produce a more intense response.

Nevertheless, if God does not control all the representatives of divinity, it is not because he or she lacks the power to enforce such heavenly censorship. It is just that to do so would be false to the divine nature. The presence of a controlled and rigid ecclesiastical monopoly would not reflect God's person accurately. In fact it would distort our image of the divine. If divinity does not limit itself to one form of life, it would be the ultimate hypocrisy for God to establish an orthodoxy among all of heaven's representatives. The existing confusion among religious speech and action tells us something about God's original intention for creatures and what life with such a divine parent must be like.

Given God's penchant for organization, it is strange that the divine allowed a degree of chaos and such a wide range of novelty to characterize the religions which celebrate the divine intent. Of course, if God is not totally identified with the life of any one religion, no priest can fully please nor any sacrifice fully satisfy all of the divine demands. No one act can alone represent God. We seek God in all our various religions. But perhaps the reason why we never find the divine, either fully or with finality, is because the total divine life is not lived solely on a religious dimension.

nly part of God is ecclesiastically oriented. Surely one who is divine is more religious than not, or else we could accuse God of being false to the various spiritual revelations that have been either allowed or given. If it is the Godhead we seek and not one particular God, no single form of religious life can satisfy us fully. Thus, it is its Acts which define the Trinity, as we have argued. But God's actions are neither always obvious nor universal. Thus, we must pursue every religious avenue open to us. All the while we know that religious forms and rituals are a human crutch which God does not need in order to bring action and decision out of the divine life. God may enjoy some ceremonies and actions, and even an occasional sermon, but that which is divine resists being fully identified with any one event, not even Jesus' resurrection -- although this does not mean that it did not occur.

4. GOD CANNOT ELIMINATE ANGER

The God who appears in the Old Testament stories perhaps cannot, or at least does not care to, control his anger. We have many accounts of God's actions which evidence this ability to become angry. These are sometimes labeled as "primitive" pictures and are said to be no longer valid for a Modern world. Newer and more sophisticated views of God's nature assume that to eliminate all anger is a sign of enlightened progress. They portray God as serene, loving, calm, or as wrapped in blissful silence. In a real sense, that which is divine is above all the world's strong passions, and such a quiet God-of-contemplation has some attraction for us all, especially when the world's bedlam becomes too much. However, is God actually able to eliminate all anger and live the easy life that some like to imagine for their divinity?.

One good reason why we want to place God above passion is that so much human anger is petty and selfish. We get mad when our egos are offended or when our pride is wounded or when our territory is threatened. When human anger stems from insecurity and a concern for our self-interest, such anger is unworthy of any divinity. We come up against enough tough, petty individuals on earth without wanting to find our Gods in heaven to be like that too. Thus, what we might say is that God neither gets angry over an affront to the divine dignity nor reacts to a challenge to divine rights and privileges. Any God worth following possesses a personal security which we do not have and engages in actions which reflect that invulnerability. The divine reaction to any threat from us is likely to be laughter rather than anger.

On what occasions, then, might God be unable to control anger? To discover what these sensitive spots are is as revealing about the divine life as it is about ours. If God never gets angry when attacked, perhaps it is only any unfairness or a brutality toward other human beings that causes an unrestrained divine fury to rise up. If God never uses another person solely for selfish advantage, any violation of human dignity and integrity will infuriate the Lord of Heaven. If anger rises whenever men or women become selfishly vicious, a great deal that is destructive in the human scene will make God mad and disrupt the tranquillity of heaven. We discover much about divinity when we learn which human acts are beyond the pale of divine toleration. Thus, we realize that there are ways in which God never acts.

We men and women hide a great deal behind a discreet smile and a locked door, but God does not blush easily. Sex surely cannot offend the divine modesty, since God is the author of that complex game. The divine is responsible for the depths as well as for the heights to which that passion so easily leads us. Sex must mean a lot to God, too, or else it would have been more muted in its prominence in our thought and in our actions. God would not let it occupy so much human emotion and energy if it were not one key to our nature. Even when sex leads us into sordid situations, this does not in itself make God angry, only sorrowful over our weakness.

As with all things, divine anger rises only when a natural desire is so misused that others are destroyed or made into slaves simply for the satisfaction of our pleasure. If we are ruthless in our disregard for the injury we cause others in the pursuit of our own self-interest, in that situation God finds sex pornographic. Only then is the divine unable to eliminate its anger over the interpersonal abuse involved. This is true whether the humiliation is in sex or in economics or in politics or in religion. Blind desire blindly satisfied begets divine anger.

Speculation about "the day God lost control of anger" would make a marvelous doomsday plot. However, it is a little beyond the mind's power to visualize the result of God's total loss of self-restraint, powerful as the divine actions have been. Anger has its satisfying as well as its humorous aspects, and there is no more reason to deny anger to God than laughter. In fact, the two should go together. When the divine is provoked, God toys, just as we do, with the vision of letting anger go. Nevertheless, entertaining as it is to contemplate such a scene, God is unable to let the divine life get out of control. We must settle for a momentary evidence of this divine anger only as well as it can be reflected in our world.

What we now humorously call "the primitive mind" understood that God's anger was embodied and was expressed all around us. A violent storm probably is not the direct expression of God's voice that some early peoples imagined it to be, but it is a better symbol of divine wrath than our more sophisticated religious piety knows how to portray. Only men and women indulge themselves in explosions as a rash expression of their emotions. Humorous as it might be to consider how God might explode, divinity laughs at such a thought even as God paints it in the divine imagination. God chooses to express anger in more subtle forms than in uncontrolled explosion. That which we call 'divine' is an artist of controlled rage, whereas we tend to be sloppy in our expressions.

5. GOD CANNOT LOSE THE DIVINE TRANSCENDENCE

We human beings fall into sheer panic at the thought of losing ourselves. This is because we know that we too easy become personally disoriented. Even when we are not aware of any explicit danger, our panic level rises over any real or imagined threat to our stability. This is due to our preconscious realization that, if once we become lost, we may not be able to find our way back home. And there are points of no return for the human psyche beyond which it loses all control. If we cross these, we may never quite regain the self we once were. This fear takes many forms, from the crying child lost in the crowd, to the student afraid that if he/she leaves one professional goal or girl/boyfriend that he/she may never find another, to the pathetic mental patient who gradually cuts himself off from the world but later consciously prefers to remain lost to himself just because her fear is so great.

God on the other hand misses the excitement of such risky human ventures. The divine self is forced to enjoy such thrills vicariously. If God had not pushed humanity into such a precarious adventure as our common life involves, the amusement world would not be such an exciting and profitable business. Certainly many seek to experience thrills and dangers even at the risk of "no return". Such daredevils make God's life and ours exciting, if often also tragic. Yet, no matter how far out God may venture, what is divine is not able to lose its own center. For us mortals, self-forgetfulness is at times refreshing. The chance to wander alone and unknown is a relief. God knows no such joys; divinity is ever-present to itself. God cannot escape or cut off the divine self. Of course God does not know (except vicariously) the human need we feel to lose some part of ourselves. We cut off our memory in the fear of being destroyed by events too strong for us to handle. God remains always in control. Divinity is unflappable even in the face of atomic explosions, whether internal or external in origin.

If we discover God's inability to lose the divine self, we realize that a person who wants to lose him or herself, or a person who is already lost, that such a one needs God. What this person lacks is the strength to remain always present to the past at the same time that he or she remains open to the future. If we could maintain self-presence easily, escape into alcoholism or drug addiction or sexual experimentation would be less widespread. Games and diversions and seductive people help us to forget. We often want to lose contact with parts of ourselves, with our past, and even with what may lie ahead. Unfortunately, our attempts at selective forgetting are not very often skillful. We lose too much of ourselves in trying to lose that part of us which we want to let go. And sometimes we lose our self-consciousness altogether, when all we wanted to get rid of was an upsetting memory or to avoid the unsettling future that looms ahead.

The power to remain ourselves, to accept all that we have been and may be, and still not to flee in panic -- that requires divine strength. Wherever we experience such a power, or whenever we encounter any action that reflects it, we are near to God. That which is divine is the most accepting being we can know, both of itself and of others. This is not because God likes everything either about the divine self or about other people. We know that God can get angry over our abuse of persons. It is just that divinity is unable to lose itself in a vain attempt to deny responsibility, as we men and women often do. God can accept all and yet remain true to the divine core.

On the other hand, we are sometimes altered beyond belief when we attempt to take in too much. God's reserve capacities are such that what is divine feels no need to lose itself. Our human tolerance level is more precarious and thus subject to sudden shifts. To hide nothing from oneself, to accept what we would prefer to hide rather than to try to lose ourselves -- to achieve such a state of openness, to avoid self-deception, as Sartre put it -- this is to reach the level of the divine and to realize something both about how God lives and about the divine source of action that can amaze.

Life in Modern Times has often been absorbed in the search for self-identity. The theme of alienation and lostness haunts modern poetry and fiction. God reads every written word and so knows how we wandering humans feel and how we express this feeling, even if divinity cannot experience such lostness in its own life. God reads the novels of Richard Wright and Thomas Wolfe and William Faulkner. In fact, Modern Man's preoccupation with lostness, plus the search which that feeling inspires, is one reason the Modern World has not been able to attune itself to God easily.

We know that God cannot drift into a lost state. Thus, if our own search to find self-identity and to overcome alienation is successful, it becomes the post-modern equivalent of knowing God. In the moment that we overcome alienation and realize our own identity, we both understand how God feels and at the same time discover the source of the divine power. God experiences self-loss only by visiting our theaters, our psychiatrists, our mental hospitals, our bars, or by listening to our desperate prayers. The divine's own self-experience is one of constant presence and self-knowledge. Yet such a contrast between the human and the divine is also the source of unease for a God who seeks to build close human relationships.

6. GOD CANNOT WITHHOLD DESIRE

The attraction of desire is present on every street corner and lurks behind every door. Given this fact, it is a little strange that so many theologians have seen fit to eliminate desire from their descriptions of the divine. True, the divine life need not reflect everything that plays a role in human life. But what drives men and women either to madness or to ecstasy, that surely must represent an important part of the divine life too. Some think that to admit that God knows desire makes the divine out to be deficient. The needs we have require something outside ourselves for their satisfaction, and the traditional goal of theologians has been to maintain God's self-sufficiency.

They thought we should allow God to depend not on others for fulfillment but only on the divine nature. It is argued that we must attribute perfection to a divine, that is, a perfect independence to God in order to secure the divine's control of our evolved creation. There is a compelling logic in the traditional demand to "keep God clean" of our faults. Human desires so often go out of control. We too easily become dependent on others -- persons, things, or drugs -- simply to satisfy our needs. We even debase ourselves in self-defeating ways while attempting to quench these thirsts. God, then, should not be forced to depend on others, as we so often do to our own disgrace.

However, if God should openly choose to accept dependence and to know desire in the internal divine life, such a decision would bring God closer to us and unfold a tale of amazing divine adventure. In this case God would feel desire just because the divine allowed itself to be put in need of other people for its own fulfillment. In such a relationship, there would be no desire from which God could be totally free. However, such a sense of God's presence is captured in some experiences of dependency more than in others. For instance, love that is offered to another is closer to the life of God than any drug experience, although both involve dependence. One acts from strength; the other out of need.

The age-old question of whether Jesus is "fully human as well as fully divine" reduces itself to this issue: Did Jesus know desire? From the New Testament story of his temptation on the mountain top, we know that Jesus reports feeling the same pulls we do when what is forbidden is offered to him. One cannot claim to be tempted by what arouses no desire or holds no attraction. We need not go so far as some do and imagine a sex life for Jesus, a "last temptation" on the cross. There is nothing sacrilegious in such a thought, since we know God was deeply involved in constructing the mechanisms of sex.

However, we fail to understand the divine if we cannot fathom how Jesus handles his own desires. He felt them, just as God does eternally and as we humans do frequently; that much is sure. Jesus probably felt the power of desire more deeply than some of us, which reflects the depth of his humanity. But he was not overpowered by those pulls; that is what makes for divinity. This does not mean that Jesus never moved to satisfy his desires. We know he did, because he ate and drank with publicans and sinners. Nevertheless, any desire that is divine in origin never allows itself to act so as to be fulfilled selfishly.

On rare occasions, we human individuals conform to this gracious rule, but such self-effacing action is an exception for us. Our acts often center on ourselves; God's do not need to. Of course, we become skillful in claiming that our desired satisfactions are also in the best interests of those whom we need for our fulfillment. We tend to argue that what is good for our satisfaction is also good for others. Sometimes this is happily true. Enjoyment can be mutual, but such coincidence is more rare than our desire-blindness usually allows us to admit.

To know a desire which requires that we take from others what they have and what we need for our fulfillment, to possess the power to coerce and yet never to fulfill desire selfishly or damage another for our own ends -- such control of desire reflects the presence and the action of a divine power. If in his relationships with others Jesus exercised this constantly, he was divine. Where we find desire unselfconsciously and unselfishly controlled, one can see God present.

Where we find raw desire powerfully felt and openly responded to, we are with humanity.

Imagine a passionless world. In many ways, to live in such an atmosphere would be a relief, particularly if you have just been driven to distraction by some desire that wouldn't quit. God is sometimes imagined to embody a state that lies beyond the reach of desire. If the divine were like that, it would leave much of the world unaccounted for. If God really is passionless, then sensational magazines and sexy novels take on proportions which nothing in the divine can explain. If God is affected by no internal passion, why does it loom so large in our created world? Of course, some see the rage of passion as solely the work of the Devil. He is the monster who walks down 42nd Street in New York while God sits quietly at prayer or in meditation in St. Patrick's Cathedral.

Yet the very existence of the Devil and his strong passions tells us something about God. Surely the Devil feels no attraction which God does not experience. But he is "the Devil" just because he cannot control himself/herself and so is driven to extreme action in a desperate attempt to gain the needed satisfactions. We sometimes think of God, then, as "in control of the Devil." Nothing any Satan conspires for or urges on us is foreign to God, except yielding to act.

God actually feels all that presses in on us and more. Divinity just does not yield or allow itself to let go. Of course, this means that God does miss the pleasure that comes with an act of absolute abandonment, except as the divine life may experience it vicariously. However, we can be sure that in the beginning God rejected a passionless world as being too unexciting to be worth creating, particularly given evolution's long and agonizing time span. Divinity opted for greater tension and for greater excitement, but also for greater destruction. God can stand it, although often it seems to be too much for us, as our frantic actions indicate.

7. GOD CANNOT AVOID EVIL

We depict the Gods, whose pictures we carry about with us, as "pure beings." If we are right, heaven should be both peaceful and easily governed. Strange, isn't it, how we censor God's portrait for our own creature-comfort when we should consider, not what we can stand up to, but what God is able to bear. And there is little evidence in history that God either can or wants to avoid all evil. After all, according to the biblical story, the rebellion against God broke out in heaven within the ranks of the divine choir. The devil was (is) an angel, as all who have ever been attracted by one agree. If God were fully pure, if divinity does not now and never has known evil, it would seem that the created world would be like God in kind, even if to a lesser degree. But we know that life in our world is not made up of various shades of goodness. Powerful and destructive forces stalk our every step by night and by day. Heaven must have its problems of law and order too.

Religious leaders and theologians have tried to prove that what we call evil is only a lesser form of good. In spite of this claim, the world we face exhibits powerfully destructive features. If "the godfather" has kindly qualities and a respect for his ancestral religion, the blood bath that spills out around him belies his innocence. "God the Father" may be more agreeable in his motives than the underworldly "godfather," but the Mafia was in God's created world-plan too. If in fact God has strong male as well as female characteristics, we cannot go beyond this aspect of God's creation either. Thus, when our world is rocked by a war between male and female forces which are identical neither in kind nor in intent, God experiences these same divisions in the divine being. What is divine is able to prevent evil from destroying its nature, but it does not avoid evil in what is created. If divinity did this, it would spread a false image of what life with "God the Father" is really like. Such life is not so much beyond all evil as that the divine actions control what otherwise would be destructive.

If we are forced to admit that the origin of the destructive forces which terrorize us lie internal to God's own nature, we may have to rethink our relationship to God radically. The experiences in which we meet the divine cannot be solely the sweet, contemplative, pastoral homecoming we desire when we are exhausted from combat. In the first place, if evil lies at the base of things, spouting both blind and shrewdly calculated destruction, we should face it just as God does and stop trying to explain it away in the name of divinity. We have to learn to treat evil as an internal tendency and power, one that requires constant vigilance and counter-pressure. If we realize that God is not able to avoid evil just because the origin of such power is interior to the divine nature, this teaches us something important about the possible success of any human moral crusade. The enemy may appear to us to lie outside, but the source of part of its power for any campaign that an evil force wages lies both internal to our nature and to God's.

Evil, then, could not wield the destructive power against us which it does if human nature were not split internally. We are so often our own worst enemy as well as our own best ally. If God cannot hold back every expression of evil and still remain honest with the divine self, at least what is divine never allows itself to become its own worst enemy, as we so often do. God knows friend from foe (that is the chief meaning of 'omniscience'), while we evidence our human frailty by blindly feeding the very flames of our own destruction. Too often we reject friends who only want to help and are misled into accepting enemies.

We will miss seeing God if we pretend that evil does not have a power of its own, or if we try to avoid evil in a blind way that God does not do. Actually, we come face to face with God when we acknowledge destruction's origin as internal to the divine life too. Yet, we alone can never counter evil in such a way that it is finally overcome. All we can do is to immunize its destructive powers temporarily. If God cannot avoid evil, how can we hope to? Answer: God alone retains the power to act for evil's total demise.

In your mind's eye, picture heaven as without evil and destruction. This is how many imagine it to be. However, the dullness of such a vision puts others off. Who wants to go on and on and on with no variation in temperature or emotional pressure? Yet all of us want one day to escape the constant threat of destruction, and the Christian symbol of the resurrection tells us that this is, or will become, possible -- "one day". But if the ongoing evil is interior so that even God cannot escape it, we can never be rid of evil -- at least in our present world -- unless we get rid of God too.

In creation, God had to allow some degree of destruction to enter in order to be honest with us about the powers raging internally internal to divinity's existence. But nothing forced God to allow for any certain degree of corrosive evil. In God's own life, that which has divine power can hold evil expressionless. The symbol of "being in God's own hands" means to be held above destruction. Our new image of heaven, then, should be one of a place of variety. It is a state where everything conceivable can be thought and felt, yet one where the control of all expression and action still remains in our hands. We can never get rid of the origin of evil, but we can do away with the kind of uncontrolled indulgence that induces destruction. God's action can always be free; ours cannot be -- yet. Nevertheless, God willing, evil will eventually be kept in bounds. That's what heaven is all about.

8. GOD CANNOT PREDICT THE FUTURE IN DETAIL

Our own uncertainty about the future leads us to attribute to God a certainty we do not have: a knowledge of future events in their every detail. Uncertainty appears to us as a disadvantage, so we remove it from God by guaranteeing divinity a security in its knowledge of future events. All this represents a gigantic projection onto God of our own wish-fulfillment. If God is able to handle uncertainty and to resist the temptation to enforce a rigid necessity on events, such an openness to the future might be the greatest divine joy. Perhaps the openness of the future and the contingencies of freedom are to God worth all the uncertainty they involve. If so, a world predetermined down to its smallest detail would neither please God nor give the divine life the feeling of power and control which theologians often think it should. Predestination might actually frustrate God, because it does not express the core of divinity's own freedom. If God prizes freedom and the contingency of decision and self-control above all else, a world which did not reflect this could not be a divine creation. A world of eternal fixity would elude God's own preferred mode of understanding and cause God pain, just because such a world is so little like the divine power which acts to create.

If one enjoys freedom and the exercise of contingent decision, nothing is more frustrating than unchangeability. Likewise, nothing could be more exciting than the risk of uncertainty. If we view our future as held open to us by our will, this creative imagination provides a basis for understanding God's enthusiasm over the uncertainties of life. In a precarious world, God sees us as acting in the divine image. The *imago dei* is uncertainty, not certainty. Only the weak, not the strong, avoid uncertainty. Nothing in the future can fall outside God's calculation of the odds for how events might turn out. Contingency presents no challenge to a divine power to act, or at least the threat is not enough to force God to slap rigid controls on human behavior. God does not feel the need, as we weaklings might, to eliminate contingent decision or human caprice even if it is malevolent. Destruction is not presently controlled by divine act. To be sure, human behavior is all too disappointingly predictable. Authentic rebels are an exception to the rule.

Prometheus is an oddity among the league of flattering conformers who hover around the divine court -- and God is a secret admirer of Prometheus' daring. God keeps open the possibility for an unusual nonconformist and hopes that humanity won't fail completely. "God loveth a cheerful rebel." Freedom can be destructive, but the rare and spectacular use of this divine power to act to open new worlds made God willing to forego plotting out and enforcing a single predictable future. That was too dull and unsportsmanlike an act for a strong being to stoop to. Of course, some persons acquire a skill in predicting and determining the future. When we are alert, very little surprises us, even if the outcome of events is different from our prediction. So too, God is not shocked by deviations from the divine calculations. Neither our capricious behavior nor the uncertainty of the future falls outside the bounds of what God expects. Our idiosyncratic additions amuse the divine consciousness as our lives unfold. There is in fact all too much predictability in human affairs.

God may be mocked but cannot be shocked. Divinity knows the limits of possibility, and the divine self is skilled in probability prediction. In fact, God invented that game. Since the divine self-confidence is high, it can afford to take risks. God feels no need to force us into a system of strict control just to secure divinity's protection. Actually, we are the ones who plead for a fixed future, not God. The divine power is fully adequate to sustain itself against uncertainty. To confront the fact that certainty is a human, not a divine, demand is to discover one central feature of God's nature and the key to the divine mode of action.

Imagine what would happen if divinity ventured to predict a date for the end of the world, and then found itself wrong. Could a divine ego live down the disgrace? I think God would probably laugh about it and explain to us that all the factors once looked as if they were headed for a destructive climax. But then all this did not go ahead to happen of its own accord, and God did not want to intervene to bring the divine expectations about, although a divine act could have. Other events also entered in which held back the final end. Imagine God with a computer of infinite size and capacity. It answers questions instantaneously on the basis of the evidence the divine intelligence gives it.

The problem in predicting the future is that we keep changing the relevant evidence. We could predict the future if we could enforce one option against all others, as God can, but what is divine seldom chooses to live its life that way. The openness of our future reflects God's self-chosen lifestyle. However, we humans make a mistake if we try to copy this openness but forget that we seldom have sufficient power to control every eventuality, something which God does just as easily as divinity moves to act. The future is more fun if we accept it as our contingent decisions move it along. Surely life is less a matter of anguish if we accept both its openness and our own limitations of control.

9. GOD CANNOT ABANDON THOUGHT

Dionysius, Meister Eckhart, and countless others with a mystical inclination have said that, ultimately, God lives the divine life above the final grasp of thought. If so, we must reach God by perfecting some method of contemplation; we must learn to surpass thought. We may reach apprehension but not comprehension, as Anselm put it, or at least we must set thought aside at some point in our divine quest. Of course, we may ask: Does rational, discursive thought, powerful as it can be, represent only a secondary level? If it does, to know God we must move "beyond thought" and its way of dividing and limiting and categorizing.

However, the way of the mystic often assumes 'unity' as God's primary characteristic. It sometimes believes that all human thought is locked in an impasse which our way of thinking itself cannot resolve. That is a Zen Buddhist claim, but it may or may not be the case. If it is not, then to learn that God is unable to abandon all thought is to discover one central fact about the divine nature. That is, God is inescapably complex both in the divine life itself and in its action in our world.

If God is condemned continually to think without letup, this is because the not-yet-fully-determined qualities of the divine nature require it. That is, a God already set in fixed ways, one who has fixed the future firmly in total control, such a God has no need to think continually. However, if indeterminacy remains and if contingency is characteristic of all that is real, then to abandon thought would be to risk losing command of the situation. The world of nature is not out of God's control, but it remains in the divine grasp only because such a will refuses to abandon thought. Instead of letting go, divine thought works to keep God appraised of all free and contingent acts. Divinity has allowed neither its own nature nor our human future to become fixed. This testifies to God's continual willingness to rely on thought as a chosen instrument of adjustment and control.

The indeterminacy of both God's nature and humanity's future requires God to hold on to thought. Our minds, then, are not such inadequate instruments for approaching God as some have said. Of course, if God is unable to abandon thought, this is partly because divinity cannot rid its life of affection and all that results from emotional attachment. Feelings are less subject to rigid control than either physical nature or human thought, a fact which Modern philosophers realized and so hoped to escape emotion's inconsistencies. But if thought is necessary for God, this tells us something about the divine existence as a feeling, willing, deciding being. Active thought is a truer expression than is the supposed image of the divine life as one of pure contemplation beyond all knowing. God needs thought, as we all do, precisely because the divine life is made up of more than thought, for example, willing and affection. Descartes may be essentially a thinking being, but not God. Emotion and will are important avenues of approach to God although such paths are not crowded with philosophers.

Thought can apprehend things of a nature other than and different from its own. Thought which is so flexible testifies to God's complex life and to the infinite aspects which inform it. The divine attributes or characteristics may not be absolutely infinite, as Spinoza thought they were, but certainly the divine nature does not hold God neatly to a rigid pattern of uniform action. God needs thought if divinity is to encompass its own multiplicity and still direct outward action with an assured measure of control.

Freedom is useless to us unless it is backed up by the calculations which constant thought can provide. Those who want necessity to control their lives begin by putting thought aside and depreciating it as representing an inferior level of human attainment. On the contrary, God cannot afford not to think. To realize why this is so is to understand something of the dynamics of the divine nature. God is God because he/she is alert to follow every new suggestion which thought offers and feelings prompt. It is said that "Zen detests every kind of intellectuality." The lesson which we are given in the classical Zen text, The Ox and the Herdsman, is this: However far conceptual understanding takes you, it can never grasp the nature of things. This is an interesting viewpoint, and Zen Buddhism is quite powerful in its critique of our uncritical confidence in the power of thought. Zen suggests that thought itself may often be our problem. However, even this position must not be adopted uncritically.

The issue is: What is reality like? Ultimately, can it be grasped by thought or not? And what is God like? What role, if any, does thought play in the divine life? What about freedom and will? The interesting thing to note is that how we answer these questions does not so much depend on the nature of thought as on the element of freedom and contingency we find in life and also on the importance we assign to emotion and feeling. If divinity is not determined but is basically free and contingent, God needs thought as an instrument of decision. If reality is partly constructed by free human action, we cannot afford to abandon thought. We sometimes wish we could restrict its role, to turn it off or to rise above it. But even when thought frustrates us by leading us nowhere, our need is to purify rather than to eliminate it.

10. GOD CANNOT DENY THE DIVINE WILL

Theologians often want to eliminate volition from the divine nature because it is such a difficult concept to handle. But think of how God must feel about all this. It would simplify the divine life greatly, as well as add immeasurably to its pleasure, if it could set its will aside and merely enjoy a secure life of self-contemplation, as Aristotle postulated. Yet, for men and women as well as for God, it is the strength of will that provides the crucial ingredient needed to keep us alert and on course. Will is that element without which human life would fall into fruitless routine. Will is that without which all our good intentions would collapse into the effortless, but also unfruitful, dreams of youth. And God is eternally young, but not in the sense that divinity can easily dream up any fulfillment it desires -- that favorite pastime of students when their professor's lecture ceases to attract them. God may feel a desire to "get away from it all," but divine maturity involves the cold knowledge that, if the divine will should relax for a moment, the best of its intentions would simply evaporate into a memory.

Will is our key if we want to mold the future to become what we intend for ourselves. God knows this with a clarity which we human beings cannot maintain consistently. We need to relax and to forget from time to time. But while we relax, like Sampson, we often have our determination subverted. God knows how to use the lightness of humor; divinity can allow itself to rest from its labors. But God's alertness still never lapses and neither can its power ever unintentionally be diverted nor its action be impeded, except by divine restraint.

While he slept, Sampson's hair was cut, and thus his strength depleted. We can say that God may smile or grimace, laugh or rest, but that he never sleeps. Men and animals alone enjoy this pleasure; God sustains constant consciousness voluntarily. The power which the divine will can release holds both itself and all of creation together. If God were ever to deny the divine will, the world would come down in shambles around our heads, like Sampson's temple. We human beings also depend on other people to maintain our good intentions in what we promise to do. We stand by and watch the various enterprises of our friends falter, along with our own, whenever we cannot sustain human determination. When we no longer have the desire to go on, or when we shift and think that some new course is more advantageous, we are in a dangerous hour. God could have a faulty will, such as some of us are cursed with, but the stability of Nature and the exactitude possible in science argue against this being the case. God's will is steadfast.

Of course, for God to change the divine will is not the same as to deny what has been willed by it before. Occasional shifts are needed, if divinity is to accommodate to the freely elected decisions which men and women make. On the other hand, some of us are stubborn and refuse to change our earlier conclusions even when circumstances have been altered. Such inflexibility gets human beings into just as much trouble as a weak will that can't remain consistent. But God has the flexibility needed to adjust to novelty. What is divine maintains an agility most of us lose with age, although what is divine never denies its will once it is committed. It will never be necessary to sue God for breach of contract or charge divinity with failure to deliver on a promise. Nevertheless, the results of what God wills are neither fully visible now nor are they entirely finished in their form. God's actions always tend toward some future climax, one which counts on the divine will to sustain it when the time arrives and a decisive act is needed.

The successors of Christ who claim the title as the head of his visible church are also the successors to the man who denied Christ three times during his trial. This symbol reminds us of the fact that, no matter how adamantly men and women protest their loyalty, the human scene is as much built on betrayal and denial as it is on steadfastness. Jesus sensed this irresoluteness in his devoted followers. Yet, he neither ranted and raved against them nor did he try to prevent their desertion. Thus, any church and its leadership is built of frail substance, but a religious community can serve a divine purpose in spite of this fallibility. Evidently God is able to accept an imperfect situation and still work with the changes and infirmities inherent in the human will. God will never deny the divine will once it is committed. But divinity has elected to work through creatures who differ with what is divine most noticeably by their lack of this quality. To change one's mind is human; to remain steadfast in decision is divine.

11. GOD CANNOT ACCEPT COERCION

God's attitude toward the use of brute force may at first seem a little strange. Anyone who possesses the unlimited power that divinity does certainly is at liberty to achieve its ends in any way that it wills. Only we whose power reserves are questionable and precarious become calculating and hesitant about employing every available power to act. We frail humans must be cautious to be sure that we do not stir up a reaction that goes beyond our ability to contain. Since God can handle any rebellion that the divine nature chooses to confront, divinity is free to use its power as it wills. Why, then, does God refuse to use coercion now to accomplish divinely announced ends? Men and women observe no such scruple, and God is a being not of placidity but of potentially devastating power to act.

In order to understand this self-restraint on God's part concerning the use of force, we must look, not to power alone, but to God's other attributes. God embodies the basic qualities of a person, that is, understanding, will, power, emotion. Thus, the divine nature is a respecter of persons. It would violate the limits which it has established for itself if the divine allowed power to dominate its actions. To use force on someone beneath its divine status might accomplish its intent in an overt way. Still, to do so would destroy the integrity of the weaker person against whom such superior force might be deployed. God could simply order each individual in the world of Nature to obey. If divinity did, the destruction which now is so rampant could be curtailed, but in the process all initiative and freedom would also be blocked. The divine will could do this, although it seldom uses such coercive power even when it is available. We humans are less scrupulous in our attempts to enforce our will.

Of course, it is clear that God does not prohibit the use of all force. The destructive powers that run wild in the world give lavish testimony to divinity's steel-like nerve. God turns lesser destructive powers loose on us, but these are only minor powers in the divine arsenal. Still, they are sufficiently destructive to annihilate millions. Why, then, does what is divine hesitate to use its personal force on us, especially when its aims are often so much more admirable than ours and thus deserve every available advantage? Because the challengers would not be evenly matched in such a game of strength. Divinity, who has the power needed to save us, ironically is handicapped in its effectiveness, because God eschews all force that involves the destruction of human integrity. God's good intentions to help us are weakened by virtue of a divine decision to forego the use of coercion. It seems a strange God who places itself and us in such an unnecessarily vulnerable position.

How can we explain this oddity? We have said that God does not allow the divine will to use force against persons to insure their compliance. Still, God does sometimes move against destruction. But for the present, divinity acts only with one hand tied behind its back. Nothing ultimately prevents God from acting to reduce all the brutality in humanity and in nature to helplessness. That which is divine can force all to come within its control, just because it remains free and in command of its will. For now, however, God attempts to reach the divine goals without the use of force, because divinity is a respecter of persons. Yet this restraint places an incredible burden on our human ability to respond to the excessive demands placed on us by any emotion, including hate. God leaves us free to face a sometimes devastating choice.

The novels we read, our newspaper accounts of crime and politics, are full of stories about the force which one person imposes on another. Even when applied for constructive vs. destructive purposes, pressure is the name of the game for those who want to get ahead. If no one used force against another, what would fill our TV screens and our police rosters each day? How can what is a monumental fact of our life be shunned by God in divinity's own activity? We know that God could win the game of power-play without even trying.

We often accomplish good things by applying pressure; sometimes this works. But as often as not we destroy or cripple someone by our use of excessive force. Our acts often misfire. God accepts the risk of using a less direct avenue to the divine goal because divinity will not damage another person for its own laudable purposes. God does this even though such self-restraint often means loss by default. God would make a poor novelist or politician. Any being which is divine shuns what we consider to be an essential part of the human way of life. Occasionally God acts in a way dramatic enough for newspaper copy, but on the whole divinity plays a quiet waiting game. In fact, God is so unobtrusive that many overlook both the divine presence and the potential power that God's will holds in trust for its future action.

12. GOD CANNOT BE CAPTURED IN ONE WAY

All that is divine is by nature elusive. We pursue human self-understanding with intensity, and out attempts to know other people are equally fascinating. Little do we realize that God is the most difficult of all beings to pin down. This is not due to sheer perversity on divinity's part. God has no fear, as we do, about being committed or confined by being understood. Of course, that which is divine may shift and move away, just as our net of understanding is about to come down around it. But this is not an elaborate sport on divinity's part which it plays simply to indulge in the art of gamesmanship. We have a horror of being tied down if we give a too open disclosure of our thought and activity. Our freedom might be compromised by too much outside scrutiny. The reasons for God's elusiveness are different; the divine ability to act is always free.

God's nature does not, as has sometimes been said, exceed our grasp because it lies beyond human conception. Humans can think any thought about God they want to. We are, however, more like divinity in mind and in affection than in body. Yet, we must begin with the body -- an aspect we often miss, a miscalculation which tends to throw us off balance at the start of our search. Although we may at first try to hold on to divinity with a single concept, whether it be Good or Unity or Holiness, God is too complex to be grasped that easily. If we could unite and hold a whole constellation of concepts and attributes in our mind at one time, that would come the closest to letting us grasp God.

The irony is that such a multiplicity of concepts has an inherent fluidity that stretches beyond the moment. A loose collection may hold momentarily but then shift and become inadequate as an instrument to grasp God, particularly if we do not constantly adjust our ideas and our actions. We need to hold our thoughts in exactly the right balance for each new situation. If God does not always choose to hold the same relationship to the world, then we need to change our fixed concepts from time to time. This required subtlety is easily overlooked if we are not careful. Oddly enough, we tend to treat God too simply, which does not do justice to divinity's vast and complex nature. This is true even though the divine does hold itself in a unity of thought and action.

In spite of the fact that God does not live beyond all thought, the concepts we use do not carry the energy needed to hold the divine still enough for our thought to grasp it. Concepts have flexibility and a capacity to create both pleasure and a powerful human insight, but we often confuse the power of a concept with the insight and pleasure it arouses, and so we do not see its difference from effective action. When we do this, we are misled if we expect to capture God simply by using the same tools that others have used. That is, we cannot simply and continually repeat a once successful formula. Yet it is disconcerting for us to learn that what once worked to lead some to God may not work for us in the same manner in our time. Then, in sullen reaction, we assert either that the formula is not valid or that the ritual is false and cannot evoke God. Actually, what happened is that we mistook the discovery of what once was for some an effective avenue as a guarantee that all can accomplish such an intricate journey successfully. We forgot that God does not always respond to the same call or submit to the same intellectual approach each time. Divinity would be false to its nature if it did.

This lack of consistency is not because God is moody and perverse. On the contrary, if divinity allowed its nature to be held in strict identification with any one verbal expression or ritual act, this would be easier for us. But we might also be misled. This is particularly true if we expect God to appear automatically when certain words are uttered or specific acts are performed. Divinity's own acts are not subject to such fixity. If they were, it might give us the idea that our concepts hold more power than they do, that words are equal to actions. However, we all know that the right words can still do wonders on the right occasion, even for God. Nevertheless, divinity cannot allow itself to be captured in any one way or domesticated by any liturgical routine. To do so would deprive divinity of its most prized attribute, freedom. This freedom which divinity guards -- for example, not to appear to us if God so chooses -- is as disconcerting to our desire for security as it is essential to the exercise of divine power. On the other hand, it also leaves divinity free to overlook the score in the human game -- if it wants to. Because divinity keeps itself beyond our verbal control, the divine will remains free to release the power needed to save us all -- if it will.

For centuries now, each new religion and each new spiritual leader has offered us a formula for capturing God. Each one tells us: All you need to do is follow the way I have outlined. Amazingly enough, many of these suggestions do work. When they do, a new religious movement is born. The perplexing thing about the formulas outlined for pinning God down is that there is more than one, and their number continues to increase. Furthermore, even classically successful ways to approach God grow cold with time. Religious fervor, once held at a fever pitch, will cool with age. Vivid religious insights fade. Even God's actions are not always recognized as divine.

God clearly intended no one spiritual path to remain open to us at all times. If we accept this conclusion, we know that we should never rely too rigidly on any past success, whether it is one we have developed ourselves or that of some earlier religious seer. We are continually forced to search out for ourselves new avenues to God that fit the time, the place, and the people. Divinity relates itself to time in various ways; therefore this does not mean that all the approaches we map out will be equally valid or successful, nor does it mean that everyone who claims to offer us a way to God has actually found the divine once and for all. All it means is that the search for God requires a constant state of alertness and a keen sense of the novel.

13. GOD CANNOT DENY THE HOLOCAUST

It is not intellectual speculation, but rather devastating destruction, that has recently raised the question of God for us. Descartes' arguments intrigue some who have a philosophical turn of mind and who are disposed to consider 'proofs' for God's existence. Saint Anselm's "ontological argument" still remains a constant source of intellectual controversy. For the public at large, however, it is the recent tales of horror and mass destruction that have most vividly raised questions about God. This is particularly true for Jews, who suffered the most dramatic and publicized holocaust at the hands of the Nazis. Still, we all know that holocausts have gone on in other lands involving other peoples not quite so marked by religion. Thus, all ideas of cultural progress, or of the gradual uplift of humanity along a scale of increased sophistication, must be abandoned. We know that horror comes from the intellectually advanced as well as from the primitive. Destruction knows no time or place. It is as much at home in universities as in rural villages.

Where God and human loss are concerned, it is interesting to note that passing through wanton destruction does not automatically remove all belief in God. However, it does not make belief automatic either. The letters and records of those who move through these experiences show us some who disintegrate and lose all semblance of belief vs. others whose belief in God is radically transformed but deepened. But as we might suspect, nothing remains quite the same after a whirlwind of destruction has passed by. But the torrent of writing, TV spectaculars, etc. which make the holocaust vivid indicate that such a devastating experience can even be productive. It is hard to imagine Solzhenitsyn without the Gulag Archipelago. Would Elie Wiesel have become a powerful storyteller if he had been left to grow up quietly in a remote East European village and not been uprooted by the winds of destruction?.

Still, the productivity of such an experience -- when it does not totally destroy those involved -- is not the most important point. What kind of God is compatible with such an experience of waste and destruction and the degradation of human life? If you live on beyond an experience of total death, certainly one result is a new view of life and God. Most obviously, all easy and sweet views of God disappear, as do all notions that somehow religious belief will protect the believer and automatically grant him or her their heart's desire. And in any holocaust the good suffer with the bad, the pious along with the disbeliever. Thus, the function of prayer must be rethought too. Thousands, if not millions, have prayed to God for delivery from threatened destruction. Only a few survived, and surely this includes some who did not even implore God to release them. Furthermore, the direct involvement of God in human affairs can't be very extensive, and at best it is infrequent. Nor can the occasional divine appearances or saving Acts be very closely correlated to times of desperate need. Divinity may make itself available to individuals at isolated times, but its direct intervention by action certainly is minimal, even if it is crucial when it does appear.

However, it is the status of evil in God's nature which forces on us a reconception of divinity. Certainly one may cease to believe in God as a result of experiencing the overwhelming evil of a holocaust. When this happens, a failure to explain the presence of evil satisfactorily may be the cause. For evil now lies close to God. Minor evils can be explained leaving God at a distance and can even be attributed to

God's intention to provide us with moral instruction. But major, wanton destruction serves no recognizable constructive purpose. And, if it is so pervasive, it must lie close to God's central design.

Some faults in our world, of course, can be explained by claiming that they do not appear as evil in God's sight but only in ours. However, surely such an event as a holocaust does not appear 'good' to God in any sense of the word. All our attempts to make evil out to be merely a product of our limited human perspective, unknown as such by God, fail now. Either God understands such devastation just as we do, or else such a divinity is of no religious service to us in trying to explain that experience. Furthermore, the notion that such waste of human life somehow serves God's ultimate purpose, at least in any simple way, is equally repugnant. The fully rational God of Descartes, Spinoza, and Leibniz becomes useless to us. By themselves, rational principles fail to explain mass destruction, even if an appeal to the great benefits derived from experiencing evil offers a plausible account of minor ills. It is hard, if not impossible, to work a holocaust into a rationally devised scheme. We must, then, be dealing with a God whose nature and actions involve a wider latitude than rational principles which, if they were to dominate, would allow.

Furthermore, any view of the world's process as being necessary" or "predestined" by God is not only unhelpful but actually repellent where holocausts are concerned. It is shocking even to consider that God not only knew about but actually plotted such destruction from eternity. We can hide some mysteries in the inscrutability of God's nature and divinity's future plan, but not a holocaust. Thus, freedom and the will to act become absolutely essential as divine attributes for any picture of a holocaust God. And contingency and chance are equally important. We must be dealing with a God who takes great risks and whose mode of control is at best quite loose -- at least presently. We face a God with a policy of noninterference, one who consciously created us with a greater capacity for evil and destruction than any aim to enhance good in the world could ever account for. And divinity did this in place of other "good" options open to it, some more preferable from a human point of view.

Such a God, certainly, is not easy or comfortable to believe in, but that need not be so great a difficulty for organized religion as it might seem. Easy and obvious as Descartes' God is, few have come to believe in such a divinity on the basis of rational necessity alone. Once our romantic views of life have been exploded by passing through a holocaust, only a God who is more difficult to deal with seems likely to account for a harsh world. Theologians who follow Hegel's lead thought for a long time thought that God might be found working through advances in culture, primarily Hebraic or Western. But since Western culture has produced some of the greatest holocausts, God must be divorced from any attachment to the achievements of any culture. Otherwise, divinity falls victim to these devastations too. Whatever advantages 'advanced' cultures bring to us, they do not save us from evil. If high cultures really represent God's intentions for humanity, then God's program must often receive a harsh evaluation.

The highest achievements of culture and science lead just as easily to death camps and nausea as they do to a comfortable God and an easy celebration of life. Religious institutions at best get a mixed score as God's representatives in a time of holocaust. Divinity may have its deputies on earth, but it is heroic individuals, and not always those highest in the church hierarchy, who exhibit what we call "the spirit of God" by their actions in the face of destruction. In fact, the higher they are in church hierarchies the less free do officials seem to be to speak out. They may represent God well in ceremony but not so effectively in the face of destruction.

Does all this mean that Christians must abandon the notion of God as loving or as entering into human life to share it? Not necessarily, but certainly the holocaust does tell us that the meaning of 'love' must be rethought. And it always has been just as much a mystery as it is a pleasure. Romantic love is surely ruled out where God is concerned, since even intense suffering is not excluded in the divine scheme. Love either does not, or perhaps will not, always intervene to prevent destruction. God may enter into our human experience, but any overtone of triumphalism in religion must be abandoned -- except where future action is anticipated. This is partly because God's presence often goes unrecognized, and surely it has little effect on the course of public life and political events. We see few overt examples of the notion that God "rules the world." If we claim this it would have to involve both what we cannot see and God's future action as yet unrealized. Otherwise we cannot make sense of that idea, given the world around us.

Any God who survives the holocaust will remain largely unseen on the face of history. If we insist on trying to see divinity there, it can only be during times of triumph, not when destruction falls on us. Any experience of holocaust returns a sense of mystery to life that can never be dispelled. Furthermore, we must be careful about romanticizing the depth of mystery in our experience of God by saying that it "explains" much. At best, our romanticizing postpones understanding; at worst, it destroys the possibility of revelation. Of course, the rationalist's impulse is to get rid of all mystery, if he or she can, but that attempt assumes that all phenomena can be given an overt and a rational explanation, which is what Freud thought true of the psyche too. Of course, "mystery" simply means that a final explanation now exceeds our powers, whereas the rationalist posture is that nothing exceeds the grasp of a modern scientifically based reason. The way God operates is something one must be divine to fathom fully, we are often told.

Neither the world nor God is in the grip of any fixed necessity, since what is fixed in its course can be explained without residue or mystery, as Aristotle noted centuries ago. Instead, our experience tells us that there must still be, in the life of God as well as in ours, indeterminate events and contingencies which depend on the future decisions of a will, both divine and human. Power must not have been clearly assigned to stay in positive channels if it can spill over into destruction so easily. Rationality thus leads as easily to evil as to good, a possibility the Rationalist prefers to avoid.

Reason may calculate, but neither in God nor in human nature does it appear of itself to specify only one right action. We are all capable of setting aside any course of action offered to us, no matter how "good" it may be, and acting in contradiction to it. God's will and power may move with considerable independence from the calculations of the divine reason. Even divinity's attraction to what is good does not control its decisions in any simple sense. What is simply venturesome must exert some independent attraction on God. It is not the good alone which moves divinity to act, neither now nor perhaps even in the future. To think that this is divinity's ultimate intent is the meaning of 'faith'.

Evidently, God moves neither easily nor automatically toward any intervention in our affairs. In this respect, the divine power of restraint exceeds ours considerably. We need not conclude that God is indifferent to human tragedy, but at least we know that the divine can keep its hand away from physical intervention in our affairs, even in the face of extreme need. Whether God is always spiritually present and available to us is another matter. If the divine is, this may be comforting to some, although it produces no mass effect on all of humanity, only on a few. And if God does work individually and not on the scale of history and cultures, the effect at present is at best minimized or reduced. Ironically, it comes nowhere near the power exercised by tyrants. It is hard to side with a God who restricts the use of divinity's own power where destructive evil is concerned, although this precludes neither God's intervention in a more public way in the future nor our acceptance of such a divine promise at any time. However, a belief in this possibility does not rest on any conclusive evidence of obvious divine intrusion in our past or in the present.

In the presence of a holocaust-God, danger always threatens. If we still believe divinity can or will save us from danger, our faith will have to rest on evidence other than the holocaust. In the midst of destruction, there are some who come to feel even more certain that God supports them, but not in the sense of their being removed from danger or spared the loss of life. Some who were part of the Nazi holocaust strangely reported an increasing sense of the closeness of God, but their lives were seldom automatically spared as a result.

The holocaust-God may not himself demand our sacrifice, in some primitive sense, but evidently such a divinity allows it. Thus, the divine sense of time and urgency cannot be ours. Although God converts some decisions to a long-range perspective in the midst of a holocaust, the outward result is still loss or destruction. To live through a holocaust, God obviously must have both great power and strength of will. The question we are each left to ponder is whether we believe this power to be strong enough to rescue us from the jaws of hell at the world's end. Can we trust in God's unwavering determination to release us with a final stroke? -- by an act perhaps necessarily more powerful than that which ordained universes to unfold into being during evolutionary ages.

14. GOD CANNOT SPEAK TO US DIRECTLY

Except to a very few, in the present age God does not seem to
"speak" to us, at least in any obvious or ordinary meaning of that term.
Still, many claim that God has spoken (or acted) in the past, and there
are individuals who assert that God now addresses words to them
directly, and they feel that sometimes divinity even intervenes. The
important point is that, even if we have heard such powerful words or
felt the force of a divine Act, these experiences are still subject to an
element of strangeness. Any voice that is heard but not seen does not
come to us in the usual manner, and the same is true of powerful acts
of an unseen origin. Whether in individual cases or in sacred
literature, the "speaking" of God may be described as the hearing of a
voice. Yet any claim to "hear" God is never asserted to be an ordinary
case of speaking. Therefore, if we are to explain what we mean when
we say that God speaks or Acts, we will have to develop a special
sense for these terms. However, if we want to rely on such unusual
"speech," (or such power to effect) we also need more extensive
justification than a mere claim.

Some critics want to restrict us to use only the ordinary meaning of
a term, but this limitation involves certain assumptions which we must
examine before we accept this restriction. On the opposite side of the
argument, it could be said that all insight that enters our life comes
from the extra-ordinary use of terms and that ordinary use yields only
common knowledge. Plato felt that a special type of "madness" was
not to be regarded as so destructive as we might ordinarily suppose.
Quite the contrary, he believed that certain kinds of madness could be
valuable and an important source of insight. And this might be the
case with God "acting" and "speaking." That is, since it is clear that no
ordinary use of these terms can apply, if we can locate some unusual
sense, this might offer us a crucial insight concerning our knowledge
of God. In religion we must always be concerned with locating new
sources of information. If a way can be found for us to accept any
words we hear or any effects which we witness as being God's, that is a
source of knowledge that we cannot afford to overlook.

The notion that the religious explorer must undertake non-ordinary
investigations is actually quite suitable. When religion accepts the
rationalistic premise that experience must be universal and common, it
has more trouble sticking to this limitation than the average secularist.

Religion's basic materials involve sacred literature and religious experience. When we examine these, neither unusual meanings (e.g., God speaks, acts) nor extraordinary experiences (e.g., miracles) can be avoided. Any attempt to reduce these exceptional experiences to ordinary forms only destroys what religion has to offer that secular life cannot provide.

In what sense, then, will God "speak" or "act" if he does so at all? Divinity's words are recorded in our accumulated sacred literatures, but when these words are spoken, or when divine acts are spoken of, some human being is the source. In this case, how did the one who first wrote them down hear the words? The first impression we have is of a multitude of voices, each one claiming to convey God's message and to have experienced divine effects. This multiplicity of sounds is difficult to reconcile with the idea of one Being. We might assume either that God does not wish to speak with one voice or that it is the human mode of transmission which develops the variety of voices. And we assume that God speaks no single dialect or language. However, since we must hear in some particular form, any "divine word" unavoidably takes on the coloring and the complexity of a particular language.

We must ask ourselves what God's reasons might be for making both divine communication and the recovery of its meaning such a complicated process. It is more difficult than is necessary, and in the end no interpretation ever receives universal acceptance. The biblical story of the Tower of Babel gives us one answer. There God imposed a variety of tongues on us as punishment for human arrogance. In any case, religious followers must explain why we have multiple religious languages and also account for why God did not elect to use one of the most adequate and precise technical languages, which we so easily develop, for divinity's important communications. In contrast, God's speaking involves the divine choice of a complicated and a technically inferior (due to its multiplicity of voices) means of communication. God's 'action' is no less complex.

Why isn't God voice clear and direct? Why doesn't divinity answer our questions? Why is God sometimes silent? Divinity is silent as to why it did not at the outset install a more efficient universal language and a clear means of communication between the designer and those who receive that divinity's words. Furthermore, God has been silent about providing keys and rules for interpreting the non-uniform "messages" attributed to divinity in a variety of imperfect languages. Since any God could easily have spoken more definitively had it wanted to, we can only interpret this silence or inaction as a sign that God preferred to leave us alone to work out our own interpretations without providing us with an absolute guideline.

With a single stroke, God could have saved biblical students centuries of probing and inconclusive results. As his own logician, she could have developed a perfectly clear and precise language. However, God's "speaking" must also contain an irremovable element of silence at crucial points. That is, God has "spoken" by giving us our imperfect plurality of languages. And divinity has also "spoken" by what it has not done -- that is, by neither creating a perfect language nor speaking out directly in order to correct our frequent misinterpretations. Actions speak louder than words -- for God too. That is why we must look for the divine in its Acts, and not simply in any of the offered impressive words.

In this sense we can say God has spoken to us, since we can learn some of the divine intentions from examining our human situation. For instance, divinity did wish to "speak" in this inconclusive and multiple way, and it does not wish to do so in a simpler and perhaps more perfect manner. Technically, God is silent as far as direct communication goes; yet the divine actions can speak for divinity here. God has left to our discovery the details of deciphering his reasons for not speaking in a single authoritative voice. Thus, our words about God's words are always subject to a certain imprecision, and this necessitates our own involvement if any interpretation is to come forth. God's Acts are sometimes more forthright (e.g., leading Israel out of slavery), but such events are rare and subject, somewhat ironically, to later verbal misunderstandings in the reports given.

15. GOD CANNOT BE VERY RELIGIOUS

"WHY I AM NOT VERY RELIGIOUS"
(An open letter to the men and women of the world.)

"Although I am often made an object of religious devotion, I have never been able to become fully religious myself. Of course, to be 'religious' means many things, and some forms attract me more than others. I have never gone in for elaborateness or formality, although papal pomp is at times spectacularly well done and entertaining to watch. I think what holds me back from the full enjoyment of religious ritual, whether simple or elaborate, is that I cannot lose myself in it completely, as the devout worshiper tends to do.

"This difference, I think, is due to the fact that I have so much on my mind that I cannot afford the luxury of shutting out all except religious devotion. The worshiper may narrow his or her field of vision, but I must remain constantly aware of the world made up of men and women and children and other living things. The stars and galaxies and every possible universe are always on my mind too. But I think what most of all holds me back from becoming completely religious is the tendency of the human religious consciousness to focus exclusively on the good in the world, while I can never escape the forces of evil or block out my painful awareness of the destruction they reap.

"In societies and in cultures the numbers who are religiously inclined vary in proportion to those who are secularly inclined. Much as I admire some who are religious, I can never forget that I am responsible for creating the a-religious population too. Actually, I enjoy secular society a great deal. I could have blocked out such non-religious ranges of interest and made the peoples of the world to be like one large church, with constant devotion and round-the-clock religious services. But that perspective seemed a little narrow, not to mention dull, and also a little unfair to the full range of potential human experience. I blush to confess that I find the pleasures of the non-religious at times as fascinating as prayer. The dangers and the risks involved in various human adventures are attractive to me. I do not think I could be a monk, or a hermit, although I can respect such single-mindedness.

"When the world at large and humanity in general are your concern, you can only devote so much attention to religiousness, important though I consider it. The tendency of the religious consciousness is to create a divinity who satisfies that image of human desire. Yet I could not afford to be limited to such a model, unless I rejected my responsibility for the whole world and all the variety created within it. Besides, freedom is so central to my nature (although it took theologians a long time to discover this) that I cannot afford to be controlled by priests. And the tendency of all religions is to determine my actions, to tell me what I can and cannot do. I created an openness to change in human existence that I do not want to take back, partly because openness to novelty is a pervasive tendency in my own nature. I would be false to myself if I tried to deny it.

"Religious writings, of course, at times catch my nature clearly and make my people aware of me. The religions of the world, when taken together, expand human horizons. They are on the whole a better avenue to me than, say, selfish hedonism. But the problem for church and temple goers is not to become too narrow in the process of finding out what any given religion has to offer. Thus, I can never go too far with one religious form or take sides in theological controversy, because so much of it is simply another form of selfish power politics. I can't afford to endorse any single path as a privileged access to divinity, although religious leaders are always trying to force an exclusive endorsement. This does not mean that I may not appear or act so as to enter into human life or offer signs of my nature, my power, and my intentions. It is just that my own view of these actions often remains different from the forms which various religions give to them, particularly as time goes by.

"My reluctance where religious practice is concerned essentially comes about because I would be false to my complex nature if I endorsed any single religious form or way of life. Such exclusiveness is for men and women but not for Gods. It is for me to propose signs; it is for human beings to give various interpretations of my actions -- and it may be by my Acts that I am best known. But since to be religious means to narrow oneself down to one form of life or theological interpretation, I can admire those who sacrifice and will go that far, but it is not for me to follow them. Of course, I do not find all religions equally attractive. I update my evaluations constantly, since any religion, or any human religiosity, changes rapidly over time.

Some become so unrepresentative of what I consider my central core -- love -- that it takes great strength not to protest against their speaking in my name. But I keep silent. I let people judge for themselves as to where they find my presence.

"At times I have thought it would be nice to be a pope or a high church official. I like the drama and the vestments, but I can't afford the time away from the world to confine myself solely to ecclesiastical affairs. Still, the outward religious authority these officials have is attractive. Since I have myself resisted the temptation to mark out any clear and final line of authority, they do it for me. I do not want to get involved in the human quarrel over who is first or who should speak *ex cathedra*. True, my full power is always ready and in reserve, but I restrain myself and seldom show it. Churches and temples and bishops' houses are nice and sometimes even godly places, but they are still only a small part of the various divine dwelling places on earth. I must stay constantly open to be in any house, in any place, at any time where I am called or choose to appear.

"Many individuals become religious in order to shut out terror, whether psychological or physical. They want to see only the good in life. I'd like to shut out terror too, with a hymn or a prayer or a beautiful ritual. But terror is so close to me that I face it constantly. By offering a rainbow I have promised not to let terror destroy the whole of creation, although it destroys enough each day to make it impossible for me to avoid grief. Most religions try to shut out uncertainty too, but I must face it. What is more, I rather enjoy the precarious and the unpredictable in life. However, I admit that I hold the power of absolute control, whereas only a few men and women are able to hold their own world on course, and then often only for a brief period of time. I understand the tendency of humans to seek certainty and all-goodness in religion, and I do not blame them. It is just that such assurance and all-goodness is forbidden to me, since I do not want to ignore the full range of my creation.

"Almost all religions form favored groups and then appeal to me to give them special treatment. True, since I am discriminating by nature, I do not treat all peoples alike, although I do offer love to all equally. Some religions represent my desires more purely than others. But I must be wary of forming an exclusive identification with any one. Almost as sure as they feel they have my favor, they grow corrupt. True, Jews have been 'chosen', but that is very different from being 'favored', as they know all too well. You often find someone speaking in your name, claiming a special status, with whom you would rather not be identified. The problem is how to give recognition without getting tied into an unbreakable contract; how to use a representative or a group without having them turn such trust into a hammer to hit or to destroy their enemies. I would like to trust religions and religious leaders. Yet, like political power, religion too easily corrupts into an arrogant self-righteousness. A God cannot be too careful with whom he or she associates, or what commitments are made, when dealing with human beings.

"Certainly, the feeling which the sincerely religious person has that I can become wholly present to him or her, that their human concern of the moment is also mine, is not false. I can become fully present in any time and place. All that is wrong is that the religious consciousness wants to confine my whole life to that. It holds me exclusively at that place long after my time of presence is past. Like Jesus, I must be about my business, and that is why I cannot afford to lead a totally religious life myself. As necessary as the religious life is for many individuals, for one who laid the foundations of our evolving world it is too restrictive for divinity to bind itself to without relief. My heart is just as attentive to those who know no formal religious life as to those for whom it makes up their whole life. I must be a God to the secular too -- whether they are aware of it or not.

"Perhaps my point would best be summed up if I said: Religion is for men and women, not for Gods. Exclusiveness and peace and rest is not a way open to a creator-sustainer being who holds a divine status. At the very least, I would have to say that a life devoted fully to religion lies outside my grasp, at least as long as the world lasts. That is, I unleashed the terrors and the powers of destruction from the bonds that prevent devastation in my own nature. I allowed them a certain scope in creation. Until such time as these forces are brought back into full control, that is, until the lion lies down with the lamb, I cannot rest -- in spite of all the theologians who think that rest is central to the divine nature and should be desired by all.

"Actually, truly religious people are those who look forward to the day when this will happen. The "religious" are those who, so to speak, live daily in an ideal world which they believe will eventually come on earth. But too often they forget that such a new order is not yet here, except perhaps internally to some. Forces other than religious devotion are now in control of the world, and some of these constantly threaten us with destruction. A God can never afford to forget that. I cannot join with the religious in celebrating an expected future day as if it were already here.

"Of course, such a new day is within reach, in the sense that it lies within my power to act so as to bring it about. Most religions are right when they proclaim that I have promised to bring an order of peace into existence. But I am stubborn. I refuse to be pinned down to a precise date. In that sense I know less than some of my religious followers, and I am also less able to join them in the advance celebration about a future world which I still have not brought about.

"Many groups, both Marxist and Christian, have thought they could themselves usher in this new world, one in which all destruction shall be halted and all wounds healed. They claim to have divined some world-altering secrets, and sometimes I feel as if they thought that my power had passed into their hands. Actually, the power to remake the world's basic plan is one I have reserved to myself alone from creation's evolution any start. Until that strength is brought into play, I cannot relax and become exclusively religious. I hope I have explained why. I blush slightly and thank all religions for the honors they give me, even if I cannot join them -- just yet.

"Most of what I have said so far involves my personal reasons for not joining any religious organization. If I consider my responsibility to others, my reason not to unite with, or to approve any special privilege for, one religious group over another is that I must hold myself open to be the God of all Christians, of all Jews, of all religions, not just some. Of course, outside the West I have religious interests other than the specifically Christian. More than that, I can't endorse any one Christian theology, because I must remain open to all religious people, Christian or otherwise.

"I do not reject the Christian claim that Jesus represents a special revelation of my nature and intent. Nor do I believe that all religions are somehow equal and have my uncritical approval. It is just that, once a group gets the feeling that I have endorsed them exclusively or authorized some one theological view, they tend to become both lax and arrogant. Then they concentrate on preserving their privileged positions rather than on promoting my causes of love and relief for those who suffer. Jesus came preaching my word of love and forgiveness, and men and women have been fighting for control over this message ever since.

"I admit that I had something to do with the vision Peter had soon after the formation of the early Christian church. That is when Peter discovered that I did not send Jesus to the Jews alone, although Jesus was thoroughly Jewish himself, but to all people open to receive my message. The early Christians fought the battle over whether or not to open themselves to the world and thus to move away from an exclusive Jewishness. They elected non-exclusiveness then, but ever since that day they have simply turned the tables on me and acted as if I now intended a message of love and forgiveness only for members of some Christian sect. I have no objection to the formation of certain churches or groups, and I enjoy some of their worship services. But I do object to any organization that tries to tie my message down to their exclusive control and representation.

"With Jesus as my voice, I tried hard to prevent any tight ecclesiastical structure from forming, or any creedal orthodoxy from establishing itself as if that were my dominant concern. I picked someone without scholarly education, not a part of any establishment, Roman or Jewish. He spoke only orally and authorized no text, although his Acts perhaps represented me better. Alas, this has not prevented authorities from trying to tie both Jesus and me down to some fixed verbal statement and formal interpretation, as if that were my primary concern. Jesus worked by Act and by loose oral illustration, but human beings seem to require more security than such an informal way of proceeding allows. Of course, their needs are greater than mine and their powers are less. Still, I cannot endorse any one religious group or doctrine exclusively for fear of simply making matters worse.

"I think of myself as a person who Acts, and not one of words only, and as a person who Acts out of compassion and generosity, not as one who is narrow. I do not enjoy haggling over who is right and who says things correctly. I do like beauty of expression and simplicity, but my life is too varied, and too much of my nature is expressed in a variety of forms and cultures, for me to identify myself with only one mode of communication. Human beings try to reduce everything to a strict unity to enable easy police action against those who challenge them. But I am a pluralist myself. I am not seen equally in all religions, but the process of sifting the true from the false I leave to men and to women. It is their human task, and I do wish they would not shift their responsibility onto me by claiming that 1 have made them my authorized, exclusive spokespersons or issued some definitive religious document. I have enough on my mind without getting involved in religious one-upmanship!".

Yours faithfully,

*
GOD

---

* Responsible for this publication (but not for the divine action): Frederick Sontag.

POSTSCRIPT I

IS GOD AS YOU LIKE IT?

By this time, you may have discovered what God is and what God is not, in other words, how divinity Acts to reveal or to conceal itself for you. But do you like what you have found? Is the divinity whom you discovered in its Acts anything similar to what you think a proper God ought to or should be like? Does God act merely to satisfy your every desire, or does divinity fall short of fulfilling the image we so often expect? Can the God of religious worship and human desire ever be reconciled with the God who created the evolving world as we find it? Perhaps no one God can satisfy us all. Or have you learned more about God than you really care to know? Is ignorance bliss where the secrets of God's life are concerned? Why won't God hold still so that we can approach the divine being easily? Like children with their parents, are we faced with a divinity who can never quite be all we would like a God to be?

Can God act so as to be both the God we want and the God who is? I think so. Certainly what is divine has the power to be both. But the issue is, can we accept God on such difficult terms, since that divinity is no longer like the God of our dreams? As the Benedictine monk said who appeared at my door in a Roman monastery midway through my first term of lectures: "I now see what your God is like and I don't like him!" We know the kinds of pictures of God which men and women like to construct when they are free to think in their own way. But if God is not as free as we men and women are who satisfy our desires by constructing a world built of dreams, could God be less than we might like a divinity to be and still accomplish the Acts we are in need of?

In any case, however you answer these questions I think we have begun to sketch what God is and what God is not, to discern some divine Acts still in process. Perhaps the most amazing thing is that God permits us to do this, that what is divine lets us know anything at all about itself. God is not afraid of our discovery, although certainly no divinity has made doing so easy for us. Even its Acts are not recognized either easily or by all, but only by those who are discerning and faithful and who often end up being merely "weary from a long journey."

POSTSCRIPT II

DOES GOD CHANGE FACES?

"Even eternity changes its face".
Elie Wiesel in Legends of Our Time

Confronted with the many faces of God, we are faced with a choice: We can deny that any one face which God offers to us is adequate or acceptable (this is known as atheism); or we can argue that the one face we find attractive is "the only true way" to see God (sometimes called orthodoxy). Behind all this is the question of whether we are going to accept or reject our assignment to try to reconcile all the various faces and actions of God which all peoples have seen. This is an unending task, and in that attempt our assurance about God often falls into limbo. Yet there is no way to force men and women to accept a difficult path when an easier way is available. God seems to have set an obstacle in the way of our pursuit of the divine, because the simplest way (that is, either one face of God or none) is not the right way.

If only one face of God were correct (e.g., Descartes' "thinking God"), or if God could be guaranteed absolutely not to exist, the issue could be settled once and for all. But if God is in fact to be found only among a whole army of faces and actions that we humans experience, not only is the pursuit of God the most difficult task ever set for us, but it can never be finally completed. This is the pilgrimage of faith. Any face of God we begin to build up out of all the pictures of God ever presented to us will be basically unstable and thus capable of no final formulation. If any picture we build up of God is to "hold still", this will require all our human strength and attention. We also know that any time we give up on our effort, the particular face of God we have discerned among the many will recede from view and lose the strength it once had for us.

Of course, behind this dilemma lies the question: Why would divinity choose to express itself through many faces rather than one? And if God does this, what does this fact tell us about the divine nature? That is, is there something in the nature of God that makes many faces, rather than one, a more accurate expression of divinity? In the divine self-understanding, God also faces multiplicity, and divinity remains balanced in nature and in control of its actions only by facing multiplicity and by meeting the threat of disintegration successfully. Thus, we cannot realize the full depth of power that lies in the divine nature if we settle on only one simple and perhaps serene face. To know God in truth we must experience some of the force of the inner struggle with the vast heterodoxy of the faces of what is divine. We must understand how a divine power works to contain this diversity and yet is able to Act to create, to sustain, and also eventually to offer to save a contentious human race.

Does our insight into "divine division" mean that one can never claim that any revelation of one face, or of one divine action, points to a core that governs God's relation to all the possible Gods we know? Can Jesus claim that God's center is compassion and not a demand for religious ceremonial sacrifice? Is that what God really wants? Can Christians claim that Jesus has himself led us to The God among the Gods or to the heart of the matter? Yes, of course. If the core we locate in multiplicity does not degenerate into the chaos of destructive warfare, we have found a controlling center. But finding such a single center would not have been necessary if we did not have to deal with the many faces and the many Acts of God to begin with.

Similarly, any claim to "revelation" would be meaningless if any one face of God, or display of divine power, were obviously right from the beginning. The world's religions confront us with many claims, with many faces, with many actions attributed to God. But no revelation would be startling if it simply presented us with what each of us knew all along. If God cares and expresses this compassion for us by entering into our suffering voluntarily, this idea should be an amazing notion to the human observer who is caught among both religion's many Gods and the violence of human action. Faced with a multiplicity of Gods, the diversity of human life and the complexity of conflicting religious claims, 'revelation' becomes both meaningful and needed if we are ever to settle on one face behind the many, or to accept one form of action as divine.

Furthermore, the face revealed to us should not be an obvious one, that is, one that results from simply fixing on one religion's God. Divinity's core must have been hidden at the beginning. Otherwise it would not need to be revealed. God's mode of operation must be esoteric rather than open to all. The easy way of universalism or of explicit knowledge that is open to all does not intrigue God. Nevertheless, a sympathetic divinity must feel a little pang of conscience when it turns down our request for simplicity and finality. God must never rest. However, we are granted momentary rest because we humans need it, not because it is an imitation of the divine life. God may have left his "traces" in the world, but it is still very easy to overlook any path to God.

Besides, every face of God we claim to have seen cannot by itself be "true", and all such faces are neither reconcilable nor manageable if compressed into one composite. God is not simply a collage of all the various faces. But if not, how do we find a criterion, or the criteria, for accepting or rejecting the various faces of divinity which are offered to us? What provides the central clue that makes it possible to find God among all the Gods without simply indulging in artificial exclusion? The trick, it would seem, is not to discover some fixed notion of God. Instead we should first find the leading characteristic of God as recognized in the Acts we and others have experienced. This begins a process of reconciliation, the acceptance of one face and the rejection of others from among the many faces of God. How can we find this needed clue to God?

Descartes offers reason's self-fulfilling demands as his clue to divinity's core. Jesus offers love and sacrifice. Ecclesiastical hierarchies offer us the institutionalization of God's relations with us. Psychologists offer an inner path, others a spiritual guide. Our test is to ask whether the key insight suggested to us operates by rejecting everything but itself. This is a luxury, we have discovered, that God did not indulge in when starting creation on its evolutionary descent.

Or, must the key Act we choose to represent God accept all that both religious and secular authorities have claimed about divinity and then go on first to indicate a way to discern a core among the multiplicity and then offer a plan of how to hold onto that vision? We should begin our quest by demanding that any key to God be able to account for all we find in human nature and in the world, not just part. God's creation of the irreducible multiplicity in which we live must have been intentional and thus be reflective of divinity's core and unusual modes of Action.

"What about God the Father, God the Son,
and God the Holy Ghost:
How are these 'Persons' to be thought of?"

Anon.

"The Christology of Jesus of Nazareth was...
implicit in his actions not in his words."

George H. Tavard

IN THE CHURCH, A COMMUNITY OF SALVATION

PART II. THE ACTS OF JESUS?

A. FIRST THE WORK, THEN THE NATURE OF JESUS

1. WHAT LIES BEHIND THE WORK?

'Christology' in the abstract is an empty academic enterprise. And it would never have come into our intellectual tradition if Jesus had not lived and begun to affect people's lives. Those around him experienced more than the usual 'man', and they responded in various ways, some positive (discipleship), some negative (betrayal). We know from the record that, although many struggled to understand him and his mission, even those closest to him were often baffled. As we all do in trying to give verbal expression to our experience, they used concepts familiar to them, such as 'Messiah', 'Son of God', 'Son of Mary'. Some eventually turned negative; even a majority did in his own time (calling "crucify him!"); but his followers kept on trying to find the right expression for their experience. Jesus' death threw their efforts to understand him into chaos. Then his experienced resurrection cast the whole enterprise in a new light.

It is important to remember that no one claimed that Jesus raised himself from the dead. Physically, Jesus is mortal. One does not "kill" infinite power. His body lay in the tomb. If anything or anyone raised Jesus from destruction, it had to be a power not originally present in the tomb at the time the body was placed there. If one experiences Jesus as risen, as Saul/Paul and many Christians have claimed, it comes only as a "later experience", not as a first impression. If this happens, as it did for the disciples, then one searches for words, concepts to explain what has occurred. Many claimed to "see", that is, to experience God in their encounter with Jesus, and they proclaimed him as 'Christ'. But more than that, they were driven to ask: How can God be present in a human person? And if this is in any way thought to be uniquely true in Jesus' case, how did Jesus' nature differ, or come to differ, from our own in order for divinity to be found fully there?

Take for example the traditional doctrine of the 'Trinity'. Roman Catholics have been told that it is a mystery incapable of final rational comprehension. Many have criticized the Trinitarian formula as being a "late doctrine", one not found explicitly in the gospels or even in the primitive church. One can speculate that such a dogma arose from abstruse theologians who were interested only in fine intellectual distinctions. But first one should stop and ask: How could it have occurred to anyone to call Jesus 'God' or to say that he is "fully divine", if he himself did not explicitly claim it or formulate that concept? Odd doctrines arise and affix themselves to a group from time to time. But Jesus' 'divinity' has been central for so long. Why?

Accidents, even human aspirations and perversity, do not account for this. What, then, were the disciples trying to say, or to account for, when they elevated Jesus' status in this way? Not so much at the time but later on in their reflections and after the Pentecost, they testified that they had felt the force of God and that they had experienced divine power in their association with Jesus' life and work. More than this: The crucifixion tragically put an end to their early optimism about Jesus as the Messiah, one who would not only speak for God, as prophets had done, but restore the lost autonomy of Israel and inaugurate a new era of peace and fulfillment.

Crucifixion ended the disciples immediate temporal hopes; then Jesus' resurrection and return restored their optimism. His departure (ascension) next made that problematic. But they still expected his return again within their lifetime, and so they had reason to think that Jesus would still usher in the kingdom of heaven on earth in expected ways -- even if the time of that fulfillment was delayed. The presence and guidance of the Holy Spirit confirmed their opinion about divine power undergirding their mission, and it also moved them to proclaim that Jesus' promised kingdom was in fact open to all. "Peter's vision" gave emphasis to the world-wide significance of Jesus' work. True,

Jesus had not told them explicitly "who he was". Instead, he waited for each to make his or her own interpretation of his person and his mission.

The basic problem was that the disciples had at first misinterpreted his role, that is, while Jesus was with them. Thus, the nature of the man they thought they knew had to be rethought. What had really been present among them? How could they account for the work of his which they had seen? How was it possible for a mission once aborted to be re-established with such energy? Surely God had been in this place, present among them. In seeing Jesus they had seen the face of God (as the line in "Les Miserables" goes), even though they had not fully grasped that fact at the time. After all, God had spoken through the prophets and no one had claimed divinity for them.

As they reflected on Jesus' work, they began to see God's power reconciling itself to the world, offering not only individual salvation (being "born again") but a restructuring of society and a revolutionary order of peace and harmony (vs. what we read in the morning newspaper). If their claims were not exaggerated, if they could still expect Jesus to complete the mission that had ended in his crucifixion, this time by a Second Coming, if he indeed had the power to control demons and to raise people from the dead, and if God had reversed the agony of death in at least one instance -- the power manifested there must have been more than any human nature as such could offer.

Thus, in the work and in the acts of Jesus, both in his life-time and as his disciples reappraised it after his death in their anticipation for the fulfillment of his promise, all this demanded an interpretation of his nature commensurate with his office and the promises made to his disciples. The full power of God must be revealed as operating there, in as well as through Jesus. If this were not so, then the offer of Christian preachers must be significantly reduced (a route many have taken in the Modern Era). But in spite of how one wants to reinterpret Jesus' role, the development both of the doctrine of the Trinity and of Jesus' divine status were a natural outcome for the early church's reflection of what they had witnessed.

Of course, what happens to any doctrine after such a start, once it has been formulated, is another matter. This is the history of the struggle between the religious spirit, its inspiration which is the work of the Holy Spirit, and its institutional or institutionalized forms. This is the place where vested interests become involved. Those without the strength to formulate their own strong experience into an intellectual form can become attached to formulas which others have shaped, whose full meaning and origins they probably do not understand. Individual security and organizational privilege become locked into promoting/defending their use. And the aim of every Reformation effort is an attempt to recover the original moving Spirit.

Of course, every individual conversion, whether to Zen or to Christianity, carries with it an overwhelming experience of the influx of a radical difference that demands an equivalent expression. This can result in the Zen art of silence; it can be expressed by Christian acts of ministry to those who suffer. And those who have experienced the effect of this inner change do not find words and formulas and creedal statements unmeaningful. Rather, they see them simply as vehicles for the expression of what they have known as an immediate reality. True, many who are without that base experience, but who have vested interests, will demand conformity to complex statements, even to the point of death. But the origin of these in an overwhelming experience must not be forgotten, especially not in the midst of their prostitution as individuals attempt to control others by demanding agreement.

Where the 'Trinity' is concerned we need to remember that it codifies God as experienced in three equally powerful ways: that is, (1) as creator, strong father, and powerful judge; (2) as exemplified in Jesus' love and compassion/passion for all of God's peoples; and (3) in the appearance of the power of God's Spirit present to them, comforting mother, supporting them in the intervening age ('till he come'). All three experiences were equally real, equally powerful in the post-crucifixion, post resurrection experience of the at-first-disorientated disciples. If there is no Pentecost, there is no vital church, no gathering of the saints, that is, those who are God's elect for special work. If there is no powerful father, Jesus' destruction cannot be overcome. If there is no mothering spirit now, we cannot hope to be sustained to carry on Jesus' ministry.

Anyone who loses the sense that God is condensed into one of these formulas may lose his or her 'Christianity', since that title means "those gathered together in his (Jesus') name". And one does not continue to celebrate centuries later, or to gather in the name of the one whom he or she has not met, unless the presence of God in Jesus' life and work is experienced in an over-powering form. One cannot believe in the commission given to the followers ("go ye unto the ends of the earth") unless one feels it as a command of God, no matter how some may distort the commission, whether intentionally or unintentionally. We must, then, ask what Jesus' "work" was (and is) and what power we feel legitimizing it. If we do this, the Trinity follows easily as a natural report on our triune experience of God's various forms of Action.

Jesus struggled, as he reported, to put new wine into old wine skins, and he decided that it could not be done. Thus, we call his message a "new revelation," and we name it as God's in-breaking for us into an otherwise inevitable history. Once doctrines were formulated as powerful expressions, our task today is the opposite. We must take the old wine skins, the inherited ritual forms and words and practices of any religion, and attempt to find new wine within them, "living water", as Jesus put it. This is not easy to do; so much self-interested distortion grows up around any vital center where a holy spirit appears and operates.

We must take the old forms of any gospel, in this case Christianity -- but it can be Zen or Buddhism or Judaism or Islam -- and try to put the old wine into new bottles. Yet we must do so without losing its power to 'save', that which all religions offer in various forms. If some have subverted religious meaning to their own interest (all officials have a tendency to do this), if we allow ourselves to be drawn into the issue on a totally technical plane of argument for (or against) a strict interpretation of a term or a formula, we have lost the religious battle at the outset. Always and everywhere that struggle means to experience once again the transforming power which first brought the practice/doctrine into being, as important to us and to all.

Zen masters, Christian Preachers, Hasidic Rabbis, prophets of every kind, have always been those who can stir the spirit within us and give it life. Of course, there are charlatans, those who offer "the pearl of great price" at bargain rates. The authentic practice of the life of every classical religion has always been "as difficult as it is rare", so that to sell it on a mass basis is automatically to render its seller suspect. (Zen Masters do not recruit.) Yet genuine, lasting conversions do occur; new life and work that is revitalizing does exist, in spite the destruction which zealots often cause. No religion as it becomes incarnate is or can be pure; humans are the only instruments available even for a divine spirit to use. Codified doctrine, words frozen in their meaning like sledge hammers, always threaten to block us, even when a fresh spirit can still be experienced within them.

Words, formulas, philosophies, even doctrines, have latent power, as those who continue to find them enlightening and inspiring testify. But the words in which these experiences are phrased, the concepts, these must never be allowed to become a block to re-experiencing the power that called them to take a stable form. Any creative writer knows this; the task is to take the insight gained and to put it into a form that can be transmitted, not to all, but at least to those who have the ears to hear. This is our situation in asking "What can Jesus do?" Many have told us stories and repeated sayings, from gospel writers to church officials to theologians. Can those words still again open the listener to the power of the experience which inspired their authors? The status we give to a novelist as 'classical' testifies to the power we find in his/her words.

In order to answer the question "What can Jesus do?", one must decide about what power was once present , and potentially is still present, in his person, which means to decide about his 'nature'. And in the case of this definitive religious figure, it means to decide about his divinity, his representation of divinity's core, and the way in which he can be for us a conduit for God's power. We need to ask about the origin of the Buddha's transforming power and the enlightenment of the Zen Masters in the same ways, but perhaps not about their 'divinity'. However, the claims that Christians make for Jesus are substantially larger, and so they require "the divine connection" for their authenticity and enactment. Until we decide about the residence of God in Jesus, we cannot know what he can do. And until we recognize the acts of Jesus, we will miss God's presence and so be unsure about what Jesus did then and can still do today and in any day.

2. WHAT CLAIMS MUST BE MADE FOR THE WORK?

Don Cupitt has analyzed the background to the claim for Jesus' 'divinity'[1], and he notes the difference between later orthodox claims and Jesus' own views of himself and of his mission (at least as recorded). Cupitt finds these to be at odds. In a traditional 'Reformed', and 'Modern' biblical position, he suggests that we return to the more 'primitive' image vs. the dogmatic formulations of faith. He claims that "for the primitive faith Jesus was not God incarnate" (p.8). But that depends on how 'primitive' one sets these dates. All admit that the fourth gospel, John, offers a "higher" Christology. And there are questions involved if one rejects this as normative, since it is possible that the earliest gospel writers had not yet fully reflected on the implications of their experience. 'Earlier' is not necessarily 'better'.

In a sense, all who come later than the first twelve (or eleven) are in Paul's (or Saul's) position. They have not met Jesus in the flesh but can only claim to have experienced him in the power of the Holy Spirit's presence to them. The "most primitive" is inaccessible to us, and thus it is not available to use as a norm to evaluate our own experience, save as the result of the highly sophisticated scholarship of biblical experts who are learned but who may or may not have experienced the spirit's power of conversion. Thus, we must ask how any later disciple, Luther, Augustine, Kierkegaard, Teressa of Avila, etc., experienced the gospel's converting power and then gave expression to it.

We begin then with words and formulas and religious practices as our only route to the historical Jesus, leaving the scholarly search of texts to the learned few. How can Christianity "become a pure religion of salvation again?" Cupitt asks (p.9). And one answer is to search out the power, the acts which were experienced, such that this could have led intelligent people to formulate it as Jesus' "divinity". Such notions are not simply constructed myths, as some stories are. They are reflections of an over-powering experience which required extravagant

---

[1] Jesus and the Gospel of God. Lutterworth Press. London, 1979. All page references are to this volume.

symbols for its expression. Jesus was encountered first as 'messiah' or 'savior'; Cupitt is right (p.8). But what relationship to God's power is required if salvation is offered to all universally, as it was then and can be still?

Cupitt's reason for recommending that we "abandon" this way of thinking is his belief that the creeds which formulating Jesus' divinity were "a severe distortion of the original faith" (p.10). But to say that begs the primary question at hand. Did no early disciple come to feel that he or she had experienced God's own power in Jesus' actions? Then, in reflecting on its immense ramifications, did they simply follow the inspiration of the Holy Spirit in proclaiming God and Jesus to be one, as the words in John's gospel had said? The exact formulation of their experience, and the power required for a universal offer of salvation, is another matter.

We can certainly agree with Cupitt and "leave the question of Jesus' metaphysical status open" (p.13). But if we are to preach the 'gospel', we have to decide how to formulate what we say about the power present in Jesus which can still be experienced by us. Jesus words are actually secondary, whereas Cupitt wants to put them first. The question is: What power is it necessary for us to attribute in order to authenticate the promises offered (e.g., new life, to become children of God)? What right does Jesus possess to make these offers, and thus in whose name does every future conveyer of the gospel speak? Such questions are not purely metaphysical but are rather spiritual, although their formulation entails metaphysical claims about Jesus.

The Nicene Creed is no longer defensible, Cupitt argues (*Ibid.*). That may be true. Baptists and Congregationalists and Mormons do not usually recite it. Therefore it must not be an absolute formulation required for all Christians, since it is not for some. Quakers avoid both clergy and doctrine, but their connection to the inspiration of the Spirit and their sensitivity to Christian presence is legendary. Nevertheless, what is the Nicene creed trying to tell us, and what experience might have caused sincere folk to form such phrases? Can a non-high-church person recite the creed in good conscience, not treating it literally, and yet still be impressed by what it is trying to report about the power both behind and in Jesus' actions?

'Messiah', as it is used in the scriptures, does not refer to a co-equal divine being. Cupitt is right about the history of messianic expectations in Judaism. But if Jesus started by gathering those around him who expected him to be a Messiah, their hopes were dashed in the crucifixion. After that, the post-Pentecostal gathering of the saints (i.e., the followers of Jesus) were faced with the monumental task of interpreting what had happened. In their attempt to justify their experience, they transformed the early notion of 'messiahship'. Jesus was no longer just "the long expected one" but one much more powerful, even if at first unrecognized.

Jesus unmistakably did feel that he had "a special mission from God" (p.15), which places him in the ranks of the prophets. But in that case we must ask: what acts are required if his 'mission' is to be carried out? What force is needed to transform our human nature and the very structure of society itself? His crucifixion seemed to put an end to those hopes; his power seemed to fail. Thus, the Resurrection does not of itself prove Jesus to be 'divine'. Rather, the act of God to overcome death, plus the influence of the Holy Spirit, become the new basis for human hope. Those who are convinced of the eventual triumph of Jesus' mission ("we shall overcome, someday") must feel the full presence of God's power in Jesus' actions. To add to this a "metaphysical equality to God" is another matter. A formula should not become a block to experiencing God's full presence in the divine power instead of simply expressing that presence. It is God's action, not Jesus' (he was crucified), that forms the basis of our hope. Yet that comes only as embodied in our present experience of Jesus' own actions.

"In Jesus God has given to men the definitive way to find salvation" (p.17). If so, in what way can God's power to do this be seen in Jesus' life; how has God become "visible to us"? The issue: Is God seen in, and fully present to, Jesus' life and work? If so, how must we then conceive of Jesus' nature? Some have answered this question by offering us formal creeds. But if Jesus' own approach was to put the burden for making declarations onto the individual, rather than telling us what to believe, we need not be subservient to classical Trinitarian formulations. Instead we ask: What power must be present in Jesus, as he acts out his life and as it is experienced by us, if God's mission is to be realized? Formulating this need not take us "beyond the New Testament" (p.22), since the gospel itself raises that question for us. It asks us, in the Kantian formulation of the question: What must Jesus be, in himself, if the promise of God is thought to be fulfilled through our belief in Jesus' power to heal us?

If our answer is that God has been experienced in three over-powering ways, this helps us to grasp the force behind the Trinitarian formulation, even if we do not accept the fact that those words fully express the experienced reality. We go back to Jesus' posture: We ask individuals to confess only what they have each experienced. We do not want to bind people to dogmas. But on the other hand, if they have overpoweringly experienced God's action as through Jesus freeing them, each must be left to express it in Trinitarian terms, if he or she finds that doing so gives an adequate form to that experience. We want to return neither to the Crusades, to forcing others by military might, nor to the Inquisition, forcing words to be spoken on pain of death. But neither do we want to set obstacles in the way of those who find that the descent of the Holy Spirit, and its effects upon their actions, forces them to express the change they have experienced when they encounter Jesus in this form. They might want to use the words from "Les Miserables" and say they have "seen the face of God".

Christianity is based on the "delay of the parousia", but this is linked with the meaning of 'faith'. And such faith is required to make belief possible, due to its non-arrival now. One believes that Jesus' life announced this for a future coming. His death and resurrection sealed that hope. To be 'Christian' is to be faithful to the hope. If "historical-dogmatic faith" and the church are in opposition (p.28), this can only be reversed by experiencing God's might again. And if this is found "in Jesus" such that it causes you to explain that "he and the father are one", you have uncovered the background of the Trinitarian formulation. The new quality of life which Christians claim to have experienced (being 'born again') is then credited to the power and presence of God, and we might find this to reside "in Jesus" (as Saul did). 'Religion' is and always was embodied in secular-style institutions, all the while God is transcendent (p.35). But we ask: In the life of Jesus are they experienced to merge?

If the "Day of the Lord" did not come, that is, when God would rise up and act (p.37), if this did not arrive as expected, can this still be experienced in Jesus' arrival, even though not as expected and as still delayed? Faith came when the resurrection and, more specifically, the Pentecost reversed the disciples natural expectation (p.42). So if we have a set of 'natural' ('Modern'?) expectations today, faith still involves their reversal, even given that our situation is different. Cupitt feels that Jesus revelation of God's saving power is "most apparent in the way he uses language" (p.44). But such words are hardly strong enough to account for the sweeping power that Christianity has exercised, both good and bad as this may be. Only the full power of God, perhaps conveyed by certain words, could be credited with the force needed to affect us so radically.

Cupitt is sure that: "critical faith must start from the Jesus of history as he and his message are made known to us by the critical historical method" (p.56). If so, we can expect only a low number of Christian converts in the future, since no more than a few can understand the "critical historical method". Furthermore, Jesus' message cannot be made known to "the whole world" in this way. However, "the Jesus of history" is another matter, as long as we do not identify this with certain scholars' picture of Jesus, or with their exclusion of some of the elements in the story of how he acted out his life.

As Saul did, each must find himself/herself transported to confront Jesus, and neither temporal distance nor cultural differences seems to be an insurmountable block, as long as these are not allowed to stand in the way of our encounter with Jesus' transforming power. Such a pursuit is never completed. Belief is a pilgrimage not a conclusion. But we must not simply bind the seeker to new dogmas, such as "the critical study of the gospels". Scholarly procedures, impressive as they may be, are not 'gospel', and Kierkegaard may be right in saying that they cannot bring us nearer either to the 'truth' or to 'faith'.

Cupitt feels that "the way Jesus showed God in his teachings has so far exercised little influence upon Christian thought" (p.51). However, that can be true only if you want to deny the identity between later verbal formulation and Jesus' specific words. But the question always is: Where is 'the real Jesus' to be found? It can be answered that this happens when God's full power is experienced as realized in Jesus' person and work. 'Reversal', which Cupitt stresses, comes about because our expectation is not fulfilled now, which causes the present to be viewed in the light of an expected, changed future (e.g., Revelations). And this certainly is not the way the sectarian world appears. It is an 'odd' way to view an unending, crass world. Yet the novice Christian believes that "we shall overcome, someday", because he or she experiences the full power of God in Jesus' presence and continues to pray for the enactment of God's new age by the descent of the Holy Spirit's pervasive influence.

"The real Jesus is not so much his person as his teaching", Cupitt argues (p.58). Certainly the teaching has been powerful, and many subscribe to Jesus' words who might otherwise avoid any commitment of being "Christian". But the issue goes beyond that, or rather it underlies it. Is the real Jesus found in his action, and is that action, as it effects us, experienced as God's action? If so, we need not claim exclusive privilege for Christianity, although many like to be authoritarian about an insecure belief they hold. Although Jesus' words are presented in John's account "I and the Father are one", even accepting that principle, which one does implicitly by locating God's power as operating in Jesus, no claim for exclusivity is entailed. One need move no further than the confession that he or she has found God there, and then invite others to share in that discovery, with no implied denial that God's power can appear elsewhere for others.

If you say "the real Jesus was much more like the Jesus of Mark than the Jesus of John" (p.58), that depends entirely on the meaning of 'real', an admittedly tricky philosophical term. If one means that Mark is closer to a live video tape recording (with sound) than John's gospel, true; it seems more earthy and simple. But if you mean 'real' in the sense of power and an expression of what in retrospect one is forced to claim as encapsulating their experience, then John can be at least as 'real' as Mark. And perhaps it is even more fully expressive of God's presence as experienced at that time and place. Jesus did preach the death and resurrection of the self as the true way to God (p.59). But for this to be believed, what must one say about the death and the divine act that raised Jesus? Was God's power fully revealed there, so that we can expect the same divine support to lift us from our spiritual and physical death, as Jesus symbolized it?

Jesus does not speak of God directly, or at least he does not do so very clearly and consistently, that is true (p.63). But does Jesus go beyond inviting us to "perceive man's absurdity" and ask us to decide where we have experienced God as fully present? The God of Christians is defined as the one whom Jesus "disclosed in his teaching" (p.65). Certainly. But did reflection on the life and work of Jesus reveal the presence of God's power and intent much more clearly than anyone originally perceived? One who has experienced this is uncontrollably led to testify to his or her belief in Jesus, although that power is shielded again -- until a future day. In the interval, it touches individuals through the presence of the Holy Spirit, not consistently but occasionally enough to be sustaining. Has "traditional Christianity imposed the risen Christ between God and man" (p.62)? Men and women may have done this, but Jesus has been found to represent God's presence, and it is not simply a shield against the shock of an encounter with God. Instead, it is both its mediator and its shield, since none can look on the face of God directly.

Jesus "did not claim to be a divine being" (p.71), Cupitt asserts. Certainly in the Gospels he is amazingly unpreoccupied with himself, which may even be taken as a clue to his divine status. But are we, have many been, forced to claim divinity for Jesus in order to express what has been encountered, what is felt to have occurred by his Action? If so, the locus of concern is not in the formula used to express this, for we know that no words can be definitive where God is concerned. Divinity eludes containment in sentences. The locus of concern is in the experience of God's power, at first in Jesus and today in the Spirit's presence, if it comes to us. Our words, Jesus' words, are only meaningful if they carry us, and others, back to re-enter that experience. Jesus' teaching did concern the suffering he must undergo (*Ibid.*). But the question was and is: How did God respond to Jesus' suffering (by forsaking him?), and do we find that God can still be experienced in this action? In Jesus, do we sense that "the Creator's work is complete" (p.73)? If so, the full power of God must be focused there.

"By the power of God which is the Spirit of God", Jesus lives in God, Cupitt professes (p.75). But Christianity was born in the belief that what happened to Jesus was only a symbol of what could happen to us all. Jesus is reticent in the words that he uses to refer to himself, and they are not conclusive in their implications. Yet does it rest upon the individual believer to phrase what he or she finds as a result of an encounter with the divine? This is no block to claiming that the believer encounters God-in-Christ. And if it is in 'Christ' as opposed to 'Jesus', the believer has taken a carpenter and elevated him in status. If doing this stems from the impact of finding God-in-Jesus, then the elevation to the role of 'Christ' is not absurd but a natural response. We search for the strongest words we can find, in order to express a profoundly changing experience for what has acted upon us. The Holy Spirit is there; Jesus fully mediates God to us.

Not all will claim any such thing. It would be ridiculous if they did; it is so 'unnatural', so much a 'reversal' of the world's way, as Cupitt

likes to stress. It is Jesus' 'work', his Acts, not his words, which his
followers struggle to express. Yet obviously we must today start from
Jesus' words. One hears his words first, today by reading the gospels
or by hearing others preach it. That is our starting point, as Cupitt
insists (p.77). But what experience do these words sometimes lead to?
And if the experience is powerful, can we declare it as a "holy place",
just as Jesus' disciples did, and claim to have encountered God there
as the events record it? To transfer the 'authority' of such experience
to an institution, to a church is, as Cupitt protests, illegitimate. Jesus
did not want to have altars built to him, the report tells us. But there is
a human instinct to build alters of all kinds, some magnificent, some
terrifying. And God must not be identified with any of these. To
identify Divinity with the person of Jesus, however, is another matter.
Jesus did not found a church; his followers did and still do, often in
testimony to their experiences of meeting God in that place.

Yet "of all the great founders of religions, Jesus is the most troubles
and disturbing" (p.81). The New Testament has, as one writer put it,
"a troubled plot". It is not simple and clear. In that sense one needs
institutions, leaders, and formulas. But if they, any one of them,
identified themselves with Jesus' 'gospel', the road to religious
corruption has begun and our call is for a constant Reformation. We
need to be referred back to the mystifying, incomplete work of Jesus to
see if we can understand why so many have found God there and
testify to it still. Inner and cosmic suffering does not cease (p.81);
absolutely not. The disciples were told that they would be persecuted
as they preached (which spiritually is more healthy than to become
celebrated). But we and they are promised that the Holy Spirit will
sustain us, until God consummates the mission which Jesus incarnated
for us.

As Cupitt reports, it is not all "done for us". "His experience must
be shared by his followers" (p.82). True, Jesus did advise us to take up
our cross and follow him, but that is not to say that by doing so we can
accomplish exactly what he did. God requires the death of ego, the
'self' to be sure, and that is important. But this cannot be the full
meaning of Jesus' work, or else we are still trapped in our own circle.
The divine Jesus is not, or need not be, "an obstacle to the recovery of
the real Jesus and his message" (p.83). That is, he is not unless we fail
to ask why he came to be given a status as divine. Did and does his
work demand that elevation in order to be understood? "Jesus'

proclamation and revelation of the Kingdom of God is... the most comprehensive religious message there can be" (p.85). But what power is needed to accomplish this project? Cupitt wants to say "each human being is as God to each other human being" (p.87). Yet we seldom, very seldom, see human beings acting that way in the world, do we?

"What is universal and absolute in Christianity is... the hope which is ahead of us, not the church but the Kingdom of God" (p.91). We certainly should never identify Jesus with any institutional structure, no matter how awe inspiring. But we still have to ask both what power can make the Kingdom of God into a social reality and whether seeing Jesus as fully God is simply a testimony to the power needed to do this. "We rescue God from metaphysical captivity" (p.92) once we rediscover what power was and is operating in Jesus' nature, what 'divinity' his work requires if it is to be fulfilled. We can start with Jesus' message, as Cupitt wants us to. But starting there, we move behind the gospel stories, and then beyond them to the future to ask: "What power was present and experienced as operating in Jesus' Acts that is sufficient to accomplish the change recommended and promised in Jesus' message?"

B. THE ACTS OF JESUS

If we are correct that one can only define Jesus' nature and understand his mission by first appraising his work and by individually encountering his Acts, then we need to outline the actions which we see Jesus undertaking, or at least those which both his disciples and his enemies have responded to. I have argued that God can only be understood, that is, his presence become real, in the same way (Part I). Thus, those who do not accept the claims for divine status made on Jesus' behalf do this in relation to their conception of God (e.g., Unitarianism). No one has argued that Jesus' actions and God's works are identical. Still, for Christians both Jesus and God become clear in their mutual relationship and by their contrast. The same will be true for the work of the Holy Spirit, of course. We need, then, to outline God's capabilities first (Part I) and then contrast them with Jesus' (Part II), as well as the incapabilities, or better passivities, in both figures as we encounter them.

If some argue that we never see God directly, that of course is true. Yet it still might be that the divine actions can be felt (e.g., in the exodus from Egypt) or the non-actions puzzled over, (e.g., in the Holocaust). Thus, we struggle with two figures simultaneously, and we will argue that we are better off that way than to deal with either one independently. Christians have claimed to see God in Jesus; therefore they are committed, or should be, to see each in relation to the other. And Christians move on to a trinity of Acts. 'God' and 'Jesus' are what Aristotle called "correlatives"; they are defined only in their relationship to each other. Each becomes clearer as the other becomes visible, or else dimmer as we lose focus on either. For Christians, there is no such thing as an "argument for God's existence" apart from establishing who Jesus is in relationship to the divine. God, of course, has and may still appear to Jews or Muslims separately, and then their understanding varies accordingly.

We will eventually move on in another account (see Part III) to extend this argument and claim that, in similar fashion, neither God nor Jesus can finally be made real for us until we understand, or perhaps have felt, the action (affective presence) of the Holy Spirit. This is not because we must begin with some Trinitarian formula as it is expressed in the creeds but because God cannot be immediately grasped. Indeed, it would be dangerous to do so; "man shall not see me and live". Jesus was here but is gone, so we must decide how, in this vacuum of the "time-in-between", God might have decided to relate to this world and to the men and women within it. Of course, God might relate to it by sending new prophets (Mohammed, Joseph Smith, Mary Baker Eddy, Sun Myung Moon). But given Jesus' lack of immediate presence to us, we need some concrete form of guidance if in fact God only becomes real as we work out divinity's relationship to Jesus, or vice versa. If there is no immediacy of the Holy Spirit, or if nothing inspires us now, we drift until some eschaton threatens us.

For some, miracles have been taken to be a form of God's presence. And when the divine comes near to us, we would expect the natural order to be interrupted, although otherwise not. Yet in the spirit of strange events recounted still, few say that God's interventions (e.g., parting the Red Sea, raising Jesus from the dead) are common today, although such events would be "uncommon" in any time. The holy scriptures of almost any religion are so designated, i.e., as 'holy', because God's presence and action have been judged to be felt and evidenced in what is recounted on their pages. Thus, due to God's contemporary distance from us, the divine power has been withdrawn and must be replaced. Otherwise, our relationship to God is disorientated, which many confess is true today. In this case we must "discern the Holy Spirit's presence" or else lose hold of both God and Jesus, a loss which has happened for many.

1. Jesus Can Suffer

Perhaps if any quality about Jesus' life is known and accepted, even by those who do not call themselves 'Christians', it would be Jesus' suffering. This may be more or less stressed in one time and place than in another. In the Crystal Cathedral in Southern California, suffering is not much stressed; it is more the Jesus-of-success. And there is a triumphal side to one's experience of Jesus, particularly for those who have undergone conversion as Saul/St. Paul did, or for those who know what it is to be "born again", as Jimmy Carter does. In the Easter Parade on Fifth Avenue, the well dressed have put suffering behind them, at least for the time. But you say: Certainly; they are celebrating the resurrection which for them has overcome suffering and the alienation of death. True, but the problem is that the miracle of "new life" can be meaningfully celebrated only if it comes as a release from suffering, from the tombs which have held us in. Suffering must precede triumph -- and not be forgotten -- else it appears simply as "good luck", as an inevitable fruition of our talents and hard work.

On the other hand, go into any rural church in Mexico and note the prominence, always, of the figure of the suffering Christ. Crosses appear in all Christian Churches, but many are so much works of art that the suffering is smoothed out of them. Father Boff concentrates on the poor in South America; Mother Teressa knows suffering on the streets of Calcutta. True, not all either in India or in South America identify their suffering with Jesus. But the Christian, before he or she can be 'reborn', must experience suffering with Jesus in order to come to any understanding of what kind of power and person he or she is dealing with. The compassion which Jesus recommends that we exhibit to all who are less fortunate, the forgiveness he suggests for enemies who have harmed us, all this is either impossible, or at least very difficult to do, without first identifying with Jesus in his suffering. To feel totally in control and successful is not an avenue either to understand Jesus or to become compassionate towards those less fortunate. We need to experience suffering and to try to comprehend how Jesus could pass through this and still live.

Those who are unsympathetic to religion often accuse revivalist preachers of "laying on a guilt trip". Sartre did say that religion was "a large laundering operation". So unless we have some dirty linen to wash, until we feel guilty in some way, we are blocked in our access to Jesus. And we need not be publicly religious in order to begin this trip. Camus tells us in The Fall that we all feel guilty simply in general, without priests and churches. Because in our involvement with human nature, we have a vague sense of responsibility for failing to help, even when we have never done any specific misdeed. "The well have no need of a physician", it was remarked. Psychiatrists deal with guilt; marriage partners can forgive each other. But if we want to know who Jesus is, the access to this understanding involves suffering over our own guilt and worrying over how we are connected to the plight of so many.

Yet, preaching "hell, fire and damnation" is not what implants guilt, although it may activate our sense of individual 'fault'. If we want to overcome guilt in order to begin a new life, identification with Jesus' suffering is the starting point for many. But this cannot be superficial; we have to take up our cross to follow him, as he advised. Yet before this can become a restoring act for us, we have to ask how, as fully human, Jesus could have suffered if he also represented God's presence among us. To suffer must be a necessary precondition to our being lifted up with Jesus. We can envisage many Gods who could not and who do not suffer. Also, many strong individuals can serve as God's instruments and handle pain without experiencing it themselves. But this does not provide us with an access to the God we find with Jesus, if the Christian account is to be believed.

Some will sense God's great difference from us in the fact that, although suffering was possible, it did not destroy divinity's power. In Jesus' case the situation lies in-between. No one denies that he was put to death under Pontius Pilot and then buried. The disagreement comes over whether he was resurrected, whether he did escape the confines of death, or whether Jesus suffered death's full indignity as all mortals must. God can "die" in the sense that for many the divine presence is dimmed or extinguished. But for God-in-itself, death is not final. It may be taken into the divine nature, felt and responded to, but this absence-of-all-life is not sustained. Jesus is different in the sense that death did overcome him with finality, at its time. But its effect was not continued, although the exact meaning of this is interpreted differently by various Christians. Some argue only for a spiritual revival of Jesus; others see the necessity for a physical resurrection of the body as an evidence of God's ultimate power over nature.

Jesus is with us, "even unto the ends of the earth", to borrow his phrase. But how this presence is present to us, and how it is connected to the disciples' experience of his appearance after death, all this is subject to no final resolution except as each of us decides. The evidence given to his disciples seems to have been sufficient for them, although it can be subjected to doubt, as Thomas demonstrated. Jesus knew that his existence beyond his evident death would always be open to doubt and nevertheless recommended "belief" in his "risen presence". Yet the simple fact that 'belief' is involved in our mode of acceptance indicates that Jesus' immunity to death is not as complete as God's. Suffering can and did affect his nature differently. Nevertheless, God's action in Jesus' case tells us at the same time that God's suffering does not go "even unto death". Only Jesus suffers that fate.

We believe that God can voluntarily enter into suffering, although divinity could remain aloof, as many theologians have thought befits the divine dignity. In Jesus' case again, he differs. He does undergo suffering, but Jesus seems reluctant to do so, and he even prays for its removal from him when death draws near. Yet in the end he accepts destruction. One can postulate that he commits himself into God's hands, when so required, because he has a more direct knowledge of God's power and God's ability to act against death. He understands, in ways that we never can, God's ability to sustain him through death. We fully-human-beings avoid suffering and avoid death at all costs, except the very brave or the masochistic. By "becoming one with Jesus" we can appropriate, or be granted, his confidence in God's protection though death; but such faith does not come naturally. Jesus shares in God's confidence; we can only pray for its support.

Suffering changes most whom it touches, even destroying many. Our powers of resistance vary, from brave to cowardly. But none of us is immune to damage. God is protected from loss, even when suffering enters the divine life. It is felt and responded to, as all important suffering must be. But God's resilience is perfect, whereas ours never is, marvelous as some human recoveries are. Jesus, again, exists at a mid-position. Suffering changes him; his body ceases life. But the change is not permanent, as in our case it usually is. The reversal of the damage which suffering causes is a divine-only action, just as those who recover from potentially annihilating suffering often see God's hand in their reversal. In Jesus' case, he at first instinctively resisted experiencing this vulnerability. But he yielded and lowered himself into God's hands, at last, sharing as he did a more than human confidence in God's restorative powers and the divine commitment to insure this by future action.

2. JESUS CAN LOVE

In talking about God, we used the phrase, "God is able to love; God is able to suffer", because nothing in God's power requires that divinity enter such dangerous territory. In Jesus' case, we have to modify the expression and change the "is able", which we use for God, to "can" for Jesus. Humans always test their power. Can we really do this? Do we possess the power, either collectively as the human race or singly as individuals? (And some commit suicide or destroy others, when it proves that they do not.) With Jesus we meet his human qualities first in the account of his work. But if we begin to experience more then human capabilities as these emerge in the accounts of his action, we leave aside God's transcendent ability and begin to ask how Jesus differs from us, in spite of sharing our humanity. When we recognize what Jesus can do, we make the connection to God's person, and the co-relativity of their natures becomes more clear.

Love is a peculiarly tricky and difficult and important concept, for Jesus but also for God. In "The Last Temptation of Christ", Kazantzakis portrays Jesus as presented with a vision of Mary Magdalene, one often interpreted as having sexual overtones. Given our transposition of Jesus from the simple role of carpenter's son to the magisterial role of 'Christ', many find such a suggestion offensive. But the creeds have insisted that Jesus must be "fully man", else he cannot identify with our nature and act to save us. And we know that sexual attraction is a powerful part of human nature; it is one which we overlook or deny at our peril. In the end Jesus did not yield, just as he did not fall into the earlier temptation to call on divine power to achieve his mission. Surely few of us can say that we have never yielded to sex as a temptation. Among those who can abuse power for their advantage, few reject its use.

Thus, we need to learn about Jesus' ability to love, and to do so in the full range of that emotion's presence in us. Otherwise, we cannot identify with him, as he suggested that we must if we are to achieve release from our own abuse of love. Classically, we have distinguished between Eros, or love as 'desire', which is what some protest attributing to Jesus, and 'agape' or the outgoing, sacrificial, non-ego-centered expression of love, concern or compassion. We know that Jesus exhibited this in a model way which has earned admiration and veneration that transcends the limited boundaries of race or nation. Yet Jesus would surely be less than human if he exhibited only that aspect of love, one which we find to be rare in human behavior.

Again, we are back to God and to Jesus' relationship to divinity. God can be an exacting judge and demand moral behavior on our part. But the divine aspect which Jesus stresses (i.e., reveals) is God as forgiving, compassionate, concerned for us -- or at least the fact that God is able to be so. The power that God evidences as the creator of solar systems and of human nature, the same overawing power which makes God both feared and revered, this can be exhibited as outgoing love -- because God is secure and not weak as we are. There is no need to protect the divine status from destruction as we must protect ours. So that if Jesus can exhibit love without a demand that we return it, he does this by sharing God's own powerful, secure, divine status, one which needs no outside support but is self-sufficient.

We human beings experience a new kind of love in both God and Jesus, one such that we need not be concerned if Jesus is portrayed as being tempted by desire just as we are. How can anyone understand us who has not felt the temptations which we do every waking and dreaming hour? But beyond the human bond we form with everyone who desires anything, anyone who is tempted and so suffers with us for this, we can see the self-sufficient love of God, secure yet offering itself to us for our support and "for our salvation". We know that love can be given without demand for return or conformity, although this is a form of love we experience but rarely. And so we may discover it to be divine in origin.

Jesus must be human in his experience of passion and desire and affection and the effects of these. But the power of God flows through his actions; it is present in his nature. That is, we feel it must be so, if he is immune to either subverting those who oppose him or yielding to every temptation, all the while remaining secure in the power of his own nature, giving love and compassion without demand or fear of loss. Love for us is a risk and an adventure. It cannot be successful unless we learn to trust, both ourselves and others. We must never cease to be able to venture or to risk. Love is as often just as damaging for us as it is exalting, it seems. On the other hand, Jesus loves without fear of inflicting loss, and we can imitate his model only by being willing to risk in spite of potential damage and a lowering of our status.

In Jesus, Christians celebrate that God "came to us", but this need not involve denying that God may come to others in other ways. Except for zealots who become carried away and always claim that any discovery is their exclusive possession. All any individual needs to or can claim is that, in the experience of Jesus, God has been known and forgiveness experienced in a way that makes life new. So God's capacity to love, as well as to judge and to demand and to test us, is crucial in our notion of divinity. But the peculiarity that makes us 'Christian' is to experience this renewed life by finding Jesus' love acting upon us.

Jesus' love and his ability to express it, then, are central for Christians -- although others may find it elsewhere -- just because this is evidenced in his Acts and in his peculiar combination of divine self-sustaining power. It is one power that is able to give itself without diminution, which we cannot. This also appears in Jesus' encounter with us and ours with him. This involves an odd mixture of human vulnerability and divine self-containment, as we experience it. God is so unlike us, in the possession of full power to sustain both the divine status and infinite universes. Such a love as that is impressive. Yet this would be unreal to us without its mediation in Jesus. It comes to us, i.e., to Christians, as that with which we can identify, even in temptation. Yet we know that the love expressed is able to save and to restore, rather than merely to exhaust and to use us, as the love of "our friends" so often does.

All this may be well and good, but the non-devout person will ask: Interesting as such an experience of love might be, as opposite from our own experience with others as it is, what difference will it make to us? What is its "cash value" in our future? Any response to this question must connect love to antagonism. Some of us are passive by temperament. But all of us at times, and many of us all of the time, find ourselves engaged in hostilities. That is the norm in our daily lives and in our newspapers, much as some pretend to avoid it. Sometimes such antagonisms are justified; the grocer has been difficult in processing our order; the bank clerk has understood our request but prefers to make life more complicated; the one in power over us wants to make it very clear that any opposition puts us at risk; someone wants what we have and is cleverly devious in the use of power to gain it. You can fool a lot of the people a lot of the time.

We respond verbally or, in our imaginary confrontations, with aggressive resistance. To be sure, to lack all capability to respond, to make one's rights clear and so to resist degradation, never to defend or to assert ourselves, that is to resign to being used, to being put down constantly by others. Yet if we consult our own psychological mood, we know that combativeness consumes a great deal of energy and that it also automatically involves us in self-centered postures. To realize how God's love is present in Jesus and thus available to us is to experience the conversion of hostile energy into divine channels. That opens us to a vocation, to a mission, to a calling, as we say. This involves not only our own self expansion but God's directed plan of action, both now and in the future.

Jesus clearly understood, experienced, and manifested for us that God's outgoing love does match the divine power of demand and judgment. The constantly ambivalent religious experience we face is to feel guilty for our brothers and sisters in general, and for our actions or non-actions in particular, all the while feeling that God's power of support is a non-demanding love that transforms our response to what otherwise might justify a hostile reaction. It sets us in the pursuit of a constructive mission instead. Such a source of energy redirected into a vocation can lead us into trouble, as it did for Jesus and Peter. Divine love never promises us a rose garden. Still, one can embark on non-self-centered creative projects all the while feeling underwritten by love.

The great problem in the governance of human affairs is to learn how to turn around the power to destroy, how to convert aggressive desire that is always restricted to "me and mine" into an instrument of peace that possesses transforming power. Such a conversion process is not often evidenced in the world, not even when it occasionally appears impressively in individuals. But its appearance is a sign, a symbol of divine care and forgiveness, a love that restores without exhausting either us or its source. To us, and to any who experience this, it arrives as a dove after a storm. It indicates God's promise not to destroy the world and, what's more, to prepare for its transformation.

It is just this aggressive but transforming love that one can experience in Jesus and that reconstitutes some to become 'Christians'. Love can then be released for non-self-centered action, or so those who experience it claim. Aggression, hostility, ambition, even envy, find constructive expression. Destruction, anger are dissolved. That which blocked the expression of our emotions is removed, and we find an outlet for it, even if this appears in sublimated ways not immediately detected by others. Like God, although only at times, one can become that contradiction: a disinterested lover. More important, this is not an entangling love, as so many of our daily attractions prove to be. Our desires too often weave a restrictive web about us that makes action difficult. However, our problem is this: Even if we come to admire such divine love, where can we find it except in the mind's imaginative constructions?

For some, Jesus proves to be this needed link. Like Saul, we need not have known him in the flesh, particularly since most of those who did at the time still did not understand what his love meant. Our insight is too often retrospective. But in recounting Jesus' work, his Acts, what he did and what some claim he does now, one finds a vivid picture in story form of operative divine love in action. In that image, in that person, God's love in the abstract can be made real, whereas ours too often remains unformed and even unexpressed. The genuine meaning of "The Imitation of Christ" is for us to be, like Jesus, transformed in the way our affections are directed, in the way that hostility and anger are turned into a divine mission of reconstruction and reconciliation. Hostility is subdued, overcome, transsubstantiated; we are reborn innocent.

3. JESUS ACTS FREELY

Most, if not all, of the world's people seeks freedom. Yet many cannot do so openly. Millions live under restraint, either internal and self-imposed or as external and enforced by tyrants, the petty or the powerful. Many probably would not voice their goal as that of finding 'freedom'. That is too abstract an expression for the humble. But if we seek food for children, shelter from oppression, protection from violence, the ability to live unhindered or to be creative of such talent as is within us -- this requires freedom. In its overt expression, there probably has never been so wide a demand for self-determination as we find around us today.

Some, perhaps most, deal with this goal in political or in economic terms. "Human rights" are also a concern, plus a system that allows food, shelter, opportunity, and education. These are day-to-day, necessary freedoms, and we will live as oppressed unless we stay "eternally vigilant" to oppose alien demands. Otherwise we will be overrun. There is also an interior freedom, much talked about in Buddhism and in Christianity, and we need to ask how this form of freedom is evidenced in Jesus. How can Jesus act to open such freedom to us, granted that he did not propose a program of economic-political reform? That was left to us to investigate, with no guarantee that any single proposal can at the time deliver enough for all.

Of course, interior freedom and external liberty are connected. Only the free in spirit can have the confidence, the self-abandon, needed to stand out against the crowd and support public openness for all. This is true because the rulers of the world fear reckless freedom; it jeopardizes their control. It is an illusion to think that many leaders really want open and free expression from in their public. At least a minimum of control is necessary for any political process to be effective, and maximum control makes tyrants more efficient just because debate is restricted. We must, then, locate our internal freedom first. Some, but not all, champions of freedom find their source for this in a religion.

In the Jewish tradition, the prophets stood up fearlessly against great odds. The champions of Jesus' gospel often had to proclaim it from prison -- from Paul, to Peter, to Martin Luther, to Martin Luther King. Once freedom is granted by God, the individual recipient no longer depends on social approval or political support. We probably would have very few public champions, only a few Joan of Arc's or Gandhi's, if some had not felt that they had become instruments of a God-granted freedom. Such magnificent examples are, unfortunately, out-balanced in number by the distorted messengers who claim to represent God, or some higher cause, but who in fact represent only themselves. All such we must eventually reject. Most unfortunately,

God's authority is more often appealed to enforce destructive self-centered ambition than to encourage openness.

Looking to Jesus again, in order to see what he seems able to do for us and so to manifest God's power, how can we understand freedom as it appears in his life and actions? Does Jesus open any doors for us which might otherwise go undetected or unopened in our individual quest for freedom? The first things to note are the Acts of Jesus, vs. the Acts of the Apostles. Next, we need to contrast this with Jesus' passivity, which was equally disorientating to his disciples both in the garden and before Pilot. But first, how do the recorded "Acts of Jesus" evidence his freedom, and do they in any way connect him to God? Are his actions models which we can, or should try to, appropriate?

He healed the sick, he fed the hungry, and he urged others to do likewise. He spoke against authority, even a religious authority which he still respected, when he thought ceremony and piety were being given precedence over the needs of individuals. He forgave without condemnation, although we forget that this did not mean that he approved of or supported every kind of behavior (He said "Go and sin no more"). Forgiveness, compassion for all who are in need -- these acts were not tied to whether he agreed with your position or even action (e.g., prostitution, tax collecting). He could speak out strongly, but his physical actions were on the whole restrained. It is hard to justify violence by appealing to Jesus. He acted in a way that is left open to all without creedal restriction. This presents us with an irony, since so many of his followers do not at all follow this openness.

This brings us to Jesus' 'passivity' and the question of whether this, when coupled with his Acts, provides the clue to Jesus' freedom and thus to how he manifests a freedom that is given and underwritten by God. The famous instance of Jesus' passivity, of his non-action, is of course his silence before Pilot. He could have defended himself, proclaimed his mission, as he had in his home town in a manner that caused them to want to stone him. He might at least have defended his followers, as we would expect him to in a US senate investigation. He might at least have tried to argue and to explain in order to get a vindication of his record. His passivity in time of crisis certainly demoralized his disciples.

Messiahs are by definition supposed to lead. They restore desecrated temples. They overturn despots. They proclaim freedom for the captive. On a socio-political level, Jesus did none of these, and many expected this from him, as many still do today. He became another messianic disappointment, and the crowd displayed their frustration and their anger by demanding his death. How then, and in what way, can such passivity be an evidence of freedom? Candidates for the supreme court must defend themselves before the US. senate or they will not be elected to the bench. Jesus must have known, he must have felt, that his own vindication was not crucial to God's mission and that, in fact, his personal defense could frustrate it.

How? In what way? Perhaps because God's freedom, and divinity's goal for our freedom as Jesus embodied it, is an ability to act for the welfare and for the release of others, particularly for those who suffer internally or externally without being fully to blame for their condition. Thus, when we are trapped in our own defense battles, we tend to make ourselves the focus; our rights and agendas are the issue. But in God's case, freedom is directed to others. Action, when it turns to self-defense, defeats God's freedom as Jesus embodied it. Passivity in this case represents freedom. But it does not do so in all cases, since in some situations the welfare of others is the central issue.

Thus, in order to understand how Jesus can be free, we must try to balance the record of the Acts of Jesus, just as we do in judging his disciples, against the Passivity of Jesus. We ask why and where freedom (as God grants it rather than by a human agency) demands action at one time and passivity at another. This tells us that even a demand for freedom cannot be pure, that it is easily corrupted into a campaign for fulfilling our own private agenda, often at the expense of the freedom of others. Divine freedom, of course, is self-assured, whereas ours is precarious. Even Jesus, as he represented God's gift of freedom, had to suffer "even unto death". Freedom is complex, dangerous, in its divine as well as in its human instances.

4. JESUS CAN ACT TO CONTROL

When we consider the power of self-control, we face the chief characteristic that distinguishes God's life from ours. This quality is sometimes translated as "power" or "omnipotence", but that puts the question backwards. Control is what we seek and what God has. Power is only its instrument. And whenever power is taken as an end in itself, the result is usually violent destruction. God could control us; theologians have called this 'predestination' and argued that God's fixed knowledge (and thus control) of the future is necessary in order not to compromise the divine power. True, some theologians want to argue for God's determination of all events, in order to give divinity the power to save us. Yet, in the argument over what preserving God's ability to control necessitates, looking at Jesus' method of using power may give us an insight into God, as has been said.

Jesus does not control his disciples; he does control himself. If he undergoes temptation, whether that of lust or over the use of power, he does not lose control. Jesus does not explode; he does not deteriorate under pressure. He does not even seek to direct his followers thoughts about him. His own control is such that he is undisturbed by their actions toward him. He does not throw Judas out from the last meal in the upper room; he does not invalidate Thomas' discipleship because he doubts. There is no evidence of a demand for rigid orthodoxy of affirmation about his mission, his nature, or the outcome of the future. To be sure, Jesus makes proclamations, but many of these are coded, stated indirectly, and so obviously are capable of various interpretations. Later on, Mohammed wants to clear up all the misunderstanding and the unclarity in the revelation. Jesus from the beginning sought not to control the words which others use. That he recommended certain actions is another matter.

The question that arises, given Jesus' intellectual openness, is to ask if all this compromises the inauguration of the Kingdom of God on earth? Revolutionaries and proponents of utopias, if they are practical and not day-dreamers, know that unity, conformity, discipline of thought and action, are the sine qua non for achieving socio-political change of any magnitude. The powers that resist change and any challenge to their dominance exploit division mercilessly. He or she in power must do so or be replaced. Thus, in Jesus we face the odd reformer, the one who announces a new kingdom, one that will revolutionize human nature and society. He does this in God's name, but he takes no practical steps of the kind necessary to institute such change. If we report that Jesus said that his kingdom was already "present within", it is possible to claim that, spiritually, our interior rebirth is in fact speeded by lack of external power but is defeated by attempted uniformity.

In this way Jesus reveals God's method of control too. By every account, our world now runs on its own, within the limits set by an evolving creation and by non-intervention, e.g., "the promise of the dove" after Noah's flood. God evidences divine control by the act of creation, as Hyden set this to music and we hear it told when his "Creation" is sung. Divine control lurks about, set in the stars, in the geological strata, in the explorations of physical structure. But God's total control is held within these self-imposed physical limits, although it can be broken when a rare miracle intervenes. Still in psychological restraint, God holds back from all thought control, although humans are driven to attempt brain washing in order to curb any diversity that threatens their goals. God dictated the entry of Jesus into the world (which is the meaning of 'virgin birth'). But once the divine act came into physical life, divine 'control' means the restraint of any determining power.

We often go "out of control". But in his test case, Jesus did not and God never does. The power of control, when one exercises it with skill, can bring new life to human beings and to enterprises. Paradoxically, then, to achieve the rebirth that many seek requires just the kind of restrained power which God exercises, just the kind of control that those who are 'insane' have lost, often little due to their own fault. If for us renewal depends on establishing control, and if God is our model and Jesus is our example, if God will not intervene except rarely and never predictably, how can control come to us for our renewal, particularly that "new life" open to us in God's Kingdom as promised to Christians by Jesus himself? The spiritual realm is not subject to the same self-imposed restrictions that operate in the physical world. With God, spiritual contact becomes an open, if not an easy or obvious, possibility. How do we locate it and experience it? The Acts of the Jesuses and the Buddhas show us the way.

In fact, we can argue that the spiritual self-control, which both Jesus and Buddha represent, provides the key to divine access and to the renewal of our inner spirit. To find this source in Jesus is to become a Christian and to testify to that as our healing source. To find it in Buddha's words and example is to become a Buddhist and to follow one of the paths that leads out from his example of achieved control. Does this leave the physical world unchanged, unaffected by the individual's spiritual discovery? It may, because everything depends on what the individual decides to attempt to do with his or her renewal. Nothing prevents this inner "rebirth" from remaining hidden from public view. On the other hand, some of our "magnificent reformers" have been driven to express the power derived from their inner control by their actions, in the public reforms they promote, in the healing they advocate and practice.

Specifically, then, what can Jesus do with his power to determine events? He can open us to see God's mode of spiritual control, which can never be seen in the stars, in black holes, or in the physiology of animal bodies. Thus, those who are oriented toward the physical world, as all but the rare ones are, may fail to discern God's spiritual life, except for a manifestation or a 'revelation' such as Jesus or the Buddha represents. Watching Jesus, we may (not must) understand how God acts inwardly, how the spiritual life can become subject to control, and how that same inner restraint can become a part of our life, although this result is not guaranteed to us. Classical theologians said that in God alone "essence and existence are identical". Sartre said God represented the ideal identity of the in-itself and for-itself, which means our projected goals are factually achieved. As translated, this becomes God's unbroken inner-control which, whether modeled in Jesus or transferred directly to us, gives us an individual and an unbroken identity, that which we now seek but were not given at birth.

God has offered to share divine control with us -- that is one form of Jesus' message. His "gospel" is that divine peace through inner-control can be ours as a gift and that, in one instance at least, Jesus is the avenue for this appropriation. Following Jesus' Acts and Works, as we have outlined them, and then sharing in his suffering, we can move beyond loss and experience a release which is divine-like in its gift to us. But if God has restricted the potentially unlimited extent of divine power, that is, placed divinity's sphere of action under inner control, we must not abuse any power entrusted to us but should rather subject it to a similar inner spiritual discipline. Jesus presents this to us as God's preferred avenue of action. Yet most of us face panic when we anticipate loss of control, something that Spinoza pointed out as a constant fear of finite beings. Can Jesus stop "the flight of panic"? Does he offer us access to divine control? His Acts evidence this.

Jesus came with promises from God, ones which were not available for sale at every drug store counter. They form the basis for our spiritual control, but only if we follow Jesus' admonitions. Yet panic invades our calm; insecurities abound. In an often chaotic world, how can this not be so in our world? -- one where it is clear that few are in control for very long and where some hardly ever are. Jesus' message has been: if we believe in the future of God, to do so offers us the basis for our present inner control, our achieved stability. Such inner calm can often lead to an outer control of events too, but this becomes true only if we are adept and if events turn out favorably. However, our newly-based inner control should make it more possible for us to "seize the day" and to control it while we can, "till he come". God advocates seeking inner control first (the Kingdom of Heaven). Then we watch to see how much can be carried over into our present action (those things that will be "added unto you"), glimpses of the Kingdom on Earth.

Nevertheless, every effective activist knows that others can seize control of the reins of the world while you are busy praying for your conversion to achieve spiritual control; the wordly ones can outmaneuver you while you struggle to find inner peace. The pressures and the shouting of those around us often make inner control a luxury. The world whirls around monastic silence. Yet Jesus manner of confrontation is an example that "opting out of the rat race", or at least of not being driven by it, represents God's plan of control as it became evident in Jesus' life and acts. Seeking first the inner kingdom is surely not a way to escape death, unless we withdraw completely from the world, which Jesus did not. All around us the merchants of control have their wares to sell, from drugs to guns. But Jesus' model of inner control is still God's own means and divinity's adopted plan. That is, it is for those who can resist the obvious promises of immediate control presented by power merchants "in the real world". Drugs and guns and money and sex are more visible and more obvious in their effect and in the action they induce now.

5. JESUS CAN BE PRESENT WITH US.

"Lo, I am with you always, even unto the end of the world" is the quoted phrase of promise. Yet one thing is certain: Jesus is not physically present to any of us now, nor has he been since the close of "gospel times". That he has been vividly present to many, including

Saul on the road to Damascus, this is clear. Psychiatrists have no need to deny that, since such experience does not depend on the presence of his physical body. Of course, here we face the event of Pentecost and the enigma of the Holy Spirit, which is to be explored later. But for now we need to explain how Jesus might be present to us, or to anyone, although gone for centuries from us in his body. First, there is his presence in the four gospel accounts. Many claim to have experienced him there, either in their own reading or as it is preached to them. Further, there is his spirit which we find present in some, although surely not in all, of those who continually tell us that they "come in his name". Not everyone who claims to represent Jesus can be so accepted. This adds to the enigma and to the mystery surrounding his continued availability.

Jesus' presence is forced on no one today, just as it was not during his life and ministry. Clearly his presence can be just as easily rejected now as it was by the majority then. This fact makes us realize that "majorities" are unreliable in matters of the spirit, even 'Christian' majorities. Jesus' disciples did experience his physical presence and, to varying degrees, his spiritual presence. But what this meant was not nearly so clear at the time as it became to them later. (Biblical scholars report this as the various interpretations of Jesus' 'gospel' which were added in by the early church, a fact which does not make these accounts wrong.) At least one disciple defected, and almost all deserted in the hour of trial. (As recent feminist theologians note: The women may have stayed closer to Jesus than the men, although they were not under the same physical threat.) Examining the indecisive, the varied responses to Jesus in his time, we should not be surprised to discover that recognizing his presence is still a controversial claim, even if it is sometimes powerful and converting.

To many, God seems distant or withdrawn or even absent. So the varied responses to Jesus' presence should not affect our estimate of his possibly authentic representation of God. If God has been with the Jews as his elected people, this has often been in less than obvious ways, and he even appears to be tragically absent at times. All are not so lucky as Job to have God engage them in dialogue over their agonizing questions (a fact which made Kierkegaard say Job could not count himself as ultimately unhappy). Odd as it seems to the orthodox, God may be fully present in Jesus exactly in the uncertainty, even in the absence and in the rejection which so many describe as their "experience of God". Of course, 'absence' and 'emptiness' are powerful terms used by mystics to describe their experience of God too, but a majority of such concepts are used negatively. Thus, the rejection of Jesus, whether by his own people in his own time or now, can be read as a mirror of God's mode of presence to us still.

If divinity does not force itself on us, that is, except by speaking through powerful, abrasive prophets, still Jesus' mode of presence is humble, even disconcerting. This is not at all to deny those who claim a powerful, transforming encounter with Jesus, or that some may, like Jacob, experience God's power by wrestling with the divine. It merely qualifies any claim to God's presence, or any assertion of Jesus' direct influence, by unavoidably linking it to the majority report of absence or disbelief. Neither God nor Jesus overwhelms us at all times, and those who do experience the presence of either do not do so in uniform, consistent ways. Jesus is able to be present to us without forcing himself upon us, which both respects our freedom and at the same time makes it difficult to evaluate the claims of those who confidently report his presence, even when we cannot deny them.

While noting the uncertainty surrounding Jesus, we have to balance this against those who claim an overpowering, a transforming encounter with him. His actions have profitably affected them. We cannot dismiss these facts; the record is too impressive, at least in its high spots. But we still must say: it is evident that Jesus can be present to us, here and now, with a power that shakes us, one that causes many to make new proclamations and to undertake new work. Although we are protected from any uniformity of response -- the full presence of God in Jesus would not unite us all but would destroy us if unmediated -- that many feel the presence of Jesus to them is beyond denial. The powerful appearance of other human beings to us, from Hitler on to our various work-a-day bosses, is usually intended to coerce us. Oddly, in God's case and in Jesus', this presence can be non-coercive. That is amazing, when you reflect on their possession of a power far beyond the human, that the divine presence has been so self-moderated as not to coerce.

God has freed the Israelites from captivity many times and still relates to that people as their liberator. And Jesus has "set us free"; that is the primary claim of those who report being affected by his presence. How can that be? How can a non-coercive presence free us, since we link freedom with the use of the power to break all inhibiting external authorities? Certainly secular revolutionaries claim that as "the only way to go". The freedom which the experience of Jesus' presence provides is neither a directed nor a controlled response. You may, of course, feel a burden placed upon you to share "the good news of the release of the captives" with others. You may respond by carrying out some of Jesus' expressed wishes. But his mere presence to us does not demand this as the only available response, whereas the use of the slave master's whip or the tyrants' torture does aim to force us to obey.

Jesus' presence should stimulate us to seek our own independence. We can recognize our encounter with him by this result, one which affects us all in the same way whether male or female, powerful or weak -- if we respond. Jesus is able to "come to us", as the phrase goes, whereas powerful temporal personalities aim for us to come to them. Others limit our freedom by their presence, an effect which the women's movement often claims to find in men. The sense in which God is wrongly conceived to be male, then, is that divinity increases freedom by its presence rather than limiting it. We face countless forces that make us uneasy almost in direct proportion to the power they exercise. But the key to 'control', as we find it in God and as we experience it in Jesus' Acts, is that it makes us able to yield, to relax in that presence, and yet to feel liberated by it.

One problem we find with those around us is that their control is untrustworthy. Even when friends/colleagues are supportive, we feel as if we might be taken advantage of at any moment. It is this fear that any male presence can turn abusive which makes many women protest male power, 'patriarchy' they label this. What they and we need to experience is the presence of a spirit so powerful, but yet so perfectly in control, that to face it is to find freedom and release. How can such a presence cause us to relax? Male power can abuse a woman at almost any time. Whether male or female, superior power can abuse either sex at any time. But the testified result of experiencing Jesus' presence is to find both peace and power so linked that fear recedes. And when fear fades and our apprehensions are calmed, we testify to experiencing a presence beyond human limits. This is why some have called Jesus' presence, for them, equivalent to the presence of God.

6. JESUS CAN USE FORCE TOO

Having noted that suffering, love, freedom, and control are abilities which Jesus can express in his actions, we also have to come to terms with 'force'. Why? Because the issue of Jesus' relationship to God is at stake, as well as the question of whether every rescue must be enacted by human hands or whether we can count on either God or Jesus for help. The Jewish scriptures are full of accounts of Yahweh's use of force. The problem is that Jesus, and those who follow him, have tended to talk more in terms of peace and love and non-violence. That is a central characteristic of Christianity, one which is also mirrored in aspects of Judaism and seems definitely central to Buddhism. Yet where Jesus and his relation to God are concerned, we have to consider whether Jesus can act with force too. Are we on our own, or does Jesus in any way make force available to us?

In approaching this question, we have to consider the technique of non-violent, or passive, resistance used by Gandhi and Martin Luther King, an approach which they partly attributed to Jesus as their inspiration. Both claim that it is a use of 'power' but that its force is moral. Gandhi and King accomplished a great deal using this method. Thus, although their approach did not involve physical force, we know that it can be effective -- at least at times. The problem is that it does not stand up well against massive violence. It can be effective only where there is civil restraint, some rule of law which inhibits massive destruction by force. It would not, for instance, have been very useful in saving Jews from the holocaust; Stalin would not have spared many from slaughter had Russians been able to demonstrate peacefully in Red Square.

It is then probable that Jesus' ability to use force, but his evident failure to exercise it or to intervene, poses the greatest religious/theological issue that remains unsolved. Moreover, there is no evidence that it can be solved except by waiting for the Day of Last Judgment and then questioning God as judge. Elie Wiesel has, it is true, put God on trial, but his The Trial of God ends inconclusively and raises as many issues as it solves. So the paradox of Jesus' power, of his failure to use force, remains the crucial test of Christian faith. Can one say with Job: "Though he slay me, yet will I trust him"?

Jesus' rejection of the use of force is celebrated in the first temptation story. He will not accomplish his mission, in spite of all the good it brings, by using a display of force. As we have noted, that protects our freedom. But the destitute and the tortured of the world might easily trade a little of this vaunted freedom for a guaranteed diet and a release from physical confinement. In that sense, we are not left free by Jesus. We are not offered the choice of asking Jesus to use force to institute God's Kingdom, even if we were willing to buy it at that price.

Jesus' refusal to use force is in a way less easy to defend than God's. Here we face the divine/human split. God's power is so overwhelming that a release of such force could devastate us. Jesus' power by nature seems more restrained, not so immense. So that if he is "fully God", it is the aspect of divine power and the use of force that are the most hidden properties of God in our picture of Jesus. He is a powerful figure, in his integrity, in his attractiveness, in the ardent pursuit of his mission, in his demands on us, in his self-confident action. But we do not see a visible display of force. Although many around us do not shy from the use of violence, no matter what its consequences, we know that employing force usually involves destruction. God may allow this; Yahweh often unleashes havoc in the Hebrew scriptures. Yet that does not seem to be Jesus' disposition, nor even his picture of God. Can force be used and destruction restrained? That is a question of divine subtlety. If toil and agony are part of Jesus' life and also of God's, we know that such a trial can lead to insight -- often but not always. Insight producing as it may be for some, the display of force makes many retire. Yet Jesus' actions, oddly, combine both force and peace.

Jesus had the option to use force. He possessed every power available to God, but he leaves us with the question of whether peace, whether it comes to the individual or to a society, necessarily involves the control of force if that peace is to survive? Force must be present; pacifists who are romantic in their idealism do not seem to understand that. But when Moses saw the burning bush, the bush was not consumed. Such a phenomenon is the sign of God's mysterious presence. That which we would expect to be destroyed by a force of powerful dimensions is not. Power is evident but its destructive consequences are not.

Of course, Jesus was crucified. In his case destructive force was not contained. Thus, it should not surprise us if naked force often sweeps us away, even while we profess Christian or Jewish belief, since it was not stopped in the case of Jesus' death. Although force used against

Jesus was not held back from destroying him, it is believed to have run its course without annihilating the human spirit. Jesus can use force -- we must assert that or else renounce his full representation of God to us. But he uses only moral, attractive force. Unfortunately, we know that this is often not enough to prevent disaster. Still, we expect the destructive consequences of force to be contained in a peace based on controlled power -- eventually.

7. JESUS CAN UNDERSTAND US

As people hear the account of Jesus' action and his gospel preached, they are told about suffering, love, freedom, and Jesus' continued presence with them. These are important qualities about Jesus which have made him attractive to millions. However, beneath all this lies the conviction that Jesus is able to understand us and our human problems. He has offered us release from burdens that are too large for us to bear individually, and the way he deals with men and women testifies that many have found consolation in him. God understands because she creates; Jesus understands because he came to us and stays with us still.

Our attempts to understand either ourselves or others or the world are so often frustrated that we have come to realize that "to understand completely" is an exclusive divine prerogative. The Modern Age thought it could and would "understand" everything. But that has not really seemed to come about. Our comprehension is blocked primarily by the depths of human nature and its motivations which we cannot fathom. In spite of modern psychology, the actions of people still puzzle and frustrate us. Yet even if God cannot be made clear and plain, we have not been willing to settle for obscurity. Many feel that, in Jesus, they have found a full understanding of God and of themselves.

Even when we understand some things, we can lose control and slip back into disorder or become unclear about much that we once understood. God is 'divine' just because this is not true in that case. Divinity controls information; it does not slip away. Yet Jesus does not express this infinity of comprehension directly. At first he seems closest to us through the limits on his understanding. However, as his story unfolds he seems more and more to be in possession of the divine ability to understand fully. Those around him fathom his purposes less and less. All the while his understanding of the human scene increases.

The revelation which Jesus brings becomes clear when we recognize in him the same saving understanding which we think God possesses. We are too often blinded by events, at least for a time. Histories are written and understood later, seldom at the time the momentous events occur. But the impressive quality of Jesus is that many find in him the same understanding which they feel God has. Compassion can be granted securely by one who truly understands, not by the larger section of humanity who do not try to understand but only to get by. Some have come to feel that Jesus looks at us and at events as one who fully understands.

We and our friends, as well as our enemies, find that even partially achieved understanding tends to slip away. Loss of memory is a sign of age, but more than that: all that we have fought to understand tends to fade away again and again, even in our youth. God holds perfect control over the divine comprehension, and we feel that Jesus' understanding of us is not subject to loss either. Events swell around us and times change. This clouds our vision of situations that we once thought we had fathomed. God faces novelty too, and Jesus was challenged in unexpected ways, but their control of understanding was not threatened.

Our search for freedom and our press not to be tied down, or to "stay loose", all this threatens our grasp on understanding. If we shift, if we move, in some sense we have to start all over again to understand. That keeps us young, if we can adjust constantly; but it also makes it difficult for us to hold on to even what once we fathomed. Experience is seldom cumulative. But in Jesus' case, we feel that there is nothing he cannot understand. In his invitation to "come unto me" if we are heavy ladened, we feel that he does, that he could understand, whereas our confidence in parents, counselors, friends is not so unconditional. (Freud not withstanding).

With Jesus we feel we are understood in ways we cannot even fully realize ourselves. Struggle clouds our vision; yet we must struggle or be lost. Jesus presents the picture of one for whom no depth or difficulty obscures. Often our self-concern blocks us and distorts our understanding of ourselves, of others and of the world. How? Our egos obscure the horizon. But in Jesus we feel that obsessive self-concern is absent, or at least that it is fully order control, which allows him to understand us without hindrance. It is this ability to set himself aside in the understanding of others that, for many, most marks Jesus out to be at one with God. This is a divine ability.

Of course, full understanding such as this is what the Enlightenment and the Modern World sought to achieve, a unified encyclopedia of all knowledge. Had they been successful, had human nature yielded its dark recesses to these inquirers, Freud would have been right and religion rendered no longer necessary. Such was not the case. We read our newspapers, but all that we read does not make clear sense. The kind of understanding that Jesus offers has still not been replaced by secular advance, although other religious avenues offer enlightenment as well. Thus, as God is understood, or as Jesus evidences full comprehension without rejection -- a rare offer -- we realize the presence of an ability to understand that exceeds human capacity. It is the kind of full comprehension that is required both to create worlds and to bring the human story to successful conclusion.

8. JESUS CAN USE POWER TO CREATE

The famous opening passage of the Gospel of John uses the concept of the 'Word' as "with God", "and the Word was God", and it was "made flesh", and "lived among us" (John I:1&14). Thus Jesus has often been made to be identical with God at the same time that he becomes God's creative instrument in starting the world on its evolving course. When Jesus is born, it is not the beginning of the Word, since it has always been co-eternal with God.

This famous Prologue to the Gospel need not be disputed, even though it has led to some of the intricate metaphysical and abstract notions of the Trinity and Jesus' pre-existence. In line with the picture we have been trying to paint, we need to see the Acts of God, the divine power to create, and contrast this with Jesus. In this way, we can understand how one divine figure acts and how another acts so that we experience them differently in their effect upon us.

Jesus need not be said to be the vehicle to create worlds and galaxies. That action can be distinctive of God. But the very power of God can be found in Jesus as we experience it or ask whether Jesus too can create. Our answer is that he can be found to hold in himself the whole power of God, the same that was used to launch the world on its evolutionary path. But now he holds this offering out to us as the power needed to recreate the world order and our human order.

This helps to explain the miracles, particularly the physical healing and the raising from the dead, which the gospel accounts report. There is no need to see these as counter-natural and thus hard to believe (although they should not be easy to believe). They are, rather, an evidence of Jesus ability to unleash that which our world's need "for us and for our salvation.

When we feel the power of God present in Jesus we have a forecast of things to come, but not as looking backward to things created through time's evolution. Jesus has many attractive features, such as his identification with the sufferings of human beings. But surely beneath much of this is our sense that, in him, there is the power to create us over again, as he spoke of and as he demonstrated this in some particular acts, usually called "miracles".

The real miracle in our experience of Jesus is that a human being could be the vehicle for such immense power, holding it in his life and demonstrating it in his Acts, a forecast of our world to come. This is our human existence as it should be, thanks be to the divine power concentrated there beyond our imagination fully to conceive.

9. JESUS CAN WORSHIP

It is odd to detect in Jesus a capacity to worship, since that which is divine we take to be the object of worship rather than a participant. And Jesus himself has certainly has been an object of worship in a variety of forms. Worship requires us to admit that a higher power is above us which deserves our attention, if not adoration. Of course, Jesus has God "above" him as his source, no matter how we conceive of the Trinity. Much as we do, Jesus can give thanks for his source of life. And he does. Like us, he can stand in awe of the power which is his source and be humble before it.

In Jesus we meet one who has the power and status to be worshipped but who himself engages in worship, since he too gives thanks to the power which supports him. And "to worship" means to acknowledge that we are begotten; we are not our own source of life. We do this irregardless of how life treats us, which certainly was the case with Jesus. We do this because we know that for our spiritual health it is necessary not to follow Nietzsche and ask to recreate, to transcend, ourselves. Jesus has a role, a mission to fulfill. He is grateful for the power given to him for this purpose, and so he can give thanks.

It is an odd reversal of roles, isn't it, that Jesus can worship while so many human beings cannot? It is humbling to acknowledge a power higher than your own which is your source of strength and thus not yours totally to command. It is this humility in Jesus which makes him such a startling and dramatic figure. As "one with the Father", he neither vaunts his privileged status nor puts us down, as so many of lesser rank do. We aspire, many of us, to positions where we can command others. Some who occupy such offices fulfill them honorably without demeaning others; but many use any power given to them to lower everyone around them whom they can.

In its fullest expression, 'worship' as an attitude is rare, in spite of Cathedrals and churches and religious services. Of course, we cannot tell for sure; some who are present may be there in a genuine attitude of worship. Yet many who engage in religious rituals do not guess how radical a true sense of worship is, or how amazing it is that Jesus can be both divine in his power and still worship the source of that power. He did humble himself to God's commands, and he did so when he was not forced to. On the other hand, we often refuse a humble pose even when it is commanded. We need to understand how Jesus can draw strength by his willingness to worship while still being our source of strength.

The ability to worship, then, tells us something about the origin of human power and its renewal. This is "power" in a special sense, because terrorists and tyrants of all kinds use power to torture and to destroy. They do not, and probably could not, engage in worship. Their power springs from the barrel of a gun, as Chairman Mao said. Brute force is located there, and it is ever present in our world just waiting to be abused. The power involved in worship is of a different kind, one less obvious and more fragile, but much sought after even when it cannot be named. It is the power of the spirit (see Part III).

All spirits are not strong. As we face what challenges us, many feel constantly weak. But we recognize powerful spirits, in art, in religion, even occasionally in politics, and we are amazed at the good their strength can produce/create. The key is to achieve a lack of arrogance. Those who feel power given to them know that it is not of their own creation. It comes as a gift to be used, an inspiration not to be neglected. We no longer feel superior due to our native self-developed strength. Power has come to us; it works through us, as a grace, as a gift; and we are thankful. Jesus' power came to him too, even if it came directly and more freely from God than ours does. Still, Jesus knows that his power is not from himself, and he worships its source all the while encouraging us to join him.

Worship may require a recognition of the burden of sin, whether it is ours individually or collectively for all mankind. Jesus surely was aware of human fault. He came to offer us release in the form of forgiveness. Yet he is said to be like us "save without sin". How can a person who knows no sin understand us and lead us in worship, we who are locked into our sense of fault? Because Jesus was fully tempted, which is the meaning of the phrase "fully human". His overwhelming sense of compassion makes him unite with us and share our grief, our remorse, as if it were his own.

Of course, this is exemplified by his passion and his experience of crucifixion. He knows sin because it became part of his own life, as well as being that force about us which concerns him most. Thus, as Jesus identifies with us in our condition, he has an added reason to worship. He prays for our forgiveness at the same time that he gives thanks to the source of his own life. To 'worship' requires one to humble himself/herself; this is why many are not capable of entering into personal devotion. If Jesus can humble himself and be present beside us for worship, we know that he has taken our faults, our weaknesses, upon himself. Yet he can give thanks even in this humiliating situation.

10. JESUS CAN ACT TO HEAL
...Else He Could not Act for Himself

Perhaps it is his very ability to humble himself in worship that is the source of Jesus' power to heal. The proud do not know how to heal the spirit, although an arrogant doctor can improve the body -- if his pride does not lead him into error. Still, how can humility enable one to heal? Because the proud listen to no one but themselves; the humble listen to others. And in order to experience compassion, one must identify with someone other than himself/herself. "Pride goeth before a fall", but it also gets in the way of real communication.

We need to be understood in order to be healed in spirit. Psychiatry aims to enable us to understand ourselves, but all healing is still an art. Its ultimate source lies in a humble spirit, one capable of giving itself without demand. The proud demand; the humble give as requested. In order to heal us, Jesus must evidence his humility as the source of his compassion and his ability to identify with us. We meet superior people all the time, and many of them do quite magnificent works. But they do not heal the spirit or speak to our suffering. That Jesus can offer healing might seem to be the opposite of what we expect from one of his divine status. Yet healing comes most effectively when the one who offers it is possessed of superior powers and does not act so as merely to impress us but so as to be present with us.

We know that God has the power to heal -- or to destroy; that is the prerogative of the divine office. Jesus amazes us because his lowly origins do not bespeak such powers. The Buddha amazes us too. In his time Moses may not have looked as magnificent (or as angry) as he does in Michael Angelo's marble as he now sits in Rome's "Saint Peter in Chains". Power used for our healing, when it comes from unexpected places, is always surprising. And Jesus did not appear powerful. Few feared him in his own time, even if Pilot showed some remorse at condemning him. Yet in Jesus' meekness God displayed the power of healing.

How can Jesus reverse the damage we and others have done to ourselves? He can do so only if we ask forgiveness, whether we feel guilty or not, since contrition is a condition for spiritual restoration. The proud struggle on against themselves endlessly. In his own spirit of worship, in his ability to love and to suffer, we find in Jesus the model that, if imitated, leads us to God's offer of constant renewal. To be spiritually 'sick' means to find our spirit unavoidably locked within itself. The key to release does not seem to lie within. Someone must reach in from outside to release us from self-obsession. To experience that is to know the hand of God in action. And if Jesus is its source, we recognize that the healing Act stems from Jesus' source of active power.

Jesus left instructions for the process of healing, just as Buddha and the other great prophets who speak for the divine each did. In Jesus' case, our restoration is dependent on following his injunctions. Since this involves moving out and away from self-concern to minister to others who are in need, whether physically or spiritually, he or she who acts in this way is already started on the road to release from inner confinement. To take up Jesus' cross need not mean to share his physical death, in spite of Kierkegaard's obsession with martyrdom. But it does involve putting one's body "on the line", being willing to risk condemnation and abuse in order to carry Jesus' healing to an often unreceptive world.

For Christians healing involves becoming "children of God", just as for Zen Buddhist it involves sitting Zazen until enlightenment is granted. Both demand intense effort. But in neither case can this be successful if it is self-centered. We see in Jesus an absence of self concern which is powerful enough to drive missionaries into difficult lands and threatening situations in order to seek out unmet needs. One is a "child of God" if, whether Jewish or Christian, one obeys the injunctions given to us that enable God's reign to be effective, first in our own hearts, then for others. A "child of God" feels that God is the source of his/her direction and power, and for Christians this is modeled in Jesus' life.

Millions of good folk attend religious celebrations, sit Zazen, follow the Buddha's path, and still find no healing, or at least nothing that seems complete. We realize that healing does not come only as a result of our action or devotion. It must be prepared for properly, else it can never arrive. From the testimony which we have, we have no reason to doubt that such healing has been experienced, for the human spirit if not for the world, even if we cannot always find it happening to our bodies in like manner. We are given no guarantees, but there is also no charge. Healing is free and unrestricted when it comes. However, God acts not of necessity, and Jesus demands only that the effort for conversion be made.

Nevertheless, the offer of healing is full and complete and unrestricted. Jesus did not divide its reception by sex or race or office. It is just that we do not control its arrival, and Jesus does not say that its transforming power will arrive immediately, only that it is promised. We are all "children of the promise", and to be a 'Christian' means to accept that promise from Jesus' hands. One learns from Jesus the conditions for healing and its dependence on a power which we do not control. Jesus was patient; he accepted God's timetable. Now those who follow him must adopt his patience. We need to learn humility as its condition and then become accepting of God's agenda and not rebellious against the divine timetable -- if we can.

11. JESUS CAN RISK REJECTION

Jesus' offer of healing has been rejected by millions, beginning with most of his own people in his own time. On the other hand, each of us spends a great deal of time trying to avoid rejection. Of course, our own offer to love or to help may not be as attractive as Jesus'. But rejection, we learn to our sorrow, does not depend on the quality of the offer. The arrogant can reject even what is in their own best interest, as factions fighting all over the world attest. We know that God does not fear rejection, but it happens to us all the time. Jesus is different.

It would seem that, if his mission to introduce the Kingdom of Heaven was to be successful, he had to gather a strong following. Those who plot political reforms must do everything in their power to gain and to keep support. God, of course, does not need our effort, but it would seem more likely that Jesus does. To be rejected is to fail in the mission. Yet since this did happen to Jesus, we must ask if our acceptance of him is really crucial to his ability to fulfill the divine mission. Jesus seems to do so little to try to win favor, even among his disciples. He must know that to accept rejection is in fact necessary for the Kingdom's coming.

How can such a paradox yield success, that is, that rejection becomes a necessary condition? How so? Because unless we experience rejection we might claim that the power was our own, that success followed on our efforts. Even in the case of Jesus, his crucifixion tells us clearly that, as an individual, he is not the sole possessor of God's power to accomplish. And even God's effort must eventually involve the Holy spirit. But for the time, it is important to see that Jesus brought neither universal healing nor the establishment of God's kingdom through the success of his own mission.

Rejection forces us to place our trust in God; we have no other recourse except cynicism or coercion. Jesus had no other option but to be placed in a tomb and to be deserted by his disciples. Of course, they experienced rejection too; their own. Perhaps that alone made them able later to proclaim what God had done, that which they thought either impossible or a lost opportunity. As long as we are triumphant, our churches triumphant, our programs triumphant, we cannot identify with Jesus or understand what his mission was. Success spoils ministers and priests and lay people, because they do not continue the experience of rejection once their initial efforts are rewarded. Without that, they cannot understand how God operates or how Jesus' rejection could mediate it.

In Jesus' case, we need to ask why the triumphal entry into Jerusalem did not lead on to success. At that high point he seemed to have everything going from him. Those along the palm paved route to Jerusalem that day, including the disciples, must have had a sense of participating in a conclusive event. When one feels so elated, reversal is hard to take and difficult to explain, because we feel personally rejected. But trying as it may be, this is necessary for each of us in order to discover that success lies ultimately in God's hands. It is not of our making, finally, even if we are participants and accomplices.

Jesus accepted his rejection; we have great difficulty in doing so. We usually complain of our innocence and claim that we are misunderstood. Often the message is the clearest just when misunderstanding is the greatest. We cannot believe Jesus' words, because it all seems too simple. Any time a sacrifice of our self-esteem is involved, we protest unfair treatment; but Jesus accepts rejection as the path needed to allow God's power to work. Healing cannot come to the proud; the successful are not sure they need it; only the rejected ones know they need something other than themselves. That is, they do if they do not listen to their own protests. Jesus does not protest for himself; thus he can be an avenue for our healing.

Rejection also makes forgiveness possible. As long as we are in control, to forgive is a foreign act. We remember everything about the climb to the heights of our full accomplishment. To accept rejection is to forget success and to search for the source of our faults, as Job finally understood and did. We need to cultivate forgetfulness. We remember far too much, and Freud asks us to recall everything, much of which needs to be forgiven and forgotten. Of course, we can react to rejection negatively and claim our innocence as victims. But Jesus' model for us is one of a lack of recrimination in spite of our rejection.

God ultimately offers acceptance to us, just as Jesus does. At the same time we are told that accepting rejection is a condition. This is because so few of us are really open to acceptance, even though we claim to seek it. We block it by setting conditions which leave neither God nor others free to operate. Jesus offers acceptance, and many have experienced this unconditionally. But one must also follow him in order to receive it, just as for enlightenment one must sit with the Zen master, or remain faithful to Yahweh's commands. Following Jesus means to pass through "the dark night of the soul"; we are rejected; we are not certain that there is a light at the end of the tunnel, but we press on in faith.

12. JESUS CAN LAUGH

It might seem like a distorted sense of humor even to suggest that "Jesus can laugh". Anyone who reads the Gospels finds him perhaps light hearted at times, but on the whole he is hardly a humorist. Yet if we are to see how Jesus can represent God to us, we must recognize his ability to laugh -- even if this ability was not much exercised in Gospel times. And most laughter should be held in reserve in the present, given the follies of human nature. Wars and rumors of wars, are no laughing matter, and that is what we constantly create for ourselves, seemingly without end.

Jesus' sense of humor must, then, be directed toward the future. He can only smile when he forecasts what lies in store for us, given God's promise to us. Our humor is of necessity future oriented; we laugh now only to escape the pain and to relieve our lack of understanding. A popular humorist makes us feel that we have insight, that we understand. Jesus does that for those who accept him, for those who feel the power of his Acts. And so a touch of lightness comes and a glimpse of laughter arrives which is to appear with the future. However, all this can only come through Jesus' gospel message, that is, to trust in the promise of God's offer to save us -- at some future time.

Of course, Jesus can laugh at our human foibles, at our ability to make ourselves look ridiculous, at our pretensions, at our attempts to take control of the world after the manner of a God. He has to enjoy our strutting about just because he understands its folly. Yet he will not really laugh now, because the transformation devoutly wished for has not come yet. He is in fact pained in the present, just as he was when he looked out on the Jerusalem which rejected him and his offer of healing.

Nevertheless, he can laugh as he thinks about how the future will be changed, "in the twinkling of an eye", as the phrase goes. One needs to be a form of God's presence to us to be able to see the drama of history in all its destructiveness and inhumanity and still be able to see beyond these to the restructured future. Only as this vision comes into Jesus focus does he dare to come near to laughter. Our time is not yet; in the present age our laughter must be at ourselves "till he come".

13. JESUS CAN APPEAR IN SMALL THINGS

You recall that the Gospel accounts report that the disciples recognized Jesus after the resurrection when he sat with them at a meal and broke bread. It was not a magnificent appearance, although it is now gloriously costumed in liturgical celebrations and all over the world on Easter mornings. Our natural tendency, even before TV media presentations arrived, was to judge importance by outer spectacle. If we do, we will miss Jesus (and God). Although we may become entranced with some triumphant, some baroque representation, "the real Jesus" only appears in small things.

Consider the modest encounters in the Gospel, other than his post-resurrection appearances. "The woman at the well" does not recognize herself to be talking to anyone unusual, until Jesus offers her "living water" which will make her thirst no more. Contrast this with the tourist bus loads I have seen rush into the supposed site of the well today and press to get small paper cups full of water to drink, completely missing the point of Jesus' encounter. Even in religion we keep demanding, expecting something tangible, some appearance of the Virgin, some liquefaction of long-dried blood, as evidence for what we seek. It is hard to discipline ourselves spiritually to look for Jesus in small things. Yet that may be where he appears most often.

If God is to be found "in the detail" of the world, and not in the grand architectonic (theories of evolution give accounts of that), then God's spirit incarnate in Jesus, it follows, will not make a big splash. Instead he will be 'marginalized' in his own time and recognized for his significant but small acts. His triumphal entry into Jerusalem was a good example. Crowds cheered him and lined the streets as his donkey went by. But they misunderstood him and over-dramatized his mission. Then, disappointed by the nonfulfilment of their exaggerated hopes, their cheers turned to rage and to the outrage of crucifixion.

So it is with most popular religious figures. The prophets were hardly accepted or listened to in their day, nor are they in any day. Hopes far beyond the possibility of fulfillment are projected by the "satellite TV evangelist". Of course, in the pursuit of some charismatic figure, one may stumble across religious meaning, pearls of great price which the crowd and the cameras miss. So that all is not lost for everyone at the religious "media event". Yet ironically, it is what the individual may discover along the way that proves to be a healing source, often not the crystal surface of the dazzling cathedral. Neither God nor Jesus employ a public relations firm, although their followers may.

In the end the "masters" we meet impress us with their control of detail, not so much by the grand design. Ironically, for the eager religious pilgrim, the reticence of both God and Jesus, which is evident in their modest manner of presentation, makes it difficult for the seeker. It is all too easy to miss the crucial appearance. The Buddha led a quiet life, by all reports. Today he has great public presence. You can visit the world's largest reclining Buddha statue. Zen masters do not advertise, if they understand themselves. Christians are prone to miss this quiet fact because of the triumph of Christianity in its outward appearance. As they realize this difficulty, each religious seeker must study the simple detail.

The God of the prophets who thunders and sends loud messages is followed by Jesus' appearance. Because many expected Jeremiah's rage, Jesus' real significance in bringing God to them was often missed by the multitudes. He fed them, apparently miraculously, but it may be that this only misled them to look at his exterior performance, which is not "where the action is" with Jesus. What the prophets predicted, he fulfilled -- but not at all in the expected outward manner of triumph. This means that our mass celebrations in Christianity, of whatever type, in St. Peters or in Angelus Temple, all risk making it difficult for those present to discover Jesus, to encounter God. The focus moves naturally to the exterior, to the grand, to the exciting. But Jesus seldom appears there.

The would-be devout follower faces difficult odds: it is easier to miss, to overlook Jesus than it is to recognize his appearance. But it is not impossible; Jesus promises us his availability. It is just very difficult, and our eyes must be trained to be sensitive to small things. Odd that a creator God, one capable for working on the scale of universes, when he lowers himself to appear can so easily be missed, so often ignored. Yet just as with our relationship to other people, we must cultivate a sensitivity to nuances, to "the little things in life", or else the friendships we form cannot satisfy.

Jesus can be called 'God', then, because like divinity he does not need pomp and circumstance to identify him. Secure in one's position, whether God, Jesus, or a fulfilled human being, each watches the triumphal parades with fascination and amusement. The stability of their nature gives them a base for their existence which does not require outward show. From early on, people identified God, or their gods, with celestial events, or even with the obvious cycles of nature. With Jesus we know, if we understand his work, that God may easily be misidentified there. Obviousness and visibility is not attractive to the truly divine. Subtlety of detail and presence in small things is. For Jesus, "small is beautiful", public display vulgar.

14. JESUS CAN STAY BEHIND THE GOSPEL ACCOUNTS

The common statement is that "Jesus can be found in the gospels", and many have recommended that we look for him there. In spite of the fact that the four gospels give us slightly different accounts of Jesus' life and work, oddly enough Jesus is not so much to be found in the gospels as in the Acts behind the gospels. First, there is the simple fact that the four gospels are composed of words, so that Jesus as a real figure may be encountered through them but not so much in them. This is not "the quest for the historical Jesus"; that was a scholarly paper chase based on esoteric theories of textual criticism.

The "real Jesus" is not even the physical man who existed or who is reported about. Many saw him, even lived with him, and still did not understand. The real Jesus is God's embodiment, the divine form of presence, which cannot be conveyed directly by word or sight. Jesus kept saying: he who hath ears let him hear, but obviously he did not mean the sound of his voice or by recording his words. He meant for them to discern the significance behind the actions only reported in words, as a spiritual occasion of insight which cannot be forced and which can easily be missed. It can fade away if not carefully guarded even after it is experienced. Blatant Gods, obvious men and women, could not do this. But Jesus can stay behind the gospels, even as they report about him.

If Jesus can stay "behind the gospels", does that mean that he cannot be recognized as God's presence to us? No, but it does mean that this cannot be forced on anyone or codified in final form. 'God' has always been said by the mystics to exceed the final grasp of word and thought. In spite of the important locus which the gospel accounts provide, this holds true of Jesus and links him to divine transcendence. But the situation is different for Jesus than for God. No one has seen God; Jesus was seen; that is the confusing factor. But just because his life was concrete and immediately experienced, we often miss its illusive quality.

We can search for "God in Jesus", as this is traditionally stated, but this will only be encountered behind the gospels, not in their literal examination. That is why the careful study of discrepancies between the four gospel records is misleading, although it is grist for the scholarly mill. Each gospel account is only a vehicle for the discovery of Jesus, if we use it properly, and we know that literal interpretation is an improper use. That tends to identify Jesus with specific terms and titles. This cannot be done, and it is blasphemy, if we seek the God beyond Jesus. Millions have found both God and Jesus by following "the gospel avenue", but their experiences are not all unified. A genuine divine encounter is often shattering, not unifying. It sets us apart as much as it unites.

Evidently Jesus is an advocate of individual discovery, not uniformity of opinion. And divinity resists being expressed in fixed creedal forms, although these may on occasion lead us to God. Yet often this result is not immediate. We do not usually hear a gospel account and then right away come to a full understanding of Jesus. We are not sure at first whom we have met. Recognition is a retrospective occurrence where important matters are concerned. This places a burden on religious institutions, because their work, their rituals, their services are immediate. This is often what makes them impressive; but if taken at face value they can all mislead. If taken pedantically, Jesus can be identified with an institution, with a 'church'. But if taken in the fullness of his office, this is inconceivable. One can be a 'minister' for Jesus, but that means to perform instructed work, to Act in specific ways.

When a 'priesthood' becomes self-contained in its function, it looses its spiritual office, although it may have a 'religious' duty in a narrow sense. If God's power is to be expressed by emissaries, this cannot be done in the literal sense of ecclesiastical function. If Jesus is said to convey God to us, it can only be in an unstable and in an illusive manner. Power of that magnitude cannot find an adequate vessel for its conveyance, nor can Jesus serve this function for us if he is taken too literally. Jesus can become our medium, embracing God for us in apprehensible form, but not if Jesus' power is treated in some obvious sense. We see raw power displayed every day, if its possessors think it will go unchallenged; or, they use it covertly if they are afraid. God, the author of that-power-than-which-none-greater-can-be-conceived, hesitates to show it openly and only lets it stand behind Jesus actions.

If all this is even possibly true, how are we to approach Jesus? Answer: With caution. And that will seem strange to anyone who has been to a Pentecostal revival service or listened to Black gospel sung. Many religious services are formal, with hardly any emotion expressed. But those whom God has swept away respond ecstatically, enthusiastically. Should we not, then, throw caution to the winds where Jesus is concerned? Must we not really shout "Yes, Lord Jesus!" with every Black congregation roused to ecstasy by the preacher's shouting or by singing spirituals? If so, either we throw caution to the wind or we may miss the essence of what it means to "meet Jesus". That does happen. He or she who will not gamble by giving an emotional response will never lose control or risk disappointment, but such a one will surely find religion dull. Where does 'caution' come in then? It comes in the careful approval and in the expression of the experience entered into, <u>after</u> the excitement has gone and the fervor has cooled.

One can approach Jesus with abandon, whether in the gospel accounts or in a preaching service offered by a "teller of the gospel". If skepticism prevents you from entering in, the Existentialists tell us, you have surrendered all possibility of finding a confirming experience. One may be reserved because one knows Jesus is not <u>in</u> the gospel, not even in its ecstatic presentation in word or song. Rather he lives <u>behind</u> it. So we must venture; one must taste the soup, sample the intoxicating wine. Then, afterwards, we may see what emerges from behind the gospels in the residue of the experience. There is no guarantee that anything will appear, else Jesus (or God) has hidden himself behind the gospels for naught, if some ritual or formula guarantees revelation. But we have no possibility of gaining access, except through the retold stories or by being caught up in an enthusiastic response that leads us to changed modes of action.

15. JESUS CAN LEAVE US ALONE TO ACT OUT OUR TASK

If we examine what Jesus can and has done for us as outlined above, it is clear that he ends by leaving us to act out our own task. His position is as a conveyer (perhaps of God) and as a stimulator (perhaps of the Holy Spirit); our position is as a respondent. In spite of all the accounts of what Jesus has done or can do, nothing forces our hand if we choose to resist or to remain blind to what is presented. God did not overwhelm his son; Jesus pled for his own release in the Garden of Gethsemane. God did not seize him or give him any recorded direct

answers. Jesus recognized what had been placed upon him as his task, ·
which is what each of us must also do, and his response was recorded
by his action, not so much in his words. If God did not force Jesus'
hand, why should Jesus force our hand if he represents God to us? Of
course, this can go so far that our response may be that "there is no
change in us".

What our task should be, it follows, is not obvious either. Our
options range from supportive tax collector to one who incarnates
doubt. Uncertainty characterizes any genuine mission. We undertake it
because we can do no other, as Luther said or should have said. We do
our task as we have been elected to it, from motherhood to the
presidency, as best we can. We do this "as if", to borrow a
philosophical phrase, we knew it to be what Jesus left us as a specific
assignment. And if Jesus is to be found in little things, our tasks need
not be magnificent but can be simple. The Quakers, the Amish report
this: It is "a gift to be simple". And if God is "in the detail", how we
perform our tasks is just as important, or even more important, than
what our projects are or their measurable success. Large scale
campaigns often need to be carried out, but Jesus does not say that our
salvation lies on that dramatically visible stage.

We need to find where Jesus resides today, as well as where he lived
in the gospel accounts. If scholars are disturbed because Jesus reflects
some, although certainly not all, of the culture of his day, then in the
present day we will all reflect some of our world too. Although he has
left us to our tasks, it may be in the needs of our day that Jesus is to be
encountered. One who tells us "Lord, he is here" is not necessarily
discovering an antichrist. In giving us his warning about false
appearances of his spirit, Jesus was not saying that he could not be
present to us; that would contradict his departing promise. But his
caution does tell us to be careful about identifying Jesus with any task
we undertake, even if we approach it in the belief that we do it in his
name.

Jesus may be found in many places and in many tasks, since the
indirectness of his original presence and the hiddenness of his nature,
which defies strict account in formulas, makes full identification
impossible. Still, we are asked to declare whom we think he is, just as
his disciples were. This means that we are asked to specify the actions
which we think he enjoins us to undertake without demanding that an
official seal of approval be given to us. It is ours to do the work, God's

to appraise us later. However, if it is done "in Jesus' name", we know that the task cannot be violent or destructive, since he rejected the temptation to use overt power. We act out our tasks in freedom, knowing that God respects our right to choose and that Jesus recommended a non-coercive way.

We know, then, that our tasks are multiple. They can't be so obvious as a particular revolutionary plan for social reconstruction in one day. Insecure humans demand that we conform and give allegiance to doctrine unswervingly. Some churches, thinking that they act in Jesus' name, press the same uniformity on us, sometimes on pain of death. They forget that Jesus stands behind, not in the gospels and that he sent his disciples into the world to serve, not to accept any authorized plan blindly. 'Dogmatic' is a human, not a divine, theological task. 'Orthodoxy' is a function of churches acting perhaps in good conscience, but it is not based on any order which Jesus left us. True, as we know him by his work so we will be known by ours, by the Acts we undertake (Jesus as Pragmatist). But these actions are not fully outlined for us, except that they are tied to serving human needs as those present themselves to us.

Does Jesus, then, support no form of social action, and can he not be appealed to gain support for our political programs? God and Jesus are constantly bombarded with requests to endorse secular programs, and some of their suitors claims to act in God's name or with Jesus as their inspiration. There is no need that all such claims be judged illegitimate; we may justify action by our appeals to God; we may argue that Jesus is the inspiration for some task we want to undertake. Our actions are supposed to be done in relation to Jesus' Acts or to God's. But both leave us alone to choose our specific action, and they resist any attempt to confine their support to any exclusive undertaking. We may claim their support, but we must do so in the knowledge of the loneliness of the Spirit and the oft-times silence of God. These conditions, which were left to us by the example of Jesus' own action, are the source of our freedom.

We are instructed to 'imitate' Jesus by following his Acts. We undertake such tasks freely, accepting responsibility for the means we elect. We may claim inspiration from Jesus, and we should. To the extent that we can see God in Jesus, we can see God in our actions. But the initiative is ours; the responsibility is ours; we define ourselves by our choices; we commit ourselves by our actions. It is of course impossible to "imitate Jesus" exactly in any later day. But insofar as his actions illuminate a way and we follow his instructions given to us, the difference is not essential. We can Act in love, forgive, heal, assist, meet need where it is -- in any culture in any time. That is why God's inspiration has been carried so far and wide on Jesus' command. The tasks he performed can be imitated wherever one or two are gathered together. They concern relations between people that are present in any culture and at any time.

Still, we are left alone by Jesus to select and to carry out our own course of action, because our settings vary so much that no one can lay down specifics for another. Jesus can be with us but not with particular instructions or authorizations. As we undertake our tasks freely, so we learn who we are. Although Jesus left us to carry this out on our own, we at the same time define ourselves as his disciples, and thus as God's later messengers, also by our Acts. "By their fruits they shall be known", which we can refine to say that we make of ourselves what we become by the Acts we undertake. If "God was in Christ", then God comes to dwell in our lives as our Acts carry out his demands. Jesus' nature is known by his work; our nature is constructed by our actions.

C. THE PASSIVITY OF JESUS

It is said that, if we cannot say with certainty what God is, we might at least acquire a negative knowledge. That is, we can be more confident about what God is not, even if mysticism or skepticism keeps us from asserting much directly about God's nature. The same situation applies to Jesus, but with certain obvious differences. Our major problem, which is the unseen nature of God, is missing. Jesus was seen; he lived a recordable life. If God lives a life, it can only be known by indirection, by speculation, and by claiming to have experienced divine Acts. True, Jesus visible life did not settle the question concerning his nature, or his relationship to God, either for his disciples then or for us now. Still, with Jesus we have a more solid factual base from which to start. Of course, the Hebrew scriptures are full of words and acts attributed to Yahweh, but these do not give us either a complete or a consistent picture.

In Jesus' case, the core of his "gospel message" is fairly agreed upon, but the words themselves do not yield an easy interpretation. Moreover, the message is little self-reflective; it centers on the life he wants to call us to lead rather than on himself. And when there are self-referenced statements, they are less than definitive and are mixed in their symbolism. On the key matter of Jesus' status in terms of divinity, we have nothing of absolute certainty to build upon, although we have stated why those who came after him assessed his work and then made the claims about his status that they did. Like other religious leaders, e.g., Buddha, claims about Jesus miracles are accumulated later. The original reports about Jesus offer us a clearer basis for conclusion than is true in God's case, yet never such as to offer us certainty in themselves.

Therefore, as with God, we need to examine carefully what we feel should be excluded from our conception of Jesus, in order to see if this "negative knowledge" in fact offers us a more complete basis for our understanding of "who he is". In God's case, we phrase this as "what God cannot do". In Jesus' case, it takes a slightly different form. If we attribute divinity to Jesus in retrospect, in spite of an absence of any direct ontological statement in his words, then all of the powers of God lie at Jesus' disposal -- and all the restrictions on God's power would also apply to Jesus. This aspect is covered in the report of the first and last temptations of Jesus, when he rejects the use of supra-normal powers to accomplish his mission and when he does not respond to the taunts to come down off his cross if he is truly the son of God.

This leads us to the notion of Jesus' 'passivity', perhaps most graphically demonstrated in his silence before Pilot in the face of his accusers. Judas and his other disciples were unnerved and dismayed at his passivity in the face of violence, a severe restriction on any plans for radical reform or revolution. This is graphically portrayed in "Jesus Christ Superstar", where Judas is presented as almost a hero. He is devastated and disillusioned by Jesus' refusal to fight for the cause of God's kingdom, and so Judas' betrayal is an attempt to force him into action, according to that musical presentation. Thus, we can know something of who Jesus is by The Acts of Jesus. Yet clearly this must be balanced by The Passivity of Jesus, what Jesus would not do even under Judas' pressure, for example. Crucial to the whole gospel story is the contrast between what his followers expected him to do and the actions which he rejected. No one can hope to understand Jesus who does not understand his passivity as well as his actions, his silence as well as his words.

In God's case certain crucial aspects of the divine nature are highlighted, that is, revealed, when we understand why God cannot do certain things. We know these to be impossible or unacceptable and so we can reach conclusions about their ground. In Jesus' case, when we can understand why he rejected certain actions and remained passive where some followers expected action, his nature and his mission, as well as his ontological office, can come more clearly into view. 'Disciples' are called such because they celebrate Jesus' actions, past, present, and future. But after the quite legitimately exciting aspects which came about when the first followers encountered him in his life, Jesus' fame fall into confusion just because of what some found Jesus not doing. His passivity becomes mystifying, and it is still a block to our understanding and sometimes to our allegiance. Thus, less the effective practice of the gospel be impaired, Jesus' disciples must particularly understand why and when he is passive, why and when he does not Act as well as how and why he does.

This question involves more than the accounts of his life as we seek to understand these. The actions of Jesus in the present and in the future are proclaimed and so must be believed or rejected. Yet if, for instance, one believes that "Jesus loves the little children, all the children of the world", one must explain what this means, since there is no -- or at least minimal -- evidence about his own action to relieve the disastrous plight of millions of children. Or if one believes Jesus' offer to "come unto me" as one that relives all suffering, for each who does testify to his or her release from suffering by an encounter with Jesus, we have perhaps more who die finding no physical relief. Jesus' passivity in the light of his recorded Acts will block our understanding unless it can be accounted for.

1. JESUS CANNOT DISAPPEAR

As we consider the world's prominent people, those who are active now and those whose actions molded our history, in appraising these "beautiful people" of thought or act, we may forget how few survive in the record in any remembered way. As happens periodically, many today want to challenge the correctness of the established canon of "very important people". Women argue that they have been "erased" from history and want to revise the historical records. In this press to admit "outsiders" to "cultural/political sainthood", we seem to forget that only a very small number survive their day and are preserved in our recorded memory or in their accumulated work, whether literary, artistic, political, military, scientific, etc. But however the lists may be revised as a result of our reappraisal in each new generation, Jesus is among those who cannot disappear.

The impact of his life and of his followers' work can never honestly be written out of the cultural-historical record. Some have tried, but Jesus' place seems beyond erasure. When women claim that their history has often been "erased", this tends to mean that it was never fairly entered in the record as to its importance in the first place. Jesus' Acts have been. Even where this importance has been exaggerated or its influence counted as negative, e.g. heresy trials, religious wars, and persecutions, it cannot be either ultimately eliminated or totally overlooked. The result of seeing that Jesus cannot make himself disappear does not establish any one belief about, or claim for, Jesus' program. But we know, or we should realize, that we are dealing with a power that cannot be dismissed. And Jesus remains passive in relation to any exertion of power made on his behalf, even if it is misused by his self-proclaimed disciples.

God's power is such, we know, that divinity cannot negate itself, cannot become nothing. Jesus' power is not that which constitutes universes, but it is similar in the sense that, like the created order, once introduced it cannot (or at least will not) be withdrawn. God's power is such that we say divinity could withdraw its constant support of the evolutionary order, but we also quickly add that God will not destroy what once has been given an independent power of existence. That which is divine is not capricious or destructive. Jesus had more uncertainties surrounding his introduction into the world of his time. He had more unclarities and uncertainties in carrying out his mission than God had in acting as a "world-class" creator, an act at once evidently simple by its result and amazingly complex to our intellectual understanding. But once his life was complete, even Jesus cannot remove its influence.

However, what we must add to this is the complexity of the 'resurrection'. That is, had Jesus' life ended in the tomb, would his influence be as persuasive as it is? We know that other major religious figures, e.g., the Buddha, Confucius, do not have immortality or the reversal of death claimed for them. It was not necessary for Jesus to have been resurrected by God's power for Christianity to be constituted. However, it is true that the belief in Jesus' resurrection has been central for a majority of his Christian followers. Thus, we must at least say that Jesus power is necessarily connected to God's power, and that we must understand both what Jesus can and cannot do in relation to God's power and the divine impossibilities. These need not be identical, but they must be held in correlation.

In the same way that we understand ourselves when we realize our limits, just so we recognize Jesus in his limitations. And bonds of self-restraint are crucial, else God would overcome us and Jesus would dictate our response. Were Jesus not passive at critical times, holding still for our appraisal just as he did before Pilot, our response might be dictated. Moreover, the destructive force of chaos is real in our world. Thus, if limits were not set and held to, we, God, and Jesus would be swept away by chaos-produced subversion. As it is, God withstands the storms of disbelief and Jesus the agony of rejection. We, however, often cave in under such conditions. Nevertheless, we have the power to sustain ourselves in many situations. And the text of Jesus' message is that, in him, we can realize that which stabilizes us against succumbing to chaos. Thus, God sustains sanity against the flood of insanity; Jesus undergirds belief against a tide of unbelief; and we are told that we can draw on both models.

God can disappear from our vision; we know that both from the spiritual dark night of the soul and from rampant atheism. Jesus can disappear in the disillusionment of one-time believers. We can become nothing in our own sight or in that of someone we love. But this experience causes us to be disconsolate, in part because we do not realize that this is just as characteristic of the divine life as of the human. Any disappearance is painful, so we know that neither God nor Jesus is beyond producing pain. This is because they can become nothing in our sight, which is the chief source of pain for religious seekers. But we also know that they too experience pain, since both the disappearance of God and the crucifixion-ascension of Jesus were as painful to their self-consciousness as to those of us who identify with them. Yet they sustain themselves. They can re-present themselves to us, for us and for their own purposes.

2. JESUS CANNOT AVOID REJECTION

One might think that a figure so positively connected to the fullness of divine power as Jesus, however that is conceived, could move to avoid rejection and succeed in doing so. But we have argued that even God cannot avoid rejection, although divinity could elect to avoid anything it wills by restructuring the entire basis of the evolutionary order. Thus, Jesus cannot avoid rejection, although he can sustain himself against it and reject that which should be excluded in his life, e.g., destructive evil. Of course, by exercising coercive power, Jesus could have attempted, as we do, to control the response of others, whether for constructive or for destructive purposes. But we experience a world which in its natural order leaves us free in our response to it, open always to human rejection. If God left the divine nature open to our acceptance, to our response or to our rejection, Jesus would exceed God's self-limitation on power if he sought to avoid rejection.

Coupled with accepting rejection comes open acceptance. We find much which threatens us, and we reject, or try to subvert, what challenges us or stands in our way. God programmed subtle built-in defensive-offensive mechanisms into the natural order, although aspects of it are terrifying as well as beautiful. Yet obviously God accepts the natural world as it evolved, whereas often we are less content with it. Jesus reflects God's approach. He apparently set no limits on his acceptance of those who came across his path (whether he approved or disapproved is another matter). Few whom we know are so open, so passive in accepting rejection. Jesus is thus not simple in nature but complex and open to varieties of approach.

We often seek a unity in ourselves. So also we look for an identifiable core in Jesus, in our friends and in those whom we love. Some theologians project such a unity into God, as contrasted with our often uncontrolled complexity. Restful as such a thought of unity is, and as much as seekers have sought rest since the time Aristotle defined it as our goal in contemplation, we see in God's failure to reject, in the divine inability to turn away from any aspect in the created order, divinity's complexity beyond our dreams of simplicity. In God's inability to reject anything, even in Jesus' universal offer for all who suffer to come to him, God's unity and Jesus' offer of rest are for now placed outside our immediate grasp as a romantic dream. The nature which cannot reject knows no final peace. All that disturbs us must disturb God. All that upsets Jesus calls for our active opposition, but not necessarily for our rejection.

God's project for the world, as Jesus presents it, leads to Jesus' inability to reject. This is the-God-after-the-flood, who gives us the dove as the sign of peace, that divinity will not reject its creation or destroy the earth's inhabitants again. This does not necessarily demand belief in a universal salvation. Souls may still be judged. But nothing is shut out, nothing placed beyond God's sight. Jesus never withdraws the universal offer of release. Its bounds know no restriction by race or class or sex or creed. Nothing is beyond redemption; everything is a candidate for salvation/restoration. The bright side of the divine inability to reject is that all avenues stay open. We close out some options through our lack of courage or in our despair. But our human tendency to reject is not reflected in Jesus constant openness.

The irony about Jesus' inability to avoid rejection is that millions have accepted him, and in doing so not only found joy in their hearts but speak of "new life" and of being "born again". The oddity is that one who, by testimony, has done so much for so many can at the same time be either silently or hastily rejected by millions. Of course, much of this hostility comes from his rivals on the religious scene. In the spiritual market place, new "messiahs" are not usually well received by the for-the-time reigning religious leaders. Part of this stems from "turf warfare" and a protection of privilege by those in power in religious institutions, who see the newcomer as a threat to their security. But much opposition also comes for the genuinely concerned spiritual counselor who is fearful that the too-easily-lead will be falsely converted, to their later sorrow.

Of course today, in the case of Jesus, his following is well established and the "track record" of Christianity, both its magnificence and its "horrors perpetrated in the name of peace" are well known. Its enthusiasts have much to point to in support of their belief; its detractors have their own tale of woe to tell. Still, one thing is clear: Jesus was not able to start his mission, or to entrust it to his followers to spread, in ways that would prevent his rejection. After all, at the crucifixion Peter, his beloved disciple, denied his lord three times, after having pledged that this would never happen. So a mission born in betrayal cannot expect to have a pure history or to be free itself from the continual possibility of rejection.

3. JESUS CANNOT CONTROL HIS REPRESENTATIVES' ACTIONS

Jesus did not attempt to exclude Judas from the final dinner party, nor did he ever reject him. He simply commented on his betrayal. There is no evidence that he wished to exercise strict control over his followers. No ordination procedures or oaths were set up by him, although he issued no injunctions against others doing so later. Privilege of office was not instituted, and when requested he denied his power to grant it. Favorites, those who seemed to him to understand his mission and its obligations best, yes. Jesus expressed approval and underlined any acceptance that indicated a knowing discipleship. Yet entry remained open to all. If he indicated disapproval, it did not involve exclusion. When Peter promised eternal loyalty only to end later in denial, Jesus delivered no lectures on the necessity for absolute loyalty among his "shock troops", as Lenin did, or as the Jesuits once did, or as passionate evangelical followers might now.

Peter was left to discover his frailty by himself without an "I told you so!" And if Judas was overcome by the implications of his betrayal, which may have been caused by his frustration over Jesus failure to carry out his mission in the expected style, Jesus was not the one who tried to tell him he was wrong. The self-discovery, the possibility of coming to realize who Jesus was and what his mission represented, that is left to each follower to uncover. Thus, since the discovery and proclamation of discipleship is an individual affair, one which is subject to constant reversal or betrayal, Jesus cannot control his representatives and seems to have made little effort to do so. Organizations instituted by his followers have done little else since, although many members silently remove themselves from organizational disputes and the arguments over who sits in the chief seats or holds which office.

We know that, when we look for God, the problem is the same. There is no final unity among the various religious leaders, and some who are the most inspirational are the ones least sensitive about not forcing us to use only authorized forms of speech. Thus, we possess a vast store of records about our human search for God, and there are any number who will offer to lead us. But in this climb, God has set up no divinely imposed quality controls or tests for correct speech.

However, in Jesus' Acts we have a statement of how God wants us to act; so if we imitate Jesus in his acts, e.g. love of neighbor, forgiveness of wrongs -- that path of action is more clearly marked out. Following deeds rather than words is more likely to lead to divine discovery than either word or story, whatever their importance. "Actions speak louder than words", Jesus told us, although the story may make the deed graphic to us. "In the beginning was the deed", and in the case of Jesus we list his Acts and follow that path. Words come, if they do so, later, and they are nowhere near as essential.

It might seem then that Jesus would still want to limit the actions of his representatives, if not their words, as a means to control church access (i.e., determine who is a believer-follower). That is true; but his "control" is that of moral example. There is no evidence of his wanting anyone punished who did not follow his path of action. Kierkegaard, of course, took what it means to follow Jesus to the extreme; he thought it required the martyrdom of the genuine disciple. It might; but as in Jesus' own situation, this must not be consciously sought. It is just a question of its acceptance, if following the missionary command of Jesus leads any individual to that ultimate decision. Again, Jesus does not prescribe martyrdom. He recommends a self-less mission of service to the need of others, both physical and spiritual. This is his recommended standard, but it is not a system of control. He also recommends carrying the gospel, the "good news", to all the world and to follow the path of the evangelical missionary.

The distinction between the authentic disciple and the sham, that we are left to discover for ourselves. Yet of course we are to use the test Jesus recommended, e.g., they shall know that you are my disciples because you love one another. Thus, hate is clearly excluded, as are other 'negative', destructive emotions, jealousy, greed, etc. So that again we can form the positive picture of the disciple by what we know that Jesus excluded as negative Acts. We really agree more as to what Acts are 'unchristian' than we do about what 'Christian' means or exactly what actions it entails. The 'ordained' ministers of a church are always possible guides, but if they attempt to control their flocks, such a use of power cannot be directly attributed to Jesus, although outstanding ecclesiastical representatives do appear from time to time. Just as Jesus did not always find the best of religion in the officials of his day, so often we find his best examples among certain laity.

Jesus is clearly not into controlling others or into authorizing his followers to do so. As Kierkegaard remarked: "I can protect myself against my enemies, but God save me from my disciples". Why? Because even with a well intentioned zeal, the follower often becomes a purist, a rigorist who acts in excessive ways that the master did not himself need to use. The weak need rigidity; the innovator seeks to open new avenues. But any lack of codified orthodoxy allows for distortion and betrayal, a fact which the religious purist always tries to exclude. That may be a noble effort, but ironically it is not one which Jesus followed for himself. Any representative of Jesus who strives to control others in word or deed must seek authorization for this attempted purity from someone other than Jesus. And the world is full of such authorities waiting to be called upon.

One important spiritual lesson we learn from all this is that Jesus does not identify the authentic religious experience with observing any creed or ritual, however beneficial these may be for the person or the institution. Authenticity lies with inward conversion which is not easily measured externally, except by its fruits in action. We have argued that Jesus is known more by following his Acts than by his words, unless his words illuminate his Acts for us. But Jesus does not want us to "put the cart before the horse". We are not to start with the word or with any rigorous observance as our measure of belief, in spite of the protest by ecclesiastical purists, but with the individual actions in so far as they are modeled after Jesus. Yet these must spring from an inner change, one that no longer sets ego-satisfaction as an assumed automatic goal.

True, when we recognize this in the great examples of Christian action and spirit, e.g., St. Francis, we also see that it cannot be controlled. Every dictator knows that action can be directed or at least coerced. Minds can be subject to 'brain washing' or to 'thought control', although with questionable long lasting success. But the human spirit, to whom every religion always speaks and which Jesus addressed, this can never be controlled by another, not even by Jesus own example. By Jesus' choice and by God's, this is due to the example of the self-limitation of divine power. Odd that what God and Jesus knew they could not control, that which would only break or destroy us in any attempt at coercion, human tyrants (and oddly even religious leaders) still try to bring under their momentary sway.

4. JESUS CANNOT ELIMINATE ANGER

When it comes to anger, we have to change our analysis slightly. Jesus could control his anger; we believe he did. But he did not eliminate it (thus he never achieved Zen enlightenment or followed the Buddha in all things.) The distinction we need to make becomes crucial and all-important: Jesus never became angry when he was attacked or misunderstood, as we do constantly. He became angry when others were abused or used for selfish purposes. Thus, Jesus can control his anger. For what more could he have had a right to be angry about than his trial and crucifixion? Yet his passivity during his trial before Pilot and during his passion so disoriented his disciples that their devotion to him momentarily failed.

What kind of person, then, does not lose control of his or her anger when abused or badly treated? One whose personal goals are not bound up in himself or herself. What kind of person does not eliminate anger, in spite of injunctions to love one's enemies? One whose concern does not lie in the healing of the suffering spirit or body of another but rather with himself or herself. Anger surges up when we have been badly treated, or at least when we think we have been. In mobs this can lead to massive destruction. Wars are still built on real or imagined offenses. Psychological warfare is still waged, because we feel slighted in our recognition or envious of someone else who succeeds over against us. Jesus controls his anger in relation to himself, but he does not eliminate it, since it is needed in order to protest any suffering unjustly inflicted on others.

In the Hebrew scriptures Yahweh seems to be angry quite a lot of the time. This is not the only emotion expressed for him, but the prophets often seem particularly concerned to express the divine anger. Other emotions are strong, e.g., compassion, concern, care. But Jesus presented a less angry picture of God, one more anxious to forgive transgression. Yet the anger of God over disobedience, or over any hurt inflicted on another, is still very much present in Jesus cries of "woe" to those whose self-concerned actions condemn them. Thus, God's anger cannot be eliminated in so far as Jesus represents divinity's presence. Jesus is secure just as God is secure, even in the face of death. For Jesus, we know that there can be moments of feeling deserted, whether by God or by his devoted disciples. But these appear as periods of testing and never explode into uncontrolled or misdirected anger as each of us might when pressed to our limit, whether justified or not.

If the sordidness and meanness of human life makes Jesus more compassionate than angry, we know by this that his anger is not based on self-righteousness or puritanical zeal or even on moral indignation. Our failure to live rightly and to listen to wisdom, whether in our human endeavors or in God's expressed injunctions, leads more to remorse and to Jesus cry of desertion, even though he has offered us release from human suffering. However, we can be angry in our zeal, angry over faults in moral behavior, judgmental about any failure in a religious life. Oddly, Jesus seems more pained than angry in these instances, that is, until someone viciously attacks or blatantly uses another for his or her own purposes. Whether religiously or for secular projects, Jesus' anger reflects Yahweh's wrath.

However, for all the talk of Jesus' love and compassion, often magnified into romantic sentimentality, we have to keep reminding ourselves that he holds controlled rage just below the surface. Fortunately, Jesus can govern his anger as we too often cannot, else playwrights and novelists and newspaper reporters would have less to write about. Our attempts at control are sloppy and vary in degree of success. Jesus cannot eliminate anger. He shares some, but by no means all, of our outrage. But it stays within his control. This offers us a key to his identity with God, one which is as much emotional as metaphysical. Jesus releases anger, but never for himself, whereas our most common spells of anger occur over frustrated plans or affronts to our dignity or to our supposed talents.

Jesus counsels us to love and to forgiveness, which are very difficult emotions to control, especially when Jesus wants these to be directed to the unfortunate who suffer and even to our enemies. Jesus says that individuals should take responsibility for his or her own condition, no matter what the circumstances. He was ahead of Sartre in recommending our acceptance of individual responsibility as necessary for human integrity. But he does say that whatever our enemies do, however responsible those who suffer are for their own state, our compassion and love must be shown. Yet this has a subtle connection with his and our controlled sub-surface anger. For not to care, to withdraw concern, is our all-too-common response. We must remain angry over the damage human beings do to themselves and to one another. This provides the heat necessary to generate compassion. The control of anger can turn it into love, although this does not happen automatically.

5. Jesus Cannot Lose Himself

One need only look in jails or in mental hospitals or in bars or in city parks to find people who, at least outwardly, seen to have lost themselves. Even if we are more sophisticated and discriminating and do not simply accept these outward signs, the numbers of those who do or who would confess their sense of being lost are immense. Jesus offers to 'find' those who are 'lost' and tells us that the shepherd has more concern for the one lost sheep than for the many who seem safe. 'Lostness' can be translated into 'alienation' or 'emptiness' and made more sophisticated, but the sense of estrangement and emptiness which many feel is at times overwhelming. We say that the blind cannot lead the blind (although we try), so it must be that Jesus cannot lose himself. If he did, we could not look to him for help. "Physicians heal thy self", we would quote.

If Jesus is incapable of loss, this is an amazing quality, and it borders on the divine, since traditionally we say that God is the only being in whom essence and existence are identical, that is, who is safe against loss. If this is also true for Jesus, it means that who he is can be defined by how he lives, whereas our actions too often are far from our (still unactualized) self image. Novels and plays are constructed by putting on paper what the author has come to understand but has not yet acted out in life. In fact, much of our desired self image never can be put into our factual lives and so requires artistic or alternative expressions. Our agony is over our fear of being a lost adult, once we have escaped childhood in tact. Jesus is amazing ('divine'?) if he does not exist under the threat of losing himself.

"Fight panic" is a sign on all our doors, although some of us are better at ignoring that constant threat than others, and some do a better job of acting out their concealment. But like the fine actor or actress, those who are most sensitive to the ease of loss are nervous to the point of panic every time the curtain goes up or every time they put pen to paper, just as every teacher who understands his or her trade never walks into a classroom sure of success, no matter how many previous compliments have been received. It could only be a "sign of the divine" that Jesus knows full well how lost so many are and yet does not have to fight the same panic within himself. If the doctor is crazier than his crazy patients, as Kierkegaard remarked, it does not give one a sense of assurance. Yet Jesus offers us unconditional assurance; he cannot lose himself.

For better or for worse, we often pass a point-of-no-return in our emotional, psychic life. We change and friends notice this, even if we do not yet realize it or cover it up well. From this self-separation from our past we often find we cannot return. Doors have closed behind us; we cannot recover our innocence (and Kierkegaard says we ought not to want to). But Jesus offers rebirth, new life. Thus, there must be nothing in his nature that is inaccessible to him or from which he is cut off. His self-openness must be complete. Ours never can be. We exercise great strength sometimes, but never continually and often only at rare moments. Those who are the most creative have found a way to hold open the doors of their personality for full expression, but only with great effort, whether this appears on paper or on canvas or on a public stage. Yet, however impressive such a performance is, it can only be in degree; it is not a divine demonstration of completeness. Talents are lost; insights fade. We may recognize our best moment as being even God-like; but we are never free of the threat of loss. Spinoza's error was to think us too much like God.

Tragedy is not in the divine life itself, although God may respond to it. Tragedy seems to be in Jesus' life, although it lies more in his concern for a lost humanity than for himself. If Jesus loses himself in the crucifixion, it is not, as it is with our losses when they happen, because the self is confused. Tragedy comes to Jesus because he does not resist the suffering imposed. And what we experience as his resurrection is our insight into his divinity, that is, that unlike all of us mere mortals, he cannot lose himself. We speak of our need for personal integration too, as well as of total loss. Our selves are split and divided and too easily fragmented. Jesus loses contact with no part of himself and, many believe, also with no part of God. Our power to prevent loss or fragmentation is quite limited, although we recognize some people as being strong spiritually and mentally as well as physically.

We are all vulnerable to loss, and we do not understand the precariousness of all human life if we think otherwise. In novels and in newspapers the contemporary man or woman is defined by the search for himself/herself. So it has always been, but it seemed to take on a more self-conscious form in the Modern World. This fact might have something to do with the loss of our sense of the presence of God, a fact which many report, although some have rejected God quite consciously. This is connected to our failure to understand Jesus full nature, for which his label as 'divine' was a powerful symbol. God is safe against loss, as no other is; Jesus is unable to lose himself, which aligns him with God; and he reaches out to offer us a secure sense of identity and purpose. This has traditionally been known as the experience of 'salvation' or as receiving 'new life'.

6. JESUS CANNOT BE OVERCOME BY DESIRE

The Church of England and many religious conservatives objected to the screening of Kazantzakis' film, The Last Temptation of Christ, because it shows Jesus as subject to the temptation of desire. Although not banned, its screening in America sparked wide protests from conservative Christians. Why? Because the exalted status to which Jesus has been raised seemed to many to exclude the temptations of desire, that to which most of us are so often prone. But in every respect, Jesus feels desire more ardently than most of us do, e.g., in his desire to save us from the tortures of guilt. To love our enemies, which Jesus recommends, must involve desire, otherwise it becomes unearthly. So we should not exclude all desire from Jesus but only what we think is "beneath his station". Still, our dilemma comes from the old formula, "what is not assumed cannot be saved". He must share our lives and emotions fully, else he cannot save us fully, no matter what the divine power.

Surely it is true that we need to be rescued or restored from the damages which our passions cause, the more earthy the more devastating they are. Thus, if in his own experience Jesus does not understand why passions threaten every day to carry us away, often against our own protest, how can he offer to rescue us from what he does not know first hand? God's incarnation could have taken spiritual form only. But the significance of Jesus full bodily presence is an indication of God's acceptance of the physically real in the divine creation and of all that this implies. It is not that physical existence does not cause us trouble as well as pleasure, but it must be experienced both positively as well as negatively before it can be brought under control. We want to avoid being "out of control". We also want to experience all that is in the world and in our bodies, as well as in our spirits, as being open to us -- which is the same as to say all that God has made open to us and to Jesus.

It is said that we must die with Jesus in order to experience his resurrection. In like manner, he must experience the depths of our desire in order to be able to accomplish our rescue from destructive excess. As we have noted, Jesus capacity for control borders on the divine. Loss of control is our Achilles heel when desire and passion sweep us away, both for good and for ill, as Plato explained in the Phaedrus. But Jesus must sink to our depths of temptation before he can offer us any effective control for our run-away desires. We say that he is like us "save without sin", because his control saves him from destructive action, whereas ours often does not. But he must experience every attraction we do, which is what it means to be 'tempted', since what one is not attracted to cannot tempt us. In Jesus' early testing, he was tempted to use power and his divine prerogatives to accomplish his purposes, as we so often try to do. Among us only the mad are tempted to use power as God does. But human desire is another matter.

If God depends only on himself for fulfillment whereas we depend on others, that would make God a figure whose existence is alien to the troubles of our lives. However, in Jesus God chose both to depend on others and at the same time to offer them a fulfillment beyond dependence. But to do this, God had to depend on Jesus, commit himself to humanity, and Jesus in turn had to depend on us. Since neither God nor Jesus ultimately controls us, both are dependent on our response and so are subjected to repeated rejection or betrayal. The satisfaction of their divine desires for us have been placed outside of their control. If so, both acquire the basis that is needed if they are to experience every desire and can exclude none. But at the same time they cannot be overcome by this. Our life is both exciting and precarious, because we constantly risk being overcome, "going out of control." Jesus risks our rejection, but he is not himself overcome either by his or our desires.

Yet, this is a strange concept for us to deal with. Perhaps that is why it is often so hard to understand the picture of God which Jesus draws for us. It is of a God who cares and loves and offers rescue; Jesus demonstrates and offers us just that. But how can one really care, really love us, and never be overcome by desire? That is "unnatural". Yet it is just this paradoxical combination that we must grasp if we want to understand both Jesus and the God he represents. To understand various concepts of the Trinity is a "cinch" compared to picturing a passionate Jesus who extends himself for us but never risks loss of control. How can such an odd being really understand our plight or experience it fully enough to help us? The issue comes down to witnessing the best exercise of control we can find among human beings, marveling at what this can accomplish and the new heights to which at times it takes its possessors -- and us too vicariously.

Now, take what we call the highest in human experience and extend it so that it does not risk loss but maintains constant control through power. This is not a cold control, ruthless and uncaring, as so much is that we encounter. Jesus experiences every passion, every attraction, every allure or thrill and even danger, but he never moves across the point-of-no-return in maintaining control. As 'unnatural' as this is to us, that is, it never appears within our experience fully, we know that it is our ideal; we recognize it and admire it. We can extend it to Jesus as his link to divinity and attach it to his offer of our rescue, sure in the fact that the rope on the life preserver he throws to us will not break. His rescue can be smooth and clean and sustained, where as our offers of rescue are often faulty and tenuous.

7. JESUS CANNOT AVOID EVIL

When we come to the unavoidable presence of evil in our own experience, we come to the problem which blocks God out of view for many and prompts us to ask if Jesus himself is free of responsibility for our tragedy. The answer of course is "no", the world was not made "squeaky clean" to begin with. Snakes and other attractions beyond our ability to resist were original with the architectural plan of The Garden, and all this supposedly came before the fascinating madness of sex complicated matters further. But if we move from the Garden of Eden and leave God to explain the divine moral responsibility to Adam and Eve, how can we say that Jesus in involved with evil? It appears to him; it surrounds him; it threatens him; it finally takes his life. But what does it mean to say that he could not avoid evil? And at the same time we want to say that he is not guilty of committing it.

Jesus could have avoided evil by remaining as a contemplative in the desert or by withdrawing to the safety of a cave with a rigorously observant group. But he did not. If you mingle with sinners, as he did, if you get in the way of civil and religious authority and yet do not bend to their control, you are not, you cannot, avoid evil. Your hands get dirty simply by involvement. This is guilt by association, which Jesus experienced then and many do still today. But this also represents the uncertainties involved in any course of action (The Hamlet Syndrome): the unavoidable tinge of evil one draws into himself or herself if one does not stay aloof but is driven to act. To care is to be involved, and to be involved is to be subject to taint and even to legitimate rebuke for not distancing yourself, or for not "correcting the situation."

Had Jesus wanted to avoid evil, he could have chosen a quite different path, joined the 'safe' people of his day. Evil is just as real as the morning newspaper reports to us every day, or as we can tell by bombs exploding in Israel and by the violence next door. Jesus could not avoid evil except by avoiding the world. Many among us reject "the world". But some learn to deal with it selectively and thus powerfully. Go for the best; associate with the right people, as many mothers urge upon their children. While still in training, one needs to look for the "right" associates. But if one seeks to care for the world and not simply seek one's own advance to positions of power and/or security, one moves among a crowd where evil cannot be avoided, although this does not mean that we need to encourage or support it. To be of real assistance to anyone, one abandons aloofness and risks being soiled. Evil is not countered by aversion.

In this dangerous venture, vigilance and counter pressure are constantly demanded. But this is the road upon which Jesus set himself, and his loyal followers must do the same. Thus, in avoiding evil we miss something important about Jesus and about his representation of God. We idealize, we romanticize, we set Jesus apart; we wash his feet clean whereas he washed the dirty feet of others. We sanctify Jesus in ways he never asked us to do. He asked only that we love and serve wherever the need is, both spiritual and physical. But in Calcutta where Mother Teressa toils, evil is ever-present and never far away. We know that this is also true in the corporate board rooms and in the seats of political power. However, it is more discreet in those settings, clothed in urban dress and clever talents, ever conscious of media presence. Jesus moved among simpler forms of evil, but they were destructive none the less.

Jesus comes to us with God's offer to raise us above destruction. But how can we understand or appreciate that offer unless we not only feel evil's destructive power but come close to its attraction, to its allure. 'Evil' means power used for the destruction of others, but the use of power is also necessary for life-enhancing work. Thus, we need to see how one can feel attracted to use power to destroy and how danger, even the smashing of bodies, can carry with it an aspect of thrill and elation. Read Gogol's accounts of the purifying effect of violence. One plays God in deciding on destruction or extinction. Thus, evil cannot be controlled until its attraction is understood. It could not be an all-negative power, else it would not find so many willing human instruments. This does not mean that destruction or the waste of life is good. It simply means that we need to associate with evil if we are to learn how power can go wrong.

Thus, we know Jesus did not try to avoid evil, else he would have excluded Judas from his circle long before the act of betrayal. But he did not return evil for evil, or counter his attempted destruction by subverting someone else, as we too often do. He took evil into himself; he allowed it around his spirit and still offered forgiveness. That at first does not seem to be an act that is a very powerful counter force to evil. And it was not; Jesus was slain. But in Jesus trial and conviction -- and he suggests the same for every follower's consciousness -- there lies his confidence that God will reverse evil's destruction for the innocent, or for those who are made innocent again by love and forgiveness. Jesus cannot avoid evil just because he comes as a divine instrument for its present and future reversal. We can only avoid being drawn into evil by identifying with Jesus, i.e., by imitating his Acts.

8. JESUS CANNOT PREDICT THE FUTURE

Even when theologians have claimed that a detailed knowledge of the future is God's distinctive possession, such foreknowledge has usually not been attributed to Jesus. Why? Even according to a "high Christology", Jesus can be excused from God's determining foreknowledge by appealing to his "fully human" nature. And surely human beings do not know the future in full detail, even if some perceptive and sensitive people border on the clairvoyant, else we would not be gamblers. Taking Jesus in himself, there is little need to give him knowledge of the future. His own words and actions appear as one who knows the uncertainties of human existence and is content not to force them. Placing the burden of decision on each individual as he does, it would be play-acting if he did not leave us a genuine contingency in decision whose outcome is unknown in advance, even by such a one as Jesus.

Of course, there are utterances of Jesus which seem to predict the future. But these are generalized predictions about human fate and are not usually connected to particular human decisions and our uncertainties. Jesus can say how the human future will go in general without feeling that every individual action must be determined along with it. This is relatively easy to accept, and it frees Jesus to make his long range predictions about our future. Nevertheless, the connection to God, however conceived, is harder to deal with. That is, if God is given predictive powers about the future, which many do attribute to deity, then in his connection to God we would somehow have to exclude Jesus from any contact with the divine intellect. Must we free God from explicit foreknowledge in order to free Jesus to accept contingency and so to free us?

Many who are religiously inclined have given God this certain foreknowledge, because it seems to them to give our world a religious security in the midst of flux. As is so often the case, many are willing to trade the burden of freedom for a sense of security. In this way humans have traded away God's freedom along with theirs. In Jesus' case it is harder to foist a foreknowledge of detail off on to him because of the way he treats his disciples and those around him. He always seems reticent about vast pronouncements and painfully aware of the uncertainties of his followers. You may say that this indicates that he "knows" what they will do. On the other hand, all we need to claim is that he "knows", i.e. understands, human nature and its inconsistencies, not each individual's particular future action.

We cannot ignore the times at which Jesus does announce his knowledge of future action, e.g., Judas' betrayal, Peter's defection. Here we need not postulate a full knowledge of all the future events in history but simply his insight into how events were unfolding and his intuition of how those close to him would respond. We could attribute these to "miracles", to a special in-breaking into nature's ways, but the notion of a keen insight into events and people as they unfold is sufficient. Jesus knowledge of our uncertainties and indecision should be given preference over any tendency to fix upon him a knowledge of the future in full. If we accept this limitation, we can take seriously Jesus' revelation to us of God's nature. We say that Jesus reveals a God who, at least for now, leaves the future free to be developed by our contingent human decision.

As with God, Jesus' strength can be seen in his willingness to live with contingency and not to try to fix it in order simply to satisfy his own desire to control, as we so often do. However, he did not need modern psychology to tell him that human behavior is unfortunately all too predictable. Still, Jesus is exceptional. He controls his own actions and his own responses, as we attempt to do at our best and as we see this embodied in the actions of our heroic models. Freedom and uncertainty are difficult to handle and often destructive. We know that. This cannot be the case with Jesus. He controls himself. But had he thought his future fixed and also known to God, and had he understood God as some say he did, his prayer in the garden before the trial and crucifixion would be needless agonizing. He should simply have said to God, with a touch of irony, "why argue; you have my future determined and have known it from eternity".

But Jesus not only does not seem to see the world "under the aspect of eternity", as God is said to do by some, e.g. Spinoza. He seems to act and to deal with us as if the future were open, as if its future shape has uncertainties, at least some of which we can resolve if we will. He understands our hesitancy and our uncertainties, and he offers assistance, just as good friends can lend strength to our determination to deal with our freedom. Jesus has insight into our human nature, its frailties and its promise, a power which impresses us still today. Yet that is a different matter from claiming any form of omniscience for him. Jesus acts as if the future is not fixed until we get there, until we see how men and women will respond to the burdens placed upon them. If this were not the case, it was unnecessary for Jesus to come to us with warnings and exhortations.

In brief, any claim that Jesus could know the future fully renders his whole mission entirely senseless. The drama could unfold without him. God can save or condemn us based solely on divinity's own power. So why offer the agony of crucifying your son unless you thought the effort might cause some to change their outlook and behave differently than expected? If we have the power to change part of the way our future world shapes up, God has an important mission for Jesus. To argue for us to "repent" is a useless waste of voice if God fully knows the future. Jesus is surely fooling us in asking us to change our actions, in any of the ways that he recommended in his words and actions, if secretly he has God as his source and knows the future with certainty. The drama goes out of the whole gospel story if the future is fixed. Uncertainty is the essence of drama.

We have argued that God enjoys an open future much more than a future under absolute control. Jesus does not so much "enjoy" our freedom as he does agonize over it, because he sees us so often making disastrous decisions. But this is at the same time the openness of freedom which allows us to respond to Jesus' call. Sin cannot be appealed to as a reason to seek change, unless the individual genuinely feels responsible for his or her own acts, decisions, thoughts. You do not understand or use good sense if you rail against a fixed series of events. You enter into the world, rather than withdrawing from it, if you feel that your effort if inserted into the sequence might have some beneficial effect -- or even a minimal negative effect. You call out warnings to others only if you feel they have a chance to respond out of their own uncertainty over the future.

9. JESUS CANNOT ABANDON THOUGHT

"Of course not", you might say. "What a stupid suggestion". But if one consults the mystics, they often see God as dwelling above the need for discursive thought. We need not go as far as Zen Buddhism to find this argued for. Eckhart discovers the central experience of God to

be one of 'emptiness'. We surely do not want to find God as full of
confused or incomplete thoughts as we are. But even if you take a
traditional approach and define 'God' as a being who possesses full
and complete thought, an intellect fulfilled and at rest, God seems to
rise above our own struggle to use thought. So we have to consider the
possibility that God might be beyond the use of, and the need for,
thought. Where Jesus is concerned, this is a more important question
than it is for God. Why? Because we see Jesus struggle with thought as
if it were the ultimate medium for communication and the path
leading to his actions. He does not try to teach us to rise above
thought, as our Zen instructor does.

This question also concerns Jesus' relationship to God and
eventually to us. If God in the divine nature existed above thought,
Jesus as he embodies God would represent an outpouring to a lower
order, that is, God in relationship, not God in himself. This can be true
and has been said, but then Jesus 'revelation' would not be of the true
God ("a God beyond God", as Tillich put it) but of a lessor God. Thus,
we are in that sense misled in following Jesus in our search for God, or
at least we will eventually have to go "beyond Jesus" if we want to find
God. Many mystics say this about any avenue of approach we might
take to God. Yet they usually do not stress Jesus' mission or our
necessity to follow Jesus Acts as a clue to our own action and to God's
nature, since 'action' , they feel, lies on a lower plane from true deity.

'Unity' has often been stated to be the central divine attribute. This
tends to place divinity beyond thought's grasp. Using Jesus as our key
to God would tend to tell us that action is a better avenue to God's
understanding than thought, as it is also for Jesus, although thought is
nevertheless necessary as an expression of action and as enabling our
understanding of it. We are not to attempt to "rise beyond thought",
but we do need to place thought as secondary, even though important
for our reflection on action. Thus, Jesus gives us no hint that God's
center is a unity that eludes or transcends the intellect's grasp. His
famous statement that he and the father are 'one' is not so much an
assertion of mystical identity as it is that he and God are in perfect
harmony over Jesus' actions and the words he uses to express God's
intentions and divinity's wish for our mode of active response.

We are then "condemned to think", as Sartre told us we were
condemned to be free, because our freedom depends on our right use of
thought in exploring alternatives, lest our will conclude us to action

blindly. The Zen monk, the successful Christian mystic, is relieved to move beyond thought. Who wouldn't be. It is an inconclusive affair full of uncertainty. But Jesus' whole life is one that dramatizes uncertainty, ours if not his. God has no ultimate reliance on thought, and Jesus knows how often words are neither heard nor understood. Yet he seems to feel that they can be a powerful instrument and can on occasion lead us in the right direction. He rejects a controlling determinism and settles for freedom and contingency with all the uncertainties of thought that go with it.

Jesus continues to think about us, even still today, he has told us, because our decisions are not yet fully set. Thus, God must constantly follow the world by using thought, even though the divine predictive capacity is phenomenal. So we ask if we can "surprise" Jesus, and the answer must be yes, at least occasionally. If this were not possible, emotion and feeling would be ruled out of their role in determining action, and we know they cannot be, because we see their so often destructive aspects. Yet God would not want us to remove emotion due to its destructive effects, even if Spinoza would, because God intended to express love in the person of Jesus. And so we must be free to love, as the phrase says, "since he first loved us". But love is risky business, even in God's case -- and especially for Jesus, as we now know and as he came to realize.

Jesus represents the saving as well as the damaging potential in love, and by his acts he tries to convey God's use of love as an expression of healing and support, rather than as pain and damage. God is not an 'intellectual'; he prefers the response of powerful emotion and action. But God cannot abandon thought, because it is necessary to the expression of emotion, and to the telling of a story, in order to report those actions to be recommended and those to be avoided. However, as it was said by the mystics that God could not be grasped by thought, so Jesus can neither be presented by thought alone nor understood solely by it. Why? First, because we have argued that "in the beginning was the act", not the word. Second, Jesus uses words to express emotion and feeling, not simply thought or concept.

In sum, the question of whether Jesus can abandon thought is tied to our problem of how to understand Jesus and who he is. If act and deed define the person, as Existentialists argue too, thought is not our fundamental instrument, but neither can it be 'abandoned'. Jesus needs thought if he is to understand our response, or the lack of it, and we need thought in order to assess his action and then to express either our response to, or our rejection of, it. So our failure to abandon thought and our insistence that Jesus cannot either, even in his relationship to God, is not due to the intellect's final centrality and supremacy. It is due to our need to express action and next to call others to it. Jesus has a 'gospel' to be preached, even if its theme is a recommended form of action or emotional response, e.g., acts of love and forgiveness.

Thought must neither be set aside nor abandoned on the claim that it is a distortion of the highest level of being, i.e. God. But neither should it be claimed as the ultimate human instrument, because it can be distorted and used for destructive purposes as well as for good. Keep it we must, frail and even deceptive an instrument that it can be. We have no choice, even though the abandonment of thought in Zen or in Christian mysticism is an attractive alternative, particularly after we have been deceived by fascinating intellectual pictures that later proved to be factually distorted. Thought can mislead, because it can misrepresent truth, and it can more easily make decisions and actions difficult. It gets tangled in webs of its own construction. But thought cannot be abandoned. It just must be used with caution. And unfortunately, it does not contain its own formulation for perfection, as Descartes and Wittgenstein hoped.

10. JESUS CANNOT DENY HIS WILL
...ELSE HE COULD NOT ACT FOR HIMSELF

Theologians often speak as if Jesus did not have his own will, or at least as if he did not exercise it. True, after due protest he bound himself to what he took to be God's will and proceeded to his trial and crucifixion. But his "garden agony" is meaningless, as is his surrender to God, unless he struggles with the desires of his own will. That Jesus, or that we, can become "obedient to God" is true if difficult, but our obedience, even if like that of Jesus, is nothing to celebrate unless it is a voluntary surrender achieved at some cost to individual desire. Thus, in opposition to the usual stress on Jesus' submission, we want to claim that Jesus could not and did not deny his will. We could not identify with him or accept his assistance if he did not struggle with his own will as we do with ours. 'Revisionist' Roman Catholic feminists might have an easier time with Maryology if they pictured Mary's "submission" along the same lines as Jesus' final obedience.

In fact, God would not want it otherwise, we feel. God's own will is central to the divine nature, and we would not find the evolved order of the universe, or universes, before us as we do in this form if God had not committed the divine will to vast architectural projects on an evolutionary course. Thus, Jesus represents God to us by bending his own will to undertake the mission of inaugurating the Kingdom. We too, then, face the project of trying to bring God's kingdom on earth "as it is in heaven", and that vast project is so monumental that only an intense commitment of the will could even make a beginning. In addition, the world of human affairs, which spreads out at our doors, operates counter clockwise to "God's time". Therefore, no reversal can be accomplished, neither in ourselves nor in others, without intense concentration of will. Ironically, this means turning the will away from its natural orientation. This anti-natural turning is a religious necessity for spiritual advance, one not much understood or accepted in a hedonistic age.

Will is not, however, easily submissive to our control. Thought is easier to direct, even if the errant school boy does not think so. Emotion is perhaps more volatile than our will, more erratic and more explosive at times. But it is easily, often too easily, moved, whereas the will is sometimes stubborn where taking direction is concerned. Will can mold the future or destroy it. It stays loyal or collapses its support and changes direction. However, if we have God's pledge not to destroy the world or to withdraw the power that undergirds our continued existence, with Jesus we can find an openness that stresses love. But this is complicated because he often uses the will's power to support those people and events we might reject, that is, unless our love can enlist the support of a strong will. We think of Jesus as never varying from his course, and we are right in that. His steady will underlies all the myriad possible variations.

Of course, today we often say of our self that we are "willful", that it is unable to undertake effective action, that we are resistant to direction or, more importantly, are self-centered. Will naturally moves around its possessor and, like the faithful dog, is responsive to the master or mistress's suggestion. Thus, we recognize that human will appears in a transformed state in Jesus. It is responsive to others, not solely to his own needs. His revelation to us is that God's will is likewise not primarily self-directed and that, as much as it does not seem so now, God's attention is on the welfare of all in the human race. The divine will is directed toward our care, in spite of the fact that the planets which God set in their orbit seem unconcerned with our concerns. God's will has been reversed to an outer-directedness; Jesus bent his will to follow this direction; our will fluctuates and waits for firm direction.

Prophets and messengers, such as Noah's dove and Jesus, report that God can change the direction of the divine will too. Anger is as possible as love; but divinity withholds revenge and wholesale destruction, as we sometimes do not. So we need to study the occasions and the conditions for God's change in the commitment of the divine will. Jesus offers this example for Christians. God's message is that divine anger over outrageous human behavior will be contained and, depending on repentance, will be converted instead to an expression of love -- a formidable undertaking if we try to imitate it. Yet we cannot forget human freedom or God's openness to novelty. So again Jesus is key: God did not force love upon us but expressed it in the Acts of Jesus, and it was so hidden and clothed that it can (all too easily) be mistaken or rejected. Jesus allows our individuality, as was evidenced in his latitude with his disciples, so that our will, like his, must stay lose in order to accommodate.

Betrayal, denial, self-centered destruction -- for us these forces challenge the will, as they did for Jesus too. The issue becomes how to stay true to one's commitment. God's was enacted in creation; Jesus' appears in his announcement of God's kingdom; ours is evidenced in various callings. Can we still stay open to adjustment as novelty breaks in or as drastic reversals occur? We postulate that God has the power to do this in spite of human obstruction; and we may believe in Jesus' commitment to do this in spite of suffering, betrayal, and misunderstanding. Jesus does not deny his will; he controls its direction, and its necessary changes. The issue is not to get rid of one's will, as some argue, so much as to maintain control and direction in spite of countervailing forces. The fact that Jesus cannot, does not, deny his will in an example to us, not only of our freedom but also of the strength of commitment required to effect any change.

11. Jesus' Actions Cannot Be Coerced

Given the number who have and do pray to Jesus daily for assistance, this fact is not easy to accept. Roman Catholics pray for saints to intercede for them. But if Jesus cannot be coerced, even his mother's plea should not be able to turn his direction, let alone those of lessor saints. Yet we must make a distinction between a 'plea' and 'coercion'. Jesus cannot be forced, but we have just stated the desirability of a strong will. Plea is another matter. We accept that neither Jesus nor God are quixotic in their commitments. Yet in line with freedom and the prominence of contingency, not to mention the chaos in our lives, we believe total inflexibility to be a defect, even in God, or perhaps especially in God. Thus, we offer our petitions to Jesus without any attempt to coerce, since that would be counterproductive. Jesus cannot be bought.

We stress the primacy of will and the need for its support in divine as well as in human decision. But parallel to a flexibility that allows for freedom, a rejection of coercion must be included, or else heaven would be besieged by public relations experts pressing their client's causes. Jesus listens; he accepts our pleas; he promises comfort, but he does not promise to be coerced by pressure. If Jesus is to be steadfast and faithful to his promise of willing our support, he must stand beyond coercion and represent God's steadfast adherence to the divine intent. Every Jew knows that God's kingdom may lie within us for some, but this becomes evident externally only occasionally. The reverse and often mysterious side of our inability to coerce either Jesus or God is their unpredictable delay in implementing their intentions. We still are ladies and gentleman in waiting.

Jesus began by refusing to use power to attain his ends. If he will not coerce us, it follows that he will not be coerced by us. Yet millions try. Jesus' offer of support and relief seems so open and so unconditional that many take it to mean that he is easily attracted to support their particular purposes. Not so. Jesus says his yoke is light, but he never says that he has no burden for us to bear. In fact the opposite. We are asked to endure persecution and being reviled. If so, why should Jesus be expected to respond to our pressures to change his will -- or God's? Jesus does not violate our freedom by forceful intrusion. Due to this fact his message is often missed or misread. But he accepts no intrusion on his person either. He rejects force as an instrument of action -- even for the good.

Of course, we see force running wild all about us. In that sense Jesus rejection of force as an instrument, whether directed from him to us or from us to him, would seem to doom his mission to ineffectiveness, or so Lenin and Mao and countless revolutionaries would argue. But that is the fascination of his mission, that is, for those who can accept its paradoxes. He claims that its offer will be made good, even if brute force is not immediately brought to bear on the powers which today seem unrestrained in defeating any opposition. This of course places a burden on the follower of Jesus, many of whom like Thomas need some proof if they are to be able to believe, as they must, against overwhelming present negative evidence. Jesus message is that God has chosen a less direct approach than the successful of the world usually adopt. But since Jesus represents God's indirect approach, the use of non-obvious means opens Jesus to our rejection too. And all this leaves God's plan open to ridicule.

Our problem is to reconcile an all-powerful God with Jesus' modest appearance and his passivity in the face of violence. Sometimes of course, following Jesus' non-violent, passive resistance can be an effective instrument, e.g., Gandhi or Martin Luther King. But on the whole the success of that approach is limited, and all around us we face power that is subtle or brutally applied to achieve its purpose, or at least to inhibit ours. This is where we need to reflect on Jesus' inability to be coerced. And this could provide a basis of faith for either Christian or Jew. If the Temple has not been restored, if the Kingdom is not yet visibly dominant, our temptation is to deny either God's power or the veracity of Jesus promise. Non-coercion at its base means that neither Jesus nor God will be deterred from their aim, even if it is delayed.

Were it Jesus' aim to fulfill our wishes by responding to coercion, it would not be hard to conceive that he might give up on the mission to bring God's kingdom to earth, since the difficulties are immense, the delays inordinate, and the natural opposition constant. We wish Jesus would bend to our pressure, and popular preachers portray him as responding to their pleas. But a Jesus who can be swayed by immediacy, even though it would be a relief at the time, could also abandon the long term mission, which would give us no basis for faith in a revised future. The question concerning Jesus' lack of response to genuine needs is constantly perplexing, and it is not fully answerable in the present day. But this unyielding quality is at the same time the basis for our confidence...odd as that often seems.

12. JESUS CANNOT BE CAPTURED BY FORMULA

It may sound strange to say this. Anyone familiar with the history of the Christian tradition, or who is involved in the struggle between contemporary churches, knows how seriously we have tried to do this. The center of this controversy has been and is the attempt to place in words (or song or ritual or story) a final expression for who Jesus is and what we can expect from him. It is admitted that the gospel accounts represent this, each in its own way, with John standing apart as having "elevated" his estimate of Jesus' status. Paul's letters, and the rest of what came to be codified as the New Testament, continue this process, at the same time that they recount bits of history of the early Christian communities. The Church Fathers carried on this attempt in more systematic fashion, as wider contact with other cultures and philosophies fed more material into their accounts. The rest of the struggles within Christianity, and the outbreak of both the Reformation and other 'revisionist' movements, all still have this question of Jesus at the center.

This whole process was set in motion by Jesus himself, because he did not provide rigid definitions or masses of his own writings, all the while still challenging would-be followers to declare who they thought he was. Following his instructions to carry the gospel to the world, rather than to isolate themselves in insular communities, each who goes out to preach or to serve must find a voice to express who Jesus was and is, at the same time declaring where the center of his message is to be found and what it entails. Of course, in the whole of Christian history we find numerous, often illuminating and even powerful, confessional, creedal formulations of who Jesus is. And the success of the world-wide missionary movement testifies to the fact that preachers and practitioners have found an often powerful voice to explain -- by acts and by works of love -- Jesus to millions. In many cases this happens with such effect that thousands accept the message, are changed by hearing it, and alter their lives accordingly.

Thus, what we know with some certainty and on a factual basis is that Jesus can be pressed into a formula and conveyed in that way to others who lack direct contact with him. And yet not all agree to any single formula for long, except by attempted coercion. This should not make us skeptical about the function of creeds, dogmatic statements, or even about our continued attempt to formulate and to construct them (that is the function of 'theology'). But it should make us realize that we are unavoidably launched on a process without end, and that this very fact tells us something about Jesus, who he is and how he can be represented. In the first place, as the mystics say about God, divinity transcends our ability to confine its full expression to words or concepts. This similar impossibility for Jesus, one which is testified to by centuries of effort, does not prove that Jesus is divine or support any given Trinitarian theory, since one might say the same thing about art, poetry, or even metaphysics.

Yet realizing all this should give us an indication of the proper way to relate to Jesus, and it also offers us a clue as to how he intended his mission to be promulgated, with an underlying suggestion of why he would use such inconclusive, non-definitive means. It is clear that he could have been very explicit and detailed in his definitions and instructions, had that been his aim. He left us with inconclusiveness, and yet at the same time challenged us to formulate our own expressions, coupled with a mandate to Act so as to carry out his mission. Jesus has asked each one who approaches him to make an assessment, whether this ends in a declaration, in a rejection, or in a skeptical suspension, and then to act according to his or her own responsibility. Obviously, we start with a massive background and not with a blank canvas, but we also come to see why it is impossible to reach any decision without formulating and acting on an individual 'faith'.

If God is by nature illusive to our grasp, at least Jesus is less so. In that sense, he can be a revelation of God to us, just as many have accepted him. The problem is that our instrument of revelation, in this case Jesus, is not fully understandable or beyond change either. However, as the Jew bases his or her relationship to God on the Exodus Event, so I have suggested Christians base their relationship to God on the Acts of Jesus. In both cases, a God who is ultimately illusive, or at least not directly seen, is made concrete for us by an act or set of actions. One problem we face in using such an anchor for our understanding of God (or for Jesus) is that the power and illumination which these events contain does not always appear, let alone stay steady or hold constant for all. From the beginning, we know that there are many who will not accept these Acts as their key to God. Yet our problem is more complicated, just because the revelatory power does not hold constant, neither over time nor for the individual enthusiast.

This fact should not cause us to claim that God cannot be discerned in Jesus' Acts. We know that millions have testified to it and that powerful communities have been built upon it. But we also know that no religious claim can be universal or asserted to hold its revelatory power constantly. In the first place, the real power lies in the Acts, which the words used to describe them can only try to convey. Our actions may revive an original event or Act too, but we know that, although the power of words to convey is amazing at times, at other times the same words fall on deaf ears. We have had multiple avenues to the divine set down for us, and we can rediscover or pioneer new spiritual paths ourselves. But the road to the discovery of Jesus, and then to verbal formulation, is always an odyssey and a pilgrimage.

13. JESUS CANNOT DENY THE HOLOCAUST

A 'holocaust', as we know simply from reading the Old Testament, means a burnt offering. Taken away from the notion of the sacrifice offered to Yahweh and often required by him, the term has more recently come to mean the Nazi destruction of the Jews, Hitler's wholesale slaughter in the attempt to reach "the final solution" to the race question. We know that some have argued that their religious faith went up in the smoke of the gas ovens that consumed Jewish children. Any outbreak of massive evil, i.e. senseless destruction without a redeeming feature, induces a crises concerning God. Job's questions return to us in urgent form. And they are harder to explain now than when Job had his privileged divine dialogue, partly because

Yahweh does not appear and respond to our pleas, nor is everything restored to us as it was for Job.

We struggle to understand Jesus in relation to the gospel accounts. But how does Jesus respond to a modern holocaust, whether in Poland, Russia, or Viet Nam? He cannot stay aloof; he cannot reject it; denial would violate his own injunction to serve every need, to respond to every suffering individual. Let us contrast this with Peter's famous denial of his Lord. When Jesus faced his own 'holocaust', Peter denied that he knew him, fearing for his own fate.

Jesus is not present to be sacrificed again today, but nothing we know suggests that he would not first be agonized and then identify with the victims. This time it is we who phrase our questions to God about all this, rather than Job. Denial is not a quality we associate with Jesus. Nothing in his own time caused him to withdraw. As he did with Abraham, God demanded that Jesus offer a sacrifice. Jesus knows the meaning of 'holocaust' first hand, and his own route to and through the holocaust can be ours -- if we elect to follow him there.

A Jew may easily believe in the resurrection, whether of spirit or of body, but it is not quite so central to his or her religious belief as it is for a follower of Jesus. I am not at all suggesting that to use the name 'Christian' one must believe in the bodily resurrection of Jesus. Our relationship to doctrine is not that definitive; it is our actions that are more important. But since Jesus' own mission and the "good news" he preached did end in a holocaust for him, every person who pursues his recommended path of action must decide where and in what way Jesus and his mission continue on in their own time and place. As indicated, this could be through any or all who imitate his Acts, not just in their assertion of belief or in their verbal expression. But how does one account for the end of Jesus' earthly mission; how should one foresees its continuance, and what should one expect from it? How is one to see one's own death and beyond? These are central issues for the searching Christian, and they define what 'belief' means for each.

First of all, we know that passing through a holocaust, whether one's own or other's, does not necessarily remove belief in God or, in Jesus case, his belief in his mission. Of course, neither does this guarantee the survival of belief; far from it. However, it is certain that nothing remains the same after the visitation of such a destructive blast, neither for Jesus' disciples at his time or today, nor for any Jew now or in the centuries of exile. Jesus' own example is proof that the fires of a holocaust descend on good and bad alike; believers and atheists are equally consumed. If God offers any special exemptions to the religiously chosen, or to Jesus' committed followers, this does not appear so at the time, although one may argue for a later restoration. Evil comes close to God in a holocaust; evil threatens to destroy both Jesus and his mission. Here is the ultimate test of belief, that is, when negative destruction is not separated away from religious belief but appears at its center.

The question of how God responds to a holocaust, one that consumes innocents, one that is not merely a sacrifice given in divinity's honor, this is hard enough. Jews can respond with the traditional Exodus recital or by intensified observance of God's commandments. Jesus' own response, and thus that of his followers, is more difficult. Just as Jesus abandons the use of power as an answer to Pilot, so his own response to any holocaust, if it is passive, adds a burden to Christian belief. However, if we shift to The Acts of Jesus, we immediately see his own service to all who suffer, and we hear his injunction to any who follow him that their actions to relieve suffering are the test of their confidence in his mission, not that they can or will prevent holocausts any more than he did. Jesus' passivity, God's noninterference even in the face of senseless destruction, these are the religious questions which a holocaust poses. Our response need not be negative; we need not curse God and die, as Job's "comforters" recommend. But pious proclamations are hard to come by and are sacrilegious if easily indulged in.

"Though he slay one yet will I trust him" is the answer of faith, one given by Job and by Jesus and also by all those who follow him through their own valley of the shadow. Obviously, mystery is never entirely removed. Years after being struck dumb by the holocaust experience, Eli Wiesel can say he is now "waiting for the messiah". But this is not a clear or an easy statement. Even after his death and the halt in his mission, Christians can call Jesus "the messiah" or proclaim him as the 'Christ'. But little in the history of those massive expectations justifies this, and his own death and eventual disappearance render all affirmations possible but also problematic. God does not follow a single "right" path; Jesus' mission was not obviously successful in his time; in fact the opposite seems to be the case. To be true to reality, all religious faith must be prepared to try to survive a holocaust.

Jesus' disciples believed that his holocaust had been transcended. Their faith that God intervened was cause for joy, but it is complicated for us by the question of why God allowed a holocaust to destroy Jesus in the first place and why such destruction was not henceforth banned in the divine-created universe. Jesus promised to return to complete the mission, but that date keeps getting predicted and then postponed. The only certainty is that Jesus left us, although he left us with a mission to carry out and his commission to Act. But to move that forward, good as any individual or group endeavor may be to relieve suffering, we must come to the conviction that a holocaust, any holocaust, does not completely destroy either Jesus, his Acts, or his mission. Not only can Jesus not deny the holocaust; he must walk through it and show his disciples how to follow in that path. This underwrites their belief, as they serve in his name, that holocausts do not consume all without restitution. It turns out that belief in Jesus is meaningless unless he and we enter a holocaust and still retain a belief that we will, eventually at least, survive.

Christians celebrate this on Easter, and we have said that the denial of the final destruction of any holocaust is at the center of any sustained belief in Jesus' role. But such celebrating must always be tempered by asking why Jesus had to die in the first place. A divine proclamation of the intent clearly stated, spread widely on the international communications highway, might have done instead. And more important: Why have millions had to die since, if Jesus' destruction really did overcome death? Could God have rendered the Easter Event unnecessary, or at least banned all holocausts after that? We have said that Jesus is understood in his Acts and that the same is true both for God and for us. By our actions we are known. So verbal proclamations, even the recorded gospel texts, are insufficient. We must follow the Acts, first those of Jesus, then of God. By undergoing the holocaust of crucifixion, Jesus' action (or passivity) tells us what his commitment is. By God's actions, if we accept them, we gain a ground for understanding the divine intent.

14. JESUS CANNOT SPEAK TO US DIRECTLY

In spite of various prophets' proclamations in Yahweh's name, we do not feel that God speaks to us directly, or at least that divinity does so in any public forum. But after reading the gospels, can we not assert that Jesus does so? We have already noted that Jesus is not completely direct in telling us "who he is". There are self-referential statements in our scriptures, true. But they are not many in number and cannot be considered definitive. Jesus speaks about God, and his use of 'father' is, although instructive, obviously not to be taken too literally. We must interpret it. Most important: Jesus tells us stories; he gives us parables; he uses symbols, and he makes references to earlier religious notions. All these help to orient us, but one cannot call this "speaking directly". There is too much indirection and necessary individual interpretation involved. In all the important senses, Jesus does not speak out clearly and definitively.

Again, we have stressed that The Acts of Jesus are key to our understanding. Significant acts, such as those recorded in the gospels about Jesus, we sometimes say, "speak to us loud and clear". Actions can be more definitive than words. Still, the actions we are asked to witness, to follow and to commit ourselves to, these may be graphic and clear to us. But we have to say that this involves an unusual sense of 'to speak' and not what we expect when we chide someone for an obscure statement and ask them to speak to us clearly and directly. Evidently, Jesus cannot do this, for all the important and impressive ways he chose to communicate. Why? In the first place, again, if it is God whom he represents and wishes to communicate to us in order to bring us into relation with divinity, Jesus knows that God is the extreme case where direct statement is inappropriate, likely to mislead, and tends to be distorted by the literal minded. In so far as Jesus communicates God to us, he cannot speak openly but must use indirect means.

Of course, no matter what the Hebrew prophets reported, today God seems to speak directly to very few. In Jesus' own time, in spite of the possible greater receptivity, Jesus does not himself present God as speaking openly. In fact for Christians, if we think about it, if God intended to speak directly to us, Jesus is an unnecessary interference. Thus, if the Christian believes that Jesus reveals God to him or her, it can only be because God has not spoken directly but has used an indirect mode. We may of course still "hear God", even if we do not assert that divinity communicates by direct speech. We often say "we hear you loud and clear" when such communication lies in an action or a gesture and not in a verbal statement. We must protect ourselves against madness, or be prepared for a "madness that is heaven sent", to use Plato's term, if we ask God for a direct intervention into our speech.

Eli Wiesel, you recall, has the figure of the mad man appear in many of his stories, and he means to tell us that God's in-breaking is often destructive of normal rational life. But when we look for God's appearance, we usually turn first to the various collections of sacred literature in which those who composed the canon and those who have studied it over the centuries claim to find the voice of God speaking to them. Certainly, collections of sacred scriptures are a prime source to turn to if we want to hear divinity speak. However, we should know in advance that we can label any voice we hear as 'divine', but that it will never be a clear and consistent and public to all. The same is true of Jesus, if we turn to the Gospels, to his Acts, and to the letters. We may find Jesus' voice present there but not without complications and qualification. Symbol and metaphor and story abound, over against Wittgenstein's preferred direct and simple sentences.

Could God have created a perfect language, avoided the Tower of Babel, aided Wittgenstein in his quest, and then allowed Jesus, and any other messengers who are sent to communicate the divine, to speak in an unmistakable voice? Yes, even if we stay to the notion that God's nature is such that it cannot be communicated finally in language, we could have been given a "more pure, a more universal" mode of discourse than we have. Ordinary language is anything but ordinary and clear in itself. The complexity of translations, and the inevitability of misunderstandings between languages, all this could have been avoided. We have to refer to the silence of God if we want to explain why God did not chose to institute such simplicity in forms of speech. We learn, or we can learn, from silence; God lives at least partially in silence; Jesus is silent about more things than about those matters which he communicates, and even this is rather slim in view of the vastness of our ignorance. True, with the Enlightenment and the Encyclopaedists, many thought that respectful silence had become a thing of the past. But as the hope of the Modern Era fades, we again find much that drives us into silence, in our awe over the origin of universes, in the depths of the human psyche, as well as with God.

Jesus, then, cannot speak to us directly, because that would allow us to misunderstand the meaning of "to keep silence before God". We all know people (including ourselves) who talk too much, when silence might be more appropriate. Jesus, then, wants us to discover the significance of silence and to learn to interpret it. If he spoke to us too directly , all silence would seem superfluous. In his crucial moments, Jesus was silent before Pilot, silent before his disciples, (to their consternation), and silent (almost) before God in his final acceptance. If Jesus spoke to us directly and fully, much that we need to learn for ourselves would be short circuited. Just as God's direct word might coerce our response, so Jesus direct speech might compromise our freedom. It might give us too great a feeling of security, which would ultimately be deceptive if we thought it characteristic both of our inner life and of God's.

15. JESUS CANNOT BE VERY RELIGIOUS

In explaining why this might be true, one obvious response would be to say that it is so just because Jesus is himself the founder of a religion and in many cases the object of worship and so not himself just another religious person. True, it is certain that, if Jesus is to be called 'religious', it must be in a sense different from that of his followers. But to understand all this involves what we mean by 'religious'. If this means to become an object of worship, we know that Jesus rejected being called 'good' and said none but God was good in any absolute sense. Thus, he rejected the status of being an object of worship, and as such he seems to stand outside the whole arena of organized, ritualized religious practice. Jesus conducted no formal services. He celebrate no ritualized mass, although he ate a simple meal.

Yet, the connection between Jesus and God, and the question of Jesus 'revelation', makes this by no means a simple question. Jesus does open us to a possible encounter with God, one that can inspire some to worship. And this can lead to the establishing of formal religions, much as Jesus' disciples wanted to do in response to his transfiguration. Thus, to the very extent that we claim to have witnessed God in Jesus' Acts, in just that sense Jesus becomes "very religious" in our eyes. And so millions have treated him. Yet again, everything depends on what we mean by 'religious'. If we mean giving honor to God, Jesus can enter into that. If it means praying for the forgiveness of sins and the experience of new or renewed life, Jesus can also lead us in that religious quest. If it means prayer, he has given us instruction in that matter. Still, we can say that he is himself "not very religious".

When it comes to elaborate ritual, vestments, outlined movements and stylized words, even inspiring organ music, there Jesus begs off as not being very religious. He advised simplicity in our address to God, and he recommends actions toward others vs. ceremony. Yet nothing in his words exactly prohibits the formation and the use of ritual. The "last supper" seems to recommend some ritual, but surely it is a minimum. Entering into it could lead to a proper religious perception and to increased sensitivity. But in the midst of any "triumphal pomp", Jesus is probably not to be found at its center, though perhaps he might be seen within it searching for the still small voice. He does not reappear to protest elaborate papal masses; he just is not very religious in that sense. And perhaps that is what it is most important to note: This may be because Jesus has equal concern for the secular as well as for the folk who are labeled as ardently religious. Thus he will not identify with "the religious" for fear of shutting himself off from the spiritually needy, those who do not express their searching in institutional or in ritual form. At ceremonial meals, he eats with tax collectors and harlots, just as well as with his disciples and his followers.

Furthermore, "the very religious" often shut themselves off from whole ranges of human experience. Since Jesus aimed his message of good news to all, he cannot accept its exclusive restriction to any single religious form. We know that the monk or nun cuts himself/herself off from much of the full range of direct human experience, perhaps for a good purpose. Although the professionally religious do not recommend this path to all (and would get nowhere if they did), their aim for a special "religious depth experience" can only be realized by concentration and the exclusion of everything but their religious aim. However, if Jesus wants to reach all of humanity, he cannot impose a rigorous ascetic discipline as the only acceptable approach. Therefore, Jesus cannot himself be totally religious, since he must stay open to be found in a wide range of secular pursuits, although it does not follow that he centers in the wild or in the destructive.

Not every human degradation is an avenue to Jesus. Some simple pursuits and common pleasures may be. He does not withdraw from bars and rock festivals, but he might more likely be found in some forms of theater and song. These avenues can become "very religious". Still, Jesus is not associated solely with devoutly religious drama or hymn. His unsuspected presence in ordinary pursuits and secular affairs keeps him from identifying solely with the formally religious and makes his discovered presence a "surprise" in its simplicity. "Love is where you find it", perhaps in a simple gesture of concern. And the same is true of "finding Jesus." Sometimes this happens in churches and cathedrals and shrines, but sometimes not. Of central importance is the way Jesus relates to "non-Christian" religions. If God is the God of all, divinity still needs not be equally present in every religious form -- that is too much self-emptying to ask and might possibly degrade God. Yet even Jesus cannot identify totally with 'Christian' churches and still represent God, as some partisan Christians want to claim. Divinity has not -- and apparently cannot -- speak with one voice.

More important, organized religions tend to get involved in politics, and churches necessarily move toward becoming institutions. There is nothing wrong with this; such mixture of the secular and the sacred is unavoidable. But Jesus cannot afford to be too closely identified with such purely "religious" causes. Jesus sought neither high religious office for himself nor self-veneration. Also, many religions celebrate the changed future they expect. Even if Jesus announced his Kingdom for the future, and even if he inaugurated its present spiritual existence within us, he is all too aware of the pain caused by the continued delay in the coming of the Kingdom, and so he cannot join in the celebration fully -- at least not yet. Thus, he is not the lead actor in the "Glory of Easter" at the Crystal Cathedral in Orange County. Religions and religious celebrations are human tasks and human constructions. In so far as Jesus does bring God to us, and in so far as he represents that office in his nature, he feels no need to be "very religious", except to join us to pray for the final victory and for the eventual coming of God's Kingdom -- one day.

POSTSCRIPT

The average person listening to a Billy Graham revival service may find that the questions we have just asked about Jesus seem strange. Graham's evangelical sermons, his preaching of the gospel of Jesus, have reached and touched millions. Few find basic fault with his approach, although one might differ on some points. For the future of Christianity, one can only be glad we have had apostles like Paul and preachers like Billy. It is clear that Jesus meant his appeal to go to ordinary persons who might find in it a relief from their distress. Why, then, should one ask questions? Do the ones we have just asked really help us to understand Jesus better? Or more important, does trying to answer these questions in any way encourage one to "receive" Jesus' message, to find relief in its acceptance, or to Act as he instructed us to do by his example?

But another issue is primary: those who preach Jesus' "good news" may not present it correctly, or at least they may phrase it in a way likely to lead to disillusion if it is not modified. All who once "accepted" Jesus have not remained ardent followers. Was there something distorted in the message they heard, so that, as time wore on, reality forced them to withdraw their enthusiastic response? If so, at some point both presenter and receiver would be well advised to ask carefully: Just what can Jesus do? What do his Acts tell us? Then, as the question is dealt with, their acceptance -- or rejection -- can be based on a clear perception of what they should expect or not expect. Moreover, it is not we but Jesus himself who placed the burden on the hearer to decide who he was, which we have translated as What can Jesus do?, or The Acts of Jesus.

For one thing, we know that all people have not presented Jesus, or received his message, in the same way. Some forms of the gospel have obviously been more successful than others, just as some who receive him report profound change in their lives while others are unimpressed or even turn hostile. But if Jesus has not been presented in exactly the same way in every age, and particularly if there are any questions about the effectiveness of any current gospel interpretations, we need to go back to the original materials and ask the question of what did and can Jesus do; how did he Act? We only need one "picture" of Jesus to be effective for us, not a catalogue of all possible interpretations. But in order to achieve that we need to go back to the early documents and search there for an account that fits our time and place and condition. This does not mean that every once-contemporary description of Jesus must change in drastic ways. The basic statements and pictures and stories are still there, plus a center of interpretation which we have come to call 'tradition'.

Yet, all this is not simply an intellectual affair of framing a definition, central a role as that may have in achieving understanding. Jesus preached love and sacrifice and healing and forgiveness. That part of his message cannot really come under challenge. By our account, he Acted in consistency with that message. So we can see the core of his gospel more in his Acts than in his words; we see it in the "good news" he preached to others and in the way his actions exemplified this. Other aspects of his life and work may be stressed. Creedal formulas and dogmatic expositions of 'Christology' may be developed, we have argued, but these should be based on Jesus Acts as the clue to our accurate understanding.

What Jesus did, then, is the key to what we can expect him to do for us. There is no reason to believe that this will be any different now than it was then, although it may be variously interpreted. Yet actions are less variable than words, and they are less subject to misunderstandings due to language and cultural differences. If you argue that what Jesus did, e.g., heal the sick, feed the hungry, was acceptable in his day but not in ours, then you have taken one particular cultural setting (ours) and made it definitive. The day when 'science' was thought to render all earlier notions antiquated has passed, and no dogmatic assertions of what can or cannot be believed should be based on some supposed uniformity of scientific knowledge, since this finality in thought did not materialize and does not exist today as fixed -- as it was once expected to. We need to express Jesus' Acts in a way suitable to the day, but no reigning dogma dictates that form in advance. No 'theory' can be equated with 'truth'. All truth is 'uncertain', subject to reformulation.

In every suggested reinterpretation, the scheme in the back of the mind of the presenter (proclaimer) of Jesus' gospel is crucial. He or she must have a careful and a powerful understanding of their answer to the question, "What can Jesus do?", else they cannot carry that good news to others without risk of eventual disappointment. If the "missionary" does not overstate what his or her hearer can expect from Jesus, disappointment can be minimized. The only true test, of course, is in the effect which the recognition of Jesus has, the realization of what he can and cannot do, of what he has and has not done, of how Jesus acted -- plus what effect all this can have on the receiver. Then, the impact on the life of the hearer may be shown by its own parallels to what Jesus evidenced in his Acts.

PART III. THE ACTS OF THE HOLY SPIRIT

"The growth of the spirit is an extraordinary thing, its the work of a lifetime."

Carmalite Monk, quoted by John Cornwell
in <u>Powers</u> of <u>Darkness</u>, <u>Powers</u> of <u>Light</u>

No, the Holy Spirit is not a dove, it is a fire...
Kazantzakis
in <u>Report to Greco</u>

"What is the divine spirit? Is the holy ghost any other than the intellectual fountain?"
W.B. Yeats
in <u>Ideas of Good And Evil</u>

Not by might, nor by power
but by my spirit, says the
Lord of Hosts

Zachariah 4:6
<u>New Revised Standard Version</u>

A. HOW CAN WE APPROACH AN UNKNOWN SPIRIT?

Paul is famous for telling "the men of Athens" that the 'unknown god' whom they worshipped had become known in their time and that Jesus of Nazareth had revealed this divinity. Although we must come to terms with Jesus before we can appraise his role as a "revealer of God", where Christianity is concerned can Jesus make our understanding of an often hidden Spirit become equally open to us? This is not an idle question if one wants to understand Christianity, not only because of the affirmations which traditional doctrine makes about the work of the Spirit, although that alone is enough to make it important. The fact is that Jesus has left us. Thus, even if a glimpse of God is possible in the Acts of Jesus, we must become more familiar with the movements of the Holy Spirit too, else the individual Christian may have little to sustain his or her belief in Jesus' still unfulfilled promises.

Reading about Jesus, hearing Jesus preached about today, still points us back to a distant time. Not many report an immediate experience of his presence. Jesus' life is still lived out in an earlier age. If we are moved by him now, this will probably be due to the Holy Spirit, so that we should try to become familiar with its activities in order to make its existence concrete for us. Even before Jesus' departure from the world stage, the Holy Spirit was important, particularly in the founding of the church after the post-resurrection experiences, as well as in the Pentecost. Had that group not felt themselves possessed, had they not felt the Spirit moving them to speak, and had they not discovered their release from provincial cultural forms, it is clear that Jesus' early group of followers might have stayed local, rather than spreading out in universal activity as they did.

It has been traditional to say that the Holy Spirit is God's form of presence with us in the "last days". Thus, since Jesus is no longer here, and if God must be mediated now by the Spirit's presence, we may lose God unless we can become familiar with the Spirit. The failure to do this may be what has happened to cause the loss of faith by so many. Thus, it may be that the distance or absence of God for many, plus the spread of public atheism, is due not to something God has done, or even what the unreligious Modern Age has caused. If we have lost our sensitivity to receive the Spirit, we have lost our most immediate access to God--until Jesus returns. But then we need to ask: Why are we less sensitive to the Spirit's presence among us, if it has been active in our past and if it is still so important to our understanding of both God and Jesus?

One of our first responses is to note that, in our age, it is more evident that evil spirits have filled us rather than holy spirits. It is not that destructive forces were not present in Jesus day; they have been at all times. It may be that violence has become more dominant, more strident today, making it harder to recognize any spirit as holy when so many are unholy. If the Middle Ages was a time of great faith, and if we are said to have lost that, is there any way in which we can see how the Medieval period was any better than we are at keeping destructive spirits in control and in allowing divine spirits a greater chance for influence? We need not point to the Enlightenment or to the rise of modern science as the cause of the Modern decline of faith, since as a matter of fact this absence may be due more to the loss of the Holy Spirit than to any intellectual or cultural fact.

We do not want to argue that the great public prominence of a powerful church was what kept destructive spirits under control more effectively than we can in a secular environment. But we do want to suggest that the prominence of the symbols of religion had a great deal to do with keeping us open to the descent of the Holy Spirit. In more contemporary terms, we might say that the key question is one of the 'ascent' of the Holy Spirit in the human psyche. Carl Jung has argued that, as religious symbols lost their power, our unconscious became more susceptible to dark forces and to their destructive effect.

Religious symbols, he argued, gave the human psyche structure and an upward focus, so that, where that is lost, the soul wanders and is much more open to destructive forces. Such a simple matter as the saying of a mass, or the giving and hearing of confession, can have the symbolic effect of lifting the soul away from destructive internal spirits.

Thus, in blocking out religious symbols we became locked into a destructive cycle. True, both humanism and science induced secularity as the rise of democracy gave people a greater sense of individual control. These events are in themselves good things, or at least potentially good. But the sense of God's presence, or in the case of Christians, Jesus' immediacy -- these are needed to balance the psyche, to keep it from running amuck and raging over its imagined powers, thinking itself to be totally independent to create worlds free of old restraints. True enough, many political restraints, and the barriers on freedom which a lack of education enforces, those we are or can be well rid of. But if our sense of the Holy Spirit and of God was lost in the process, the destructive forces in the soul, its dark side, can run amuck without opposition.

Certainly many would agree to the fact that there has been a rise in mental illness, plus the increase in crime and crowded prisons. We live in an age of violence and terrorism, not in a time of utopia as was predicted. This need not lead to a call for rightist political-social control; ours has also been the era of the absolutist, the totalitarian regime, and this makes individual liberty seem all the more prized to us, if we can protect it. But what we are asking is whether the rise of the use of violence as an instrument to enforce a social plan is connected to the loss of our sense of the presence of the Holy Spirit, which was left to us as God's vicar -- not to any priest or Pope except as he is a symbol of the God's presence in spirit. The release of evil spirits, which are destructive in our psyche, in our homes and in the public square, is a factor we need to try to counterbalance. Our suggestion -- one suggestion -- is to attempt a reconnection of the Holy Spirit in our lives.

One irony in this is that, with the decline of the influence of overt religious symbolism which once gave the Spirit's presence a sense of focus for us, we have even more trouble today in understanding the Holy Spirit and its methods of operating than we do with God. In the day of the absence or silence of God, the Holy Spirit may seem even more distant. And this must be so, given our appraisal of the destructiveness dominating the public stage. Thus, it is even more difficult to revive the sense of the Holy Spirit's presence, which is needed to balance the destructiveness of our age, than to make God's presence vivid to many today. This is true with a single important exception: we are powerfully aware of the forces which are latent in our collective psyche, and we simply need to refocus on a sense of inner divine presence.

We are, then, painfully aware today of the acts of evil or destructive spirits. We have suggested that Jesus was best understood by his Acts. Can we focus on the not-so-obvious Acts of the Holy Spirit and in so doing find a way to restore its positive power in our private and in our public lives? Given the "wars and the rumors of wars" all about us, so that even the fall of oppressive regimes often seems only to lead to further chaos, it certainly seems worth "giving it a try". In a real sense we have nothing to lose. If Jesus is controversial to some, and if God has been used by others to support their selfish or even destructive causes, the Holy Spirit has "a pretty good reputation in the market place." Certainly it is often associated with artistic and creative energy. Its record in the Christian church is as an inspirer and, most important, as a force overcoming differences. This reconciling presence is important in a day in which every group seems intent on gaining isolated independence with no compromise for the sake of mutual union.

True, the Holy Spirit has been said to cause strange phenomenon too, such as "speaking in tongues." But even if one does not participate, or if one finds this practice not edifying, it is usually not destructive. If the Tower of Babel divided us by language and made us incapable of understanding one another, the descent of the Holy Spirit on Pentecost enabled those assembled to "understand foreign tongues". Nothing seems more needed for us today than for each to be able each to speak in his or her own native tongue but to be able at the same time to understand what others say in theirs. It is the division-overcoming quality of the Holy Spirit which most needs to be explored and revived today, among religions as well as among differing political and social groups.

We need to build a statue to an "Unknown Divine Spirit", perhaps in Moscow or Beijing or Johannesburg today more than in Athens, and then, like Paul, find someone who can make that spirit known to us. If Jesus made the unknown god known to the men of Athens, then to follow our outline of Jesus Acts and non-acts might lead us to the re-discovery of the healing, binding power of the Holy Spirit for us all. And since the Spirit was given to us as the form of God's presence "till he come again", it fits our understanding of Jesus role not to look for his dominating presence among us now (since "he is risen") but to find signs of the work of the Holy Spirit as a way both to understand God more fully and to contain evil spirits more effectively in this day. They are in the world and in our souls, and the powers at loose seem capable of destroying us all, including our religions.

Formal churches cannot create this sensitivity in us of themselves, although some may bring the Holy Spirit closer to us than others. Why? Because every religion is of necessity institutionalized and practically structured. This must be so if a group is to function. But the Holy Spirit is by tradition free and unconfined by conventions. That is the source of its strength. Thus, as much as religious institutions may do good or serve a needed function, as much as they hopefully stimulate us to search for God's spirit, this will only be found in the individual's inner heart or in a wind that blows us free of confinement. If the Holy Spirit is discovered by our awareness of it in its Acts, and if it can increase our sensitivity to God's presence once again, this will be to a God of power, one not contained by formalities or subject to the control of any individual, male or female, priest or lay person -- let alone by institutions, secular or utopian.

What happens when the Holy Spirit does not move Christian peoples? We express a coldness, a hostility, a lack of compassion toward those who differ socially or morally, even leading to violence and repression. The history of religions show us that all are subject to the perversion of their highest ideals. "The letter of the law killeth", we say, and so it is with any rule or code or creed. If spiritual compassion goes out of any law's implementation, human destruction, and particularly the destruction of the human spirit, can follow. Hence the Quakers are good models for us, although our need to keep the world's affairs running will probably not allow us all to become Quakers. They remain as our instructive minority. But all who know them recognize that they operate their meetings and make their societies as structureless as minimal governance allows. Those speak whom the Spirit moves. It does not therefore follow that every word uttered is golden, or that the Holy Spirit would claim the authorship of every phrase a Friend utters. But observing periods of silence does give the spirit an opportunity to move souls -- if they stay alert and sensitive, and non-ego centered.

When the words of any Friend prove particularly inspiring, an old Quaker saying is, "Friend, thee hath been used". And we all are used by many forces, but only a very few of them are 'holy'. However, the aim is to become "ego empty" so that a Spirit has a chance to inspire, to "speak through", to "use" the individual. We know, our psychiatrists know, our priests are all too aware, that the forces roaming around in the souls of most of us often drive us toward ego-bound destruction. So in any age, even in an Enlightened one, or perhaps particularly in an "Enlightened" one since it is so self-proud, the main project is or ought to be to make room for the divine under whatever name or guise. We need to be "much used" by such a Spirit, rather than to center on ourselves and on our interests. To allow ourselves to be dominated by self-concentration locks out every other concern, surely the Holy Spirit most of all.

Let us consider the well known "social gospel" and its connection to the Holy Spirit, or its possible disconnection from it. We need not believe Hobbes or Nietzsche's account of human nature, or even follow Machiavelli's political advice, to realize that nature is little altruistic in its human forms. Often survival dictates a self-centered stance, else we die. But the best of the human spirit has not always been at war with itself or with others; it can and has risen to heights of compassion for those who suffer, e.g., in Jesus or the Buddha. Out of this rare accomplishment come the mystics and those in pursuit of a higher life, and they are an inspiration to many. But from this unnatural compassion, which needs constant nurture and training if it is not to fall back to self protection, comes Gandhi, Martin Luther King, Florence Nightingale, Mother Teressa, and a host of other mission-driven spirits many of whom are not so publicly visible.

In many countries of the world we see socially conscious people arguing, and working for improved conditions for those who suffer politically or physically. Why? Live and let live (or let die) is an obvious response to misery by many. We are not "our brothers keepers", unless one accepts Jesus definition of 'brother' and his injunction to serve, or unless one is moved to join the Buddha in compassion for all who suffer. Amnesty International, the Red Cross and countless other groups and individuals labor for compassionate causes to relieve all who suffer. Yet interestingly enough, few today would claim to do this under the inspiration of the Holy Spirit, or of any spirit other than the human spirit, in spite of the fact that their effort is by majority count in the world at large "anti-natural". Relief of suffering is not at all obvious conduct for an astute human being, if he or she understands "the principalities and powers" which make the world go round.

The carry over from the original movement of the Holy Spirit, which animated first Jesus and then his gathered disciples, the compassion which the Buddhas and others have taught -- these inspiring spirits must be given credit for a great deal of what we term "the zeal for humanitarian relief of suffering." But a problem comes with this good: If the animating Spirit is lost, or if its origins are forgotten, all the "good causes" in the world quickly become just another campaign which puts self-promotion first on the line. This turns into a demand to have the world see things our way, our particular utopian or idealistic reform. But societies are not likely to do this except superficially, unless to espouse "good causes" seems socially acceptable and economically profitable, or in some cases even to be the best base to use to gain political power. If the Spirit's animating power is lost, what is to turn us from natural self-seeking? The "good" causes lose their altruistic force and even the best spirit can corrupt. "The salt has lots is savor", as Jesus mentioned.

"Social Gospels" never stand alone. There is no more reason to feed the starving in Africa or to rescue a desperate child than to built an addition on your house, buy a new dress, etc. And millions prefer the latter course, unless coerced or converted. When we see "good causes" corrupt, when they are merely used to further the political or financial interest of an individual or group, then we know that no Holy Spirit blows on them. "Thee hath been used", but not by any good spirit. Thus, whenever a religious group takes its "good causes" for granted and fails to work closely to keep the Holy Spirit alive and inspiring in their lives, they risk corruption, and becoming self-seeking in the name of virtue. They have lost animating zeal or a "God connection."

This takes the Christian back to a misunderstanding about the Trinity, about the origins of the church, and about our relationship to God and to Jesus in our time. In the case of the Zen Buddhist, this makes the devotee aware of the need to continue Zazen, for the Jew his or her need to pray and repeat observances. And so on for every religion. Religious beliefs and practices are not 'natural'; they do not self-start or continue to run unaided. Reformation is a constant need, like the "continual revolution" or the "eternal vigilance" needed to preserve liberty. In the Christian's case, God did present divinity's face in Jesus of Nazareth, and it can be discovered there still. But Jesus has withdrawn. Had not the Holy Spirit descended and inspired his followers on Pentecost, there might be no authentic Christian spirit preserved to be present for us now. Jesus absence from our immediacy leads to the constant need for the Holy Spirit and to our prayers for its inspiration.

Even the many who still claim a direct relationship to Jesus as their inspiration forget that it can only be the inspiration of the Holy Spirit which leads them to "see Jesus", since he is still unseen by the vast majority all of who hear the same words. Thus, even if you have experienced Jesus offer of "new life", as many claim, there is a risk of its evaporation, or of the perversion of its source, if the Holy Spirit is forgotten. Oddly enough, the Holy Spirit, that most neglected and actually least understood 'person' of the Trinity, is the one we most need today, or in any day after Jesus withdrawal from his disciples. It alone, in spite of many false claims to divine inspiration, is the sole avenue for our relationship to God and also to receive our inspiration from Jesus in any age after God's immediate presence was withdrawn in its physical form.

In the case of Jesus, we have argued that the way to understand who he is, his nature and what he can do, is to study the Acts of Jesus. In the case of God, this is also true, e.g., the Jew's celebration of Exodus as what God has done. Somewhat ironically, this becomes even more true in the case of the "third person" of the Trinity, for we do not have the background of the claimed acts of God, e.g., in sending the Prophets and Messiahs, or in offering us the Saints and Mystics. In Jesus case, we have the record of his life and of his Acts, even if these require study to realize their significance. In the case of the Holy Spirit, we have the least "evidence" of all. And yet we have argued that it is the most important form of God's presence in our age and that the animating Spirit is likely to go out of every "good" cause, if the source of the inspiration for this "counter natural" force is lost. The Spirit must be maintained; it is the easiest to lose.

How, then, can we "connect" with the Holy Spirit by its 'Acts', if the evidence for its presence is the least substantial of all the forms of divine presence? There is a good reason why every conservative

Christian clings stubbornly to the literal words of Jesus. Even though we have claimed that the New Testament is only enlightening if the reader is inspired by the Holy Spirit, many prefer to cling to the literalness (or so they suppose) of the words, just because the Holy Spirit is far less concrete in its presence. Yet it is the Spirit, one can argue for Judaism, Christianity, Muslim and for Buddhism, which animates the religious life, keeps it from going dry and from being perverted. One must study the Acts of the Holy Spirit or else lose God, supremely difficult as this may be to accomplish.

We can study a contemporary example in "Liberation Theology", in Socialism, or even in Marxism in its secular form. These each represent a great passion for the relief of the lesser privileged. But each can also turn into "just another political venture" if the animating spirit is lost. Marxism is a particularly telling example of an ideal that corrupts when there is no Holy Spirit to animate the revolution. Liberation theology correctly sees Jesus as a liberator. Its problem lies into transferring this to a particular political program. Of course, compassion must be translated into deeds, else it is hollow. Our theme is: By their Acts only shall be known, whether God, Jesus, the Holy Spirit, or any individual who follows their inspiration. With liberation theology, the question is: Is it motivated by a compassion to liberate those who suffer, or does it tie itself to any particular existing political program? For many who were originally Christian who were inspired in their goal to help the poor, the animating spirit has been lost; it has been traded for political achievement.

This is not an easy but rather a tricky question, since the Spirit must be made flesh, as happened in Jesus case, if it is to be effective in its goal. The "good will among men" must become good deeds. The animating Spirit of course must become known in its Acts, but Liberation Theology requires action on the social, political front. Individual aid is not sufficient. Their zeal stems from the utopian vision of our possibility to reform whole societies and social orders. That laudable aim should not be negated. But if in the political involvement required, if the contact with the animating Spirit is lost which alone can hold liberation theology from an identification with secular forces, its energy may be distorted for ulterior purposes. Only if we learn to identify and to appropriate "The Acts of the Holy Spirit" can we hope to maintain any purity of intention.

B. THE ACTS OF THE HOLY SPIRIT

And who could ever have known your
will, had you not given Wisdom? Who has
learned thy counsel, unless you sent your
Holy Spirit from above.

As for your intention, who could have
learnt it, had you not granted wisdom and
sent your holy spirit from above?

Book of Wisdom IX.

1. THE SPIRIT CAN SUFFER

We know this must be true. For any animating spirit, whether Christian, Jewish or otherwise, is obviously capable of exhaustion by individual manipulation, by corruption, and by being turned to a selfish purposes under merely religious banners. In this case just as Jesus' mother suffered for him when Jesus suffered for God, so the Holy Spirit must suffer frustration, at bear minimum, when it sees its intentions fail or become misdirected. If we have zeal, and if it is frustrated in its employment or misunderstood so that it is subverted, we suffer. Thus, given the everyday sacrifices we must make in order to promote our "good intentions", the Holy Spirit, God's primary inspirer, must suffer intently to see its inspiration fail to direct human aims toward enhancing construction.

Theologians have been split over whether they can allow God to suffer (meanwhile, of course, God does suffer). And there are compelling reasons why God's power, which is crucial to salvation, might be compromised if divinity were simply overcome by suffering. However, if the Holy Spirit is God's "official representative" in all post-Jesus ages, it must suffer to see how the Gospel has been subverted again and again. And if the Holy Spirit is also a source of inspiration to us for the renewal of God's kingdom, the Spirit must suffer frustration whenever the building of God's kingdom is abandoned. We are not forced into the Spirit's clutches, as some maintain we are with God's programs. But we know from totalitarian regimes and revolutionary councils that, unless strict control is maintained, the reform fails. Thus, the Spirit suffers most by knowing that coercion alone could guarantee the success of that which it inspires, all the while it advises against the use of force.

Since God is often said to be distant from us, 'transcendent' in the technical term, it would not be strange for a far off divinity to stay aloof from suffering, even ours. But in the case of the Holy Spirit, we know its office is defined by its relationship to us in God's absence. Like Jesus, whatever draws close to us must suffer in this connection, even if it is an inspiring Spirit. God's power was sometimes thought to be diminished by suffering; thus theologians protected divinity from this experience. But for the Holy Spirit, its inspiring role cannot be diminished by any relationship, since its function is to sustain others. Thus, it can uphold us in our projects only if it suffers with us, touches us here, and yet still inspires us to press on with God's causes. Its strength comes in its involvements, whereas ours is often diminished by spirit attention.

Yet if we are often changed negatively by suffering or even destroyed by it, the presence of the Holy Spirit can renew us under persecution, not always, but this effect is evident in enough cases to be accepted. The "prison literature", e.g., Martin Luther King, Dietrich Bonhoffer, testifies to how a human spirit can be strengthened by suffering. So either the Holy Spirit can suffer with us or else it cannot reach us where we most need inspiration. Yet if destructive suffering made some feel that God had to be excluded from such an experience in order to protect the power of divinity, in the case of the Holy Spirit its whole claim to be divine in status comes exactly from its ability to be present in our suffering. There is no other way to explain how some sustain themselves while others collapse. Do we experience the Holy Spirit in our suffering, realizing that it itself undergoes suffering, enters with us in, while still remaining powerful enough to inspire us to resist destruction and to heal every wound wherever we can? If such is not the case, the Holy Spirit will remain absent and unknown to us.

2. THE SPIRIT CAN ACT IN LOVE

Love is another quality which some find hard to attribute to God, at least in the familiar sense of passionate desire and our constant need for another. In Jesus, God is said to love the world, and that claim is easily acceptable if we study the Acts of Jesus and accept his witness. Still, God has often been kept distant from the distorting passions we know that love involves. This can include destruction, as happened in Jesus' case and with countless others. Thus, we instinctively protect God from love's passionately reckless qualities. We attribute love to divinity, if we do, as a very pure outgoing emotion, distinct from the desire and passion which so often dominates us in love. For the Holy Spirit, however, its center must lie in love or else it has no religious office. Jesus' function is clear to his followers in their imitation of his

Acts. The Holy Spirit itself has no immediately visible acts. We can see its inspirational effects only if they are mediated. Like God, no one looks directly on the face of the Holy Spirit. It can only be felt by those sensitivity to its presence.

But wild spirits and demons can be destructive too. We feel and see their effects every hour, even if we are not ourselves possessed by them. Thus, the core of our experience of the Holy Spirit must lie in a felt act of love, compassion so overwhelming that it demands a response, an expression, from us. God's own relationship to us is more indirect, covered more in mystery. The Holy Spirit's activity is mysterious too, but whenever it is felt, the embrace of love is at its core. Mystics in pursuit of God express, at the culmination of their odyssey, an overwhelming experience of love. In this case, it is actually the Holy Spirit they experience as God's intended guide since Jesus' departure. Hate, even rage, so fills the world's stage that any inner experience of being overcome by love must be taken a sign of the nearness of the Holy Spirit, even if it is manifest in a human spirit or in a body.

On the other hand sometimes, perhaps often, our problem is that we cannot express love adequately, either physically or verbally. So whenever the poet sings, whenever compassion flows into word or song, we should recognize the inspiration of the Spirit. Otherwise we remain mute, frozen and inexpressive. The Greeks appealed to the gods for inspiration and guidance, and their gods were symbols of this human need for added stimulus in order to be creative. On Jewish, Christian, or Buddhist terms, there is no need to deny the Spirit's variety of forms. In fact, its origin as 'Holy' is testified to by its inability to confine itself to one form or even to one person. In any case, when creativity and expression flow outward, we know that the Spirit is near. Love can be expressed and there is a joy in fulfillment. Yet the Spirit does not dominate, as love often does in its many forms and in the persons we meet. The Spirit that is holy liberates us to greater expression, activity, and structure building That power stems from its divine connection.

The amazing thing, however, is that the love conveyed in the Holy Spirit's presence is not entirely 'disinterested'. Meister Eckhart claimed to discover 'disinterest' at the core of God. That might be true. But God's expression in the Holy Spirit, as it represents and relates us to God in the days after Jesus, moves us to compassionate action. It offers new direction, even a change in our previous activity, not a passivity. God has been said by some not to change. At least in the sense of the preservation of divine power, that is true. But wherever the Holy Spirit is present -- since it is not confinable or predictable -- it induces change; it is the inspiration for constructive change. Thus God acts; divinity is involved in change every time the Holy Spirit descends into a life or into a group. It inspires; it does not destroy; it encourages; it does not damage; it heals suffering; it does not cause it. That is its distinguishing and crucial characteristic.

3. THE SPIRIT CAN ACT AND STILL OFFER FREEDOM

When love consumes us, we are often made captive; we become most driven, feel the least free, and become irresponsible, reckless. The Spirit evidences its "Holy" origin because it can express love abundantly and still maintain a freedom of direction. It is not bound. This may sound easy, but it is not. We meet many inspiring figures, and most of them tend to dominate us by our attraction to their zeal. We become willing captives, even, "slaves for Christ", as one expression goes. All inspirers are not Hitlers, although his crowd attraction is legendary and cannot be denied. Sports heroes take us captive at the same time that they inspire us, as teachers of all kinds do. How is it, then, that the Holy Spirit can inspire, exude love, and still leave us free? That is amazing, so divine. Take Jesus' example: If we commit ourselves as "slaves for Christ", we do so freely or else our allegiance is not genuine. Thus, the Spirit may inspire, but it does not in itself commit us. That is the distinctive difference.

'Freedom' is everywhere sought for, it seems today more than ever. Yet it often comes associated with anarchy, with a lack of commitment or direction, even license. The Holy Spirit is 'holy', because it inspires us to seek our liberty in creative expression, in overcoming political repression; yet it carries its own discipline. It is not anarchic. How can this be? Because it inspires us to goal-directedness without dictating the goal, to creativity without specifying the form; it moves us to acquire discipline of expression without controlling us. It ignites the fuel; we give the direction. Other loves that inspire us too often seek to control us. Whether intentionally or not, we feel caught, even when we love the pressure. We can feel ecstasy, but only if we abandon self-control. A spirit that attracts us away from a love that is commanding is known by its fruits, that is, autonomy and creativeness, and it gives evidence of its source, God's post-Jesus presence with us.

From Greek times to the Enlightenment we have thought universal education to be our route to freedom. "You shall know the truth and the truth shall make you free" -- even if this motto was not at first extended to all women, classes, and races. Education can liberate, and yet we are cautioned by observing Germany's pre-Hitler high level of education and the fact that his student-faculty-intellectual following was large. Intellectual facts dominate intellectuals just as much today, even without a dictator, and we recognize our "slavery" no more than the intellectual Nazi did. Such "captivity" is usually only recognized later on.

Totalitarian ideologies do 'educate'; what they do not do is genuinely free their followers. We really are not "born free", so we feel the need of an inspiring spirit to cause us to seek our independence. Many who could live free fall into traps of addiction and violence. So if the spirit that encourages us to seek an education in order to become free is a Holy Spirit, it supports our weakness but does not subjugate us to its control. Freedom is frightening too, as Sartre noted, so the Spirit that is holy inspires by undergirding us with confidence. It does so, however, without demanding control.

All freedoms are subject to being lost. Our "eternal vigilance" lapses. The freedom which the Spirit brings is not an easy freedom, but it encourages us to "fight stagnation" and to stay alert in order to protect our liberties. Our very need for this support indicates that freedom is fragile, else no power other than our good intentions would be necessary. Such is not the case. "The path to hell is paved with good intentions". Thus, the Humanism that replaced God with its high ideals is precarious in that our good intentions toward one another are not enough to guarantee freedom. A strong spirit is necessary; our individual commitment too often is not enough. Ultimately we are able to be free as human beings because the Holy Spirit, which alone is "born free", offers us the power needed to support our good intentions, which individually fail too easily and too often.

4. THE SPIRIT CAN CONTROL

But: it controls itself, not others; it inspires but does not demand. That is, the Spirit "controls" only by its inspiration, which can be either at first not received or later rejected. It is false to think that its appearance is always overpowering. God's might be. And this lack of force is due to the fact that the Spirit controls fully only itself, not others. This is a distinctive quality and indicates its divine link. No other source of inspiration can guarantee such control, try as we may, succeed as we do for a time. The Spirit's inspiration, then, is not a demand, which is the way so many other powerful and captivating forces present themselves to us. This is an odd quality, a fact which means that many fail to see that the spirit which inspires them is Holy. Why? Because there is no demand felt in its inspiring presence, only support and encouragement for our openness to exercise our creative or our healing powers where others are concerned, or spurring us to the relief of suffering where there is need.

We often lose control over ourselves. But more important for the health of the world, we lose command over our creative, healing powers which we could extend to external projects or to other people. We "lose our grip", as we say, and "the best laid plans of mice..." In fact, the calm, the steadiness of the inspiration, its evidence of control, and the way that it allows us to get a better grip on our own self control -- this is what distinguishes a divine Spirit from "Dionysian frenzy". We are familiar enough with that kind of inspirational excitement, but too often it is characterized by our inability to control neither ourselves nor others. We see visions, but we are exhausted by them; they distort as much as they inspire. The divinity of this inspiring Spirit evidences itself in its control, in its lack of demand, in its support for our talents, by its enabling us to achieve a greater sense of control over our own powers. Our response is uncoerced. We are inspired both to be free and to be calm.

We may find God in this experience, but we also become particularly aware of our difference from divinity. God's control could dominate and overpower us.("Man shall not see me and live"). But in the Spirit's presence, we sense the divine power, held back, transformed to suit our condition so as not to destroy. Of course, that is just the reason the presence of a Holy Spirit is so often unrecognized. It seems too mild, too congenial, to be divine. Jesus presence was like this, which is why so many failed to recognize him for who he was. Thus, the Holy Spirit is a fitting form for God's presence to us in the intervening age. It too can be misread as to its revolutionary powers. We need to feel its inspiration, as most who knew Jesus did at least to a minimum degree, except of course those whose response was to destroy the source of God's annoying presence.

We know that God has restricted the divine power so as to leave us free and the future open. This too makes the Holy Spirit a fitting divine representative for us in God/Jesus' absence. It is here, around us, never absent; but it is not determinative, often missed in discerning its presence, yet recognized as inspiring by those who sense its origins. Like Jesus, it does not force an interpretation on us. We are subject to the influence of many spirits, and we are left to ourselves to discover and to identify those which seem divine in their source. We were not given God's name in detail; we were not told who Jesus was. We were never made unavoidably aware of a Holy Spirit's presence, because of its amazing self control and its lack of coercion. We feel something has inspired, perhaps even transformed us, with a vision we had not had before. But its recognition and naming are left to us. All around us today we see, by contrast, a thousand examples of dominating, controlling, even destroying forms, of spirit inspiration.

5. The Spirit Can Be Present With Us

Jesus has promised to be present with us, even unto the ends of the earth. Some see and feel that. However, many do not realize that Jesus' form of presence is not in his own immediate appearance but by the gift of the Holy Spirit's constant attendance. Thus, to "see Jesus", as many have claimed to do since Saul's Damascus road experience, is really to recognize the Holy Spirit's movement and to give it a name. Of course, the problem for all who are religiously possessed is to explain: (1) why so many are, and can remain, unaware of the Spirit's presence if it is constantly there; and (2) why so many are more aware, even more attracted to, destructive spirits and allow themselves to be controlled, even possessed, by them, sometimes destroyed by the ecstasy. One answer lies in the lack of an overpowering control exercised by the Holy Spirit vs. the "demon possession" of others.

One other puzzle we face is how, if the Spirit is the form of God's presence with us, so many who seek God can miss divinity, which they do, even when it is so close. That is the mystery of spiritual 'presence' which we have to solve if we want to approach God, or rather to allow God to approach us. Every other presence, from rock music to domineering individuals who pressure us, makes itself all-too-immediately felt. They are unavoidable. That is divinity's hidden key: it can be avoided. The Spirit is there, but silence is its preferred mode of presence. It impresses us only in its power of inspiration, which is even made to seem to be ours because it flows through us. We look for God, for an inspiring Spirit, too often in the wrong, in the obvious places. Just as in architecture, God is "in the detail"; so the Spirit is found in the quiet, subtle voices within, never in rage.

Even religious people, who claim enthusiastically to be aware of God's presence, can lose that sense and become unsure of God. Just so with the "divine delegate", the Holy Spirit. There are times and places which men and women have felt they must dedicate the place or the moment to commemorate their feeling of a divine presence. Yet we know we can close off that feeling, that God can withdraw into silence, and that the Spirit seems to lose inspirational power. These are the dry periods for the Spirit. Yet this is not a clear indication of total absence, as we are tempted to declare in our disillusion. The Spirit's ability to be fully present, but yet to be non-coercive, fools us into labeling this as "absence", if we forget its nature and return to demanding obviousness. The Holy Spirit does not seem interested in uniform human response, even though its presence is constantly available to all. Our freedom, the freedom which the Spirit grants to us, makes it possible for us to become disoriented. We lose ourselves in non-being, in emptiness, as Kierkegaard reported.

One problem is that, even under divine inspiration, our response to the movement of the Holy Spirit is all too often to try to coerce, to dominate others. This leads to artistic quarrels over the "control" of one's work, as if any creative product were ultimately subject to control. Ironically, those who are the most creatively possessed are often the hardest to live with. This can only be because they think that their inspiration, their creative product, is self-produced. Examining the lives of creative people, we see that they are often mundane, even sordid, so that nothing distinguishes them from their uncreative neighbors but the product of their work. It cannot be we, as individuals, who are creative in major or even in minor ways. It is the presence of a Holy Spirit with us whose inspiration we feel. Yet too often we think that it is we who are the source.

6. THE SPIRIT CAN ACT IN FORCE

Contradictory as it may seem, after saying that the Spirit's presence was non-coercive and always leaves our response free, it has to be admitted that the Spirit is at times capable of being overpowering. Because it is not a predictable spirit but lists where it will, we can provide no guidelines, produce no formula, in our search for inspiration or tell another how to go about preparing for it in any exact way. The Boy Scouts are right: "Be prepared". We can only make ourselves ready. We study how spirits seem to have guided others. We follow the via negative as with the search for God. That is, we can much more easily tell which spirits to avoid, due to their record of dominance and destruction, than to advise any individual on how to find the right spirit. That is in a sense what it means religiously to seek 'purity'. We work to void our lives of any destroying, interfering spirits.

Once the ground is prepared, waiting and maintenance and daily routine are our only possible posture. But then, even in cases where we are not ready, in situations where the person seems poorly equipped to be a divine receptacle, we see and may even feel a divine force descend that is overpowering, first to its recipient and then to us in our response to his or her work. The creative force seems hardly contained within the words, the song, the art, the political acts. We are amazed, but possibly the recipient is even more amazed. "Why me?" But the force with which the Holy Spirit can visit us, although admittedly and fortunately only on rare occasions, is such that even a "lowly vessel" can receive and convey it. The Spirit does not by any means always descend on "the most likely candidate." We quote: "How odd of God to choose the Jews."

The violence of the world around us dictates that the Holy Spirit must be able to use force, even if that is not its typical posture. Otherwise it could be drowned out to our ears by the high volume noise level, the physical destruction all around us. There are of course "peaceful places", and many who are religiously inclined retire to them in the hope of divining the Holy Spirit more clearly. Such can be the case, but there is nothing necessary about it. Because of its capability to use the power of its infinite source, it can be heard in mid-Manhattan, at rock concerts as well as on Walden Pond. Silence is its "dwelling place". But when the Spirit moves out of that onto the world stage, which it does on occasion, its force is such as to achieve its effect even on the spiritually deaf and the blind. That is the message contained in Jesus healing of the blind.

The subtle and revealing difference here is that the Spirit's use of force does not destroy. "And the bush was not consumed". It is an overpowering presence whose power knows no equal but which leaves us whole in its passing. No other presence of such great power leaves us totally unwounded. That is the problem with power as we use it. The use of force is necessary if the opponent is vicious. But this is never simply good, and it is often self-destructive. In the Spirit's case alone, when it arrives with force it is converting, often revolutionary, in its change, but it is not destructive in its effects. We are left whole, as is not the case with drugs. We worry about the negative side effects of even powerful medicines which can heal. In contrast, when the Holy Spirit comes in force, it is known by the absence of destructive side effects in its passing through.

7. THE SPIRIT CAN UNDERSTAND

Those around us in power all too often seem either unable or unwilling to understand us or our petitions. We know the spirit that confronts us is 'holy' if we feel totally, wholly, understood. We confront others around us, seeking not only for ourselves to be understood, as well as our needs and our desires, but to understand the world around us and those in it. There come moments of rare understanding when we no longer "see through a glass darkly". But these are rare; they do not seem available to everyone and often cannot be sustained. In any case of total understanding we are in touch with the divine, however fleeting. And we can credit this to the power and presence of the Holy Spirit, since (as Sartre knows) only God is capable of total self-understanding without self deception. It takes a divine Spirit to understand fully without reservation.

Given the Enlightenment and Modern Science, all this may seem to be a human accomplishment, not necessarily connected to any divine source. It is true that the Modern Promethians thought they could now steal all of God's fire, and they did collect quite a bit. But the mood of neither science nor of the intellectual world today is one of confidence in our complete understanding, neither now nor in the future. That goal seems to be permanently outside our grasp, no matter how powerful the theories are which we may formulate and use. Thus, full understanding and its use has returned to God's possession. It is no longer a violation of secular learning to see those moments of complete understanding as a divine disclosure, as the power of the Holy Spirit not only present to us but enabling visionary insight, since this is no longer thought to be a compleatable human project.

Novelty, and the search for freedom for ourselves and for those around us, often seems to interfere with what understanding we do achieve. The world does not unfold as a necessary dialectic, despite Hegel's dream. Thus, our understanding is constantly thrown off balance, interfered with by the eruption of chaos. God is God because the divine intellect adjusts instantaneously, constantly and perfectly. It is not that God's understanding is outside of time, as some have thought but rather that divinity is known by its complete adaptability. We are aware of the Holy Spirit's presence when novelty, change, confusion arises and should throw us off, but we report that we adjusted "intuitively". The Spirit is able to increase understanding without limit. Yet for us it must be a borrowed gift. However, some have claimed that this can happen only if we are part of the divine mind and thus have such a capacity. But: What raises us to participate in this; is it not the power of a Holy Spirit as present to us?

We know from the failures in our educational systems that, to achieve understanding, we need more than simply the presence of schools and books. Teachers, as they inspire, represent the spirit as it is holy. But when we face crowds that do not seem able to understand, or even want to understand, we need to pray for the descent of the

Holy Spirit, its inspiration and its sustaining power. Otherwise, our efforts to educate fail. The Greeks knew the necessity to invoke the gods to carry them over the ever-present barriers to understanding. We implore the gods for aid too, but it is for the inspiring descent of the Holy Spirit, for its presence with us, that we plead. It is there; it is available; it offers to lift us up; but it must be allowed to take hold.

8. The Spirit Can Act to Create

We have already marked this as the chief power of the Spirit and the major indication of its presence. Creation takes place in evolutionary time. God created out of nothing, nothing other than the divine unlimited nature. We create out of ourselves too, but our resources are severely restricted. So we ask: how is it that the Spirit should be able to cause us, or anyone, to create? We do not possess new world plans or world visions inside of us. From whence do such new worlds, and new views of our created world, come? We call this source 'divine', because, out of minor material, art and visions come. Thus, the Spirit is able to create, or to inspire us to create, because it represents the inexhaustible source of creation itself, the absolutely infinite store of possibilities and possible worlds. We have already said that not all creative people recognize this as the source of their power. The Spirit's presence is so subtle that it is easy to overlook.

Yet, we know that we are just as much tortured by what we feel we might create, but do not, as we are by the Herculean effort to give birth to what we do produce. Yet the result is not proportional to the effort. We drive ourselves; we "Climb every mountain". Yet what results from our exertion often seems as much to come from unconscious effort as from conscious trying -- a lesson we gain from Zen and Carl Jung. Therefore, the power of the product seems not to be directly proportional either to our intent or to our effort. We feel used as a conduit. We are filled, we say: we must "let it flow". The Spirit can create, then, because it is able to offer disproportional assistance and results that never seem to be fully simply our personal production. However, it is important to realize that this cannot happen without our own prior disciplined effort, but neither can it be done by our efforts alone. The Holy Spirit can transform infinite power to fit finite, lower powered, agents.

God creates conflict-free, we know. Nothing impedes the growth of a universe, even if the internal forces produce "big bangs". On the whole, our creativity must face conflict, from within and from without, although the picture of the tortured artist is often either over-drawn or overly dramatic. Our main conflict is often with ourselves, although that conflict is so constant and so draining that we project it as a combat with named and unnamed people and forces. Paranoia seems to be the artist's anvil. But there are times, probably more than our constant fight with the world allows us to admit, when the creative product seems to slip off the pen or to fall easily from the hand. "How to succeed in artistry without really trying", this is the Holy Spirit's motto. However, when this moment comes, like the Zen archer we allow the arrow to release itself to hit the target. Yet this can happen only after numberless hours of discipline, even though it does not follow as a direct result of our effort.

We also hide our talents, fearing our "great capacity", as Blake put it. The world would be a different place if every latent human talent were realized. The dark side of the teacher's role is to witness a parade of unrealized potential. It is not always "wasted", in the strictest sense, but too often it never comes to full fruition. Wasted talent is obvious, but it is "the Tomb of the Unknown Talent" over which we mourn silently, because we know not what lies buried in the interior tomb of so many of us. God wastes nothing by incapacity. Humans cause disasters by trying to live beyond their capacities, 'hybris' as the Greeks named it. The Holy Spirit is the source of the power which settles on even weak reeds, although it responds to the beauty of a light spirit or to the awe of a powerful talent, just as we do, and can settle to empower it. However, this visitation is usually only realized after it has passed, by recognizing a creative product whose result seems beyond the power of simple human invention.

9. THE SPIRIT ACTS BY WORSHIPPING

God is often the object of worship; Jesus is the occasion of our worship, although we have argued that both are able to join us in worship. The Holy Spirit much more obviously belongs in every worship service, since we know that inspired services are said to be due to the powerful presence of the Spirit. One does not have to be Pentecostal (or a "Holy Roler", or in a charismatic movement) to believe this. We say of theater performances, of athletic events, that the performance was "inspired". In revival tents in the American South, the Spirit has carried whole crowds away. But in simple Quaker meetings, the Spirit also leads us in worship. If the inspiring Spirit is the form of God's presence in the intervening age, then such worship celebrates, and anticipates, that Coming Age. Thus, the center of action in any service of worship should be the inspiring Spirit.

Can we be sure it will always guide worship when we want it to? No, we know it descends when it wills. It is not subject to our control by pleading or even by ecstatic activity, in spite of the claim of control by some. We can tell, only after all our pleas for guidance have died away, whether our prayers were answered, although this is not always outwardly discernible or uniform in the recognition of all present. In fact, just because the Holy Spirit can worship, it may, like God, join us silently. In fact, if silence involves contemplation of God and is central to worship, we must be careful about too much shouting or public pleading. The possession of the Spirit may be visible in signs, in the movement of people, in the loud "Amens". But the Spirit may also worship with us silently.

In order to worship effectively, we have to admit our inferiority. Boasting is not an appropriate posture, although it is much engaged in irreligious circles. Yet if God can bend to worship, and if Jesus humbled himself, then the chief power of the Holy spirit in worship may be the gift of humility. "Tis a gift to be simple...". Thus, in addition to lifting us up like Prometheus to grasp a share of God's creative power, the Spirit alternately humbles us along with itself, since we know that the possession of power corrupts, even -- or perhaps maybe particularly -- in creative people. "Ego is seen running naked through the halls." We need to surrender our positions of superiority, whether great or small, in order to worship; this may be why so few are skilled in its practice. They do not check their egos at the church door. But the Holy Spirit can humble us by its presence.

Some have called religion a "guilt trip". Sartre called it a "vast laundering operation". It is true that the one who feels faultless has no reason to worship. So that the preaching of human sin is not such a bad thing, if it leads to confession and to new direction, something we all need. The Spirit's presence, then, lightens our sense of fault and humbles our spirit, that needed experience before worship is possible. We need a sign pasted on the door of every service of worship saying: "let only the humble enter here." We look to the Spirit to provide that attribute too, as well as its creative inspiration. It's presence can be so overpowering as to make us feel humble, an experience rare on the world's public stage. So we pray for that gift to descend from the Holy Spirit, since otherwise proper worship is not possible for us. We think too much of ourselves. We need to experience the fact that real power comes from beyond our control.

10. THE SPIRIT IS ABLE TO HEAL

We credit the Spirit with occasional amazing creative or physical powers, and we credit its presence with our ability to worship, since it is not always in our power to place ourselves in that posture, particularly if we are feeling successful. But to create the humble spirit, the contrite heart, really leads us nowhere beyond ourselves if no healing takes place. We talk mostly about the healing of the human spirit, of "the sin-sick soul". But there is no need to deny the possibility of physical healing. Any power, e.g., that in Jesus, which can offer new birth to the human spirit -- such a task requires divine power, although counselors may assist. Our new birth can influence the body as well, if the Spirit wills it. And that is the point: the instrument of healing in our present world is always the Holy Spirit's work, although Jesus demonstrated this in his time.

How can the Holy Spirit heal; what is the form of its presence; and are its healing powers ever placed under our control? First, it can heal because it is God's form of presence, and God-with-us is always a healing encounter, or at least it can be. Second, its presence is not seen, although it may be felt, and its movement is only known by its results. "I only know that once I was blind but now I see". We must listen to the testimony of change, of restored life, of new spirit. Third, without question, the Spirit's healing powers are not in our control, since those powers stem from God's presence, and the ultimate blasphemy is to pretend that we control God or that we can predict the divine response. Nevertheless, difficult as it is, when we see the results of healing beyond our ordinary powers, we say "The Holy Spirit has been here".

Ultimately, 'healing' means to bring under control all that wastes or destroys either the body or the human spirit or the natural world. That requires the power to reverse damage. And this we do not possess, although some utopian dreams of social engineering thought we could recreate ourselves. These visions have now withdrawn beyond our reach, sometimes disappearing in brutal attempts that result in tragic destruction. Thus, only the power of the Holy Spirit can go beyond our highly developed skills to reverse damage and restore, and then move on to contain all that can destroy. The presence of the Spirit sometimes offers this unexpected healing in the form of God's presence with us and is a testimony to a healing process promised for a future day, one when God's direct hand will replace the Spirit's presence with us. This involves future time, which indicates our belief that God can control the future, just as the Spirit operates in the present.

All healing which we experience now, much as we testify to the visitation of a divine Spirit, is for us but a direction to the future. Thus, God's gift of the Holy Spirit's presence may show us works of spiritual or even of a physical healing, but this is only given to us as a sign of the healing of the world, of its restructuring, which God anticipates. Since that is not yet here and seems further off every time we read a morning newspaper or find ourselves betrayed or used by "friends", the healing potential of the Spirit is largely given over to sustaining us toward that future day. The Spirit moved Job when he said, "Though he slay me yet will I trust him". It takes the presence of a more-than-natural-power to sustain our fragile spirits through the holocausts visited upon us. And when ever we are still able to retain our confidence in the healing future, it is a testimony to the Holy Spirit's present power.

11. THE SPIRIT CAN RISK REJECTION

We know that Jesus faced rejection and did not try to prevent it. We tend to think that God could not be rejected; how could someone with the power to create galaxies be rejected? Almost everyone whom we know with even limited power works to prevent rejection, and he or she moves to acquire more power in order to increase their strength to resist all opposition. But Jesus in his Acts revealed a startling fact about God as the source of all power in the world: An infinite power can lower itself to rejection -- but only for our sakes. If the world was created to bring human beings to fruition, how can it be that this involves submitting to rejection if one has the power to prevent it? And how can doing so help the weaker party (us) in any way? If the Holy Spirit is God's form of presence with us now, can this help us if the Spirit accepts rejection too?

In dealing with these questions, we sometimes put off too much as due to "God's regard for our freedom". And our independence as finite spirits is important. But where evil is concerned, the world is a more damaging place than it need be. We do not live in the best of all possible worlds. We can leave divinity with its share of responsibility for the evil and the destruction in the operative world and accept the share that results from our own actions. Given our situation and the often dire situations we are plunged into, if God does not directly intervene at any time, how can that divinity best help us now in the age before the world is reformed? What kind of presence would assist us and give some indication of God's concern and eventual intended action?

Whenever we are in trouble, we quickly learn that, in distress, you find out who your real friends are. Affluence, success, the need of others for us, does not prove it. In the depths the question is: Who stands by you? -- that is the test. In answer, the Holy Spirit does not so much exalt you to new heights, though it can induce creative work, as it functions to undergird those who are friendless, those who lack the power to protect themselves. "God with us" means the spirit's presence to us even in our depths. However, the Spirit can be with those whom the world's powers reject, only if it risks rejection for itself. One gains acceptance by being seen with "the right people", which is as true in religious circles as it is in the social/business world. Even in religious groups, you risk rejection by not conforming, by being a "loser", a non-conformer. So in the time of rejection by one's own people and by one's religious group (a traumatic event which Jesus experienced) one should look about for the Spirit's presence.

Fast friendships are established by being with someone in time of trouble, not in their time of success. So if God wants to express divinity's concern, and more than that to say, as was said with Jesus, that God supports "the despised and rejected" of the world (which seldom includes church officialdom or even seminary professors), the Spirit must allow itself to risk rejection by being found among "the wrong crowd". Only when the society around you chooses to misunderstand you and to reject you on the basis of non-conformity, only then is the support of God's Spirit likely to be felt with real power. True, even those to whom its support is offered may reject it, but it is the mission of all Jesus' disciples to carry the message of God's acceptance, and the availability of the Holy Spirit's support, to all without discrimination. Then, in their freedom, they can accept or reject the Spirit's offer.

12. THE SPIRIT CAN LAUGH

If the Holy spirit risks rejection in order to come to all who suffer as despised or rejected, how in the face of such serious, even tragic, business can we talk about laughter? Because: The 'gospel' is the "good news". Thus, what the Spirit brings to those who accept its offer of comfort is 'joy', and we know this to be true. How can African slaves in America develop joyous, ecstatic services of worship in the face of their repression? Because they found the support of God's Spirit. In accepting it, they believed its message that God relates to them in their misery through the presence of the Spirit as a promise of their future restoration which God intends to accomplish -- "one day". The Spirit's message is to expect joy. The ecstatic religious spirit often declines with success; it comes to seem unnecessary.

Looking at the world and its human suffering, you say, "It isn't funny". And so it isn't. Massive misery is never anything but tragic for the compassionate, although many are indifferent or even gloat if they benefit from another's loss. But the Holy Spirit alone can laugh when all the rest of us are in tears, because it knows the future, not in the detail of our responses, but in God's intentional outcome. Since it is God's form of presence to us, the Spirit must sometimes show us a face of smiles -- like the tragic/comic face of drama. Why? Because that is its testimony to the future, of what is God's intention and of what it is in God's power to accomplish. The angels said to the shepherds, "fear not". Yet ironically, at the time of that amazing birth we still had centuries of fear ahead. Nevertheless, the announcement of Jesus' coming was a revelation of God's entry to try to overcome our fears in the-age-in-between.

Of course, many centuries after the Christian message was first proclaimed, fear is still in every newspaper, on countless faces, and on most street corners. Jesus' departure, and the lack of his immediate presence now, plus our inability to hear his words from his own mouth, all this leaves us with the Holy Spirit as our only guide in all things religious. This applies both to our reading of the scriptures and to our attempt to decipher the Gospel message from the recording words. The Spirit has long been said to be our guide for understanding, which some scholars of the scripture's interpretation must learn again as the Enlightenment's "final solution" projects fade. True, the Spirit's guide to the joy found in the Gospel message can lead us to laugh in the face of paralyzing fear, but this will never be a uniform and a universal result. The Spirit's inspiration is too individual, too willing to allow us our idiosyncrasies.

But again, the Spirit is able to laugh, because it knows that it represents the final triumph of the Gospel promise. And except for the Holy Spirit's comfort and the change in us which the Gospel announcement can bring about, the full Gospel still exists only in promise. The outer world reflects the Gospel's good news only occasionally and in rare moments. On the whole, since Jesus' departure it has been "business as usual" on the secular plain. But the Spirit's availability to us in our despair can raise us up in strength, due to the laughter found within the Spirit's center of confidence. It knows; we only believe that the intent of God which it represents is fulfillable. It smiles for the future, as Negro spirituals always shouted joy in the midst of repression. That the Holy Spirit can laugh is a sign, not that God does not understand what goes on in the world or ignores the pain in our lives, but that God will have "The last laugh".

13. The Spirit Can Appear in the Detail

We have noted that God can be found, if you do discover the divine location, in the detail of the world, not in its grand design. If taken in its broad picture, the world does not argue to a loving or to a forgiving God. Nevertheless, to one sensitive to the detail, God can be encountered. Jesus was more literal in his appearance, at least physically, so that we argue not so much over where he lived or even how he appeared but about the significance of his spirit and the transforming power of his Acts. The Holy Spirit, as representing God's continued presence, is also not self-evident, ironically far less so than Jesus was, and it is much less talked about than God. So if the Spirit's presence is to be felt, if its comfort and healing and promise are to be believed, we must become sensitive to the detail. There is much in any existing organized religion to put a spiritually sensitive person off religion for good. But where, within that outer shell of churchly activity, do we find the detail in the Acts of individuals that signifies the Spirit's presence?

Every other force in the world that we can name is more evident, whether sports figures, movie stars, politicians, or even our friends and, most of all, our enemies. Odd that God, who is said to have wanted the divine presence represented in the world and made available to us "after Jesus", should have made the form of the Holy Spirit's presence too us so non-obvious, so easily missed. Every major religious figure, e.g., Buddha, Jesus, has spoken of the necessity of becoming inwardly sensitive to the divine presence, or even to our own spiritual presence. Every mystic has told us how we must be emptied out of ourselves before God can enter in and how painful the process of this self-separation is. But given the noise all around us, how else can we become aware of a guiding Spirit's presence, especially if it is present only in the detail?

God is in control of subtle detail; that is the Spirit's message. In that sense "He's got the whole world in his hands". If the devil seems more evident on the Big Scene, we must look for God far more sensitively, which is why Jesus told the rich young ruler to sell his wealth. In spite of the universe which God created with ease, although with agony over time too, the stars and planets were finally fixed in their course for all to see and man descended, God is little accessible there. That is too obvious a place for a subtle God. And besides, if God is a Spirit who must be "worshipped in spirit and in truth", how are we to distinguish this spiritual God from Plato's demiurge, the maker of worlds? We must be trained in different ways, to understand silence, to appreciate detail, to accept subtle messages, not blatant frontal attacks on our belief system. And the Spirit's major purpose is to increase our sensitivity.

How can the Spirit's continued availability to us make us sensitive to God's presence, when that is in no way obvious once Jesus has withdrawn? The answer is that, just as we must distinguish the spirit of a friend or someone we love from their physical presence to us, and just as love is too easily taken for a physical relationship (and there is a beauty in the physical for itself), our increased sensitivity to spirit vs. body, to the non-visual over the visual, or perhaps treating the visual always as a sign for what cannot be physically presented -- this increase is the Spirit's "gift" to us, if we accept it. For none can make us more sensitive to the spirit of another, not even God, or perhaps especially God, unless we are willing to open ourselves and risk being unprotected and vulnerable. This is the Spirit's constant message to us from God: "Open yourself. You have little of real importance to lose".

14. THE SPIRIT CAN ACT BEHIND THE GOSPEL

Jesus seems evident in the Gospels ('Christ' less so). He has the lead part in the drama. But when millions have tried to appraise him, they have found him to be more behind the printed word than evident on its surfaces. God had only a "behind the scenes" role in structuring the Gospels, and yet it is the aim of these accounts to reveal God to us. Odd, then, that God does not appear at the end of the drama which the Gospels recount, although many have discerned the divinity behind the story and found themselves closer to God by that hearing. It is not so odd, then, that God's form of presence to us in the Holy Spirit should not be an obvious presence either, since Jesus left us and the God who sent him took no final curtain calls at the story's ending. The Spirit introduces us to an unseen God.

Of course, we remember that Paul told the men of Athens that the unseen God whom they worshipped had now appeared in Jesus, and many have heard that and believed. But it was not a physical presence in any observable sense (no one screamed "God!" when they saw Jesus). Our entry to God, via the Spirit's presence with us now and continually, cannot be one of obviousness. The pain involved in this fact, in this decision of God to act behind the Gospel and not to place the Spirit's presence "up front", accounts for the fact that God's concern for us can be so easily missed. And the Spirit's comfort, as well as Jesus' promise, can be confused with some external paraphernalia or social cause. To be sure, the Spirit can be present in a social cause -- even as presented by "religious people" -- that concerns the relief of suffering; but again, it is not identified with specifics.

If our view of God is dim even after Jesus' "revelation", just because Jesus' words about God are at best indirect, Jesus' revelation of God's 'Spirit' in the gospel stories is subject to even more indefiniteness. Jesus use of the familiar term 'father', in his description of God's love and concern for all who suffer; these are dramatic images. When Jesus says, " I am with you even to the ends of the earth", we know this must be in the form of God's presence, i.e., the Spirit's presence, since Jesus has not been physically present for centuries. However, if you say that Jesus has been spiritually present, that is true, because he did say he would be wherever two or three were gathered together in his name. (He did not say that he would attend massive assemblies, but he made no special promise not to appear there either.) Thus, we look to see the Trinity emerge in the Spirit's descent. For if it is the Holy Spirit which is present to us, that is the same as Jesus' spiritual presence, and also of God's. The Trinity is most easily seen in its spiritual form of presence, but this is not at all easy to discern.

When we think of Jesus in his historical life and work, and if we think of God in the divine massive creative project of the evolving universe, it is hard to see how one can argue for the self-evidence of a trinity as three persons in one. But actually, the emergence of the formal doctrine of the Trinity can be most easily understood from the perspective of the Holy Spirit. If in God's hiddeness from view and in Jesus' withdrawal as the gospel story closes, if one has trouble seeing a unity in those enterprises, then any experience of a Holy Spirit's presence to us and its effect upon us seems immediately identifiable with God's presence. And for Christians this is the same as God's presence in Jesus. The two can be experienced as immediately present in the third.

15. THE SPIRIT CAN LEAVE US WITH OUR PLAN OF ACTION

After all that we have outlined as what the Holy Spirit can do, and all that we may have learned about the nature of the Spirit by acknowledging what it cannot do, in spite of all the power represented and all the promises made, this account still leaves us each with our own task. We develop, each of us, our own plan of action. This is not so strange, if we face a powerful but also a free God, if Jesus went to his death for us and departed before his mission to install the kingdom "on earth as it is in heaven" could be completed, and particularly if the Spirit which was left to be present to us takes such an unobvious role. Jesus never led his disciples in a pledge of allegiance to a specific creedal affirmation. He said much that we can interpret, but the specific formulations were left to us. Were it otherwise, the scandalous fighting within Christian denominations could not take place. "Jesus came preaching peace and forgiveness and love, and Christians have been fighting about it ever since".

A forced confession is not God's desire, although many a tyrant in a church or in a state has pressed for one. What is voluntary is hard to commit to, hard to express precisely or to pledge to. That which is not necessary can be easily withdrawn or argued about. Even God does not indulge in coercing us, although many who use the divine name do. This causes us agony and religious uncertainty, and God could have avoided placing that burden on us by establishing a series of divinely funded indoctrination centers. Divinity is responsible for some, but not all, of our suffering over uncertainties. For many, this indefiniteness argues for no God or for a God who does not care. Yet Jesus' presence argues for a God who reveals his case to those who have the eyes to see and the will to accept. But the function of the Holy Spirit is to inform us that God does care, even in the midst of continual uncertainty, even destruction.

If God is not obvious, even after the coming of Jesus, particularly considering his unfinished project of establishing the Kingdom, does the Holy Spirit make God's nature any more clear or certain to us and so make faith more possible? Faith is often said to be the gift of the Holy Spirit, and so it must be the Spirit's presence which renders belief possible, whereas our lives and experiences seldom do so on their own. Even when we hear the "good news" preached or see the face of God in the compassion of another, unless we are supported by a Spirit we deem 'holy', that belief is not likely to remain vital. Or more importantly, it is not likely to sustain us in order to move us to carry the gospel out to others, to serve the relief of suffering. Thus, the key to Christianity's flourishing in the present day lies with the Spirit, with our ability to sense its presence and any decision it makes to grace us with its power.

It can be dangerous to feel that one knows God absolutely. Man and woman kill while claiming divine support, and they can subject people to tyranny in God's name. Thus, God's lack of concreteness is a divine self protective device, although ironically some of the world's tyrants have acted as if God were absolute in the divine endorsement of their acts. Jesus' Acts can represent and reveal God, as Christians claim, and there is no need for other religions or agnostics to deny that possibility. But in our understanding of the Holy Spirits' Acts, we can come closer to God in our own day. That we have overlooked this is also why God has so often been thought to be absent of late. True, God can undergo 'death' in our awareness, just as Jesus did. But in times of spiritual bleakness, coming to some realization of the Holy Spirit's presence, its message and its potential gifts for us, can enable God to be reborn in us and Jesus to be raised for us from his death.

C. THE PASSIVITY OF THE SPIRIT

PREFACE

In an agnostic age, we need to become sensitive, if we can, to the movements and to the power of the Holy Spirit. In times when men and women thought God more obvious, or when some established ecclesiastical structure seemed to make the Holy Spirit's presence visible, we did not need to pay so much attention to this. We could allow the Spirit to descend where it would and to withdraw when it cared to. Now, in a time of God's silence and Jesus' absence from us, either the Spirit that will represent their presence to us or else God will not feel very near and Jesus' offer of new life will not seem possible. Just as God is potentially available in all times and in all places we can postulate that the Spirit's presence can always be felt by us and move us. But this can be so only if we become sensitive to it and learn the modes of its presence. To do this means to understand the Acts of the Spirit, that is, what it can do.

Ironically, this also requires us to understand what the Spirit cannot do, or more accurately, its Passivity. Were it at all times active, its presence would be hard to miss. Were it not limited in its presence to us by its Passivity, its power would be unavoidable. Those things which God cannot do, which contradict the divine nature, plus Jesus puzzlingly silence at crucial times, all this is hard to accept until we understand the necessity of Jesus passivity in order to represent God as he does. Thus, as God's presence to us and as our link to Jesus "till he come", we should expect to learn just as much from the Holy Spirit's passive role as from its activity. It may be present in every time and place, but it is not active at every time and place; and it should not be, if it is to represent God/Jesus accurately. The religious consciousness is always puzzled when it encounters passivity where it expects, and yearns for, activity. So to understand divine passivity is key to our acquiring religious sensitivity.

1. THE SPIRIT CANNOT ACT TO BECOME NOTHING

On the surface this may sound like a contradiction, but that is why it must be understood if the Spirit is not to pass us by. When we are serious we do not really expect the Spirit to be visible to the eye. But its seeming total absence and its lack of felt force by so many millions, this requires us to ask how the Spirit can apparently reduce its presence to zero level. Of course, you can say that it has other presences than a Christian presence, and that is true. The Buddha's spirit is felt by millions, as is Mohammed's revelation and Confucious' Analects. And there is no reason not to see these as forms of the Spirit's presence, even if they are not directly connected to Jesus. The Jewish sense of the presence of God is immense, although we know that God's Spirit does not appear to Christian and Jews in like form. Yet it does appear. Zen's 'emptiness' is a close approximation to our experience of the Spirit's verge toward nothingness, and western mystics have found silence and nothingness to be an avenue to God.

To be constantly present to us would deny the Spirit's freedom, and we know that it is free to descend and to withdraw as it chooses. It would also limit our freedom if the Spirit's presence could not be withdrawn. This necessitates dormancy; it must be capable of approaching nothingness. Of course, the Spirit must also be capable of reversing its movement from out of nothingness, if it is 'Holy', although this causes us great uncertainty as we try to relate to it and to follow its lead. We can prepare our receptivity and stay alert to the signs of spiritual activity, but we cannot control or predict the spirit's coming or going. This takes constant attention and a cultivated sensitivity, and many miss the Holy Spirit's presence because they cannot hold faithful against such odds.

As a divine presence, the Spirit sees its own limitations; it knows it would not represent God to us accurately unless it did seem to disappear into nothingness from time to time. Though this may appear "unnatural", we need to learn from the Spirit's absence, understand its verge toward nothingness, if we are to find in it God's presence to us. On the other hand, like God, the Spirit could be actively present to us constantly. Even so, its divine withdrawal toward nothingness is an act of freedom. Otherwise, the power of its presence would be overpowering. We can learn a lot from voluntary silence. Yahweh frequently speaks to Jeremiah in a loud voice. But Jeremiah's relationship to God is unusual. To be a prophet means to hear the voice of God very often, or in this case to feel inspired frequently by the Holy Spirit. But we cannot all be prophets. Most of us must learn from God's silence and from the Holy Spirit's frequent absence which leaves us to experience nothingness.

Yet this absence, this Spirit's actual presence in nothingness, need not be destructive. Many spirit's we meet, and some we would rather not meet, verge constantly on violence and destruction. Thus, we have one negative check on whether or not a Spirit is holy: Does it ever press us toward violent activity? Does it ever place us on the edge of destruction? If we press these negative tests, we learn the constructive, the inspiring, the sometimes even the creative qualities of a Spirit which is holy. In its absence, in its silence, in the move toward nothingness, the Spirit can still represent God to us, that is if we can "decode" the message and reject the obvious absence. But the violent or destructive spirit, although easier to discern, has unholy intentions and is not "from God".

2. THE SPIRIT CANNOT REJECT ANYTHING

We think of a 'holy' Spirit as being highly selective, as the ultimate in religious orthodoxy, as always able to select its time and place to appear with those who are pure in their religious piety. The Spirit does not reject the ultra religious rigorist, of course. But the odd thing is that this is because, ultimately, it rejects no one. It's divinity is shown in its acceptance of all who seek its presence and its inspiration, although we know that it does not respond simply to our command, to our biding. "Come unto me all..." Jesus said, and in doing so he represented the non-discriminatory policy of the Holy Spirit. To say this is quite different from saying that the Spirit approves or responds fully to all who seek its presence. Jesus has told us that divinity responds to a humble spirit. Yet it is still open to all and rejects no one *per se.*

This is odd behavior for a Spirit that is holy, since every religion we know is characterized by exclusivity, some even violently so. All base their group membership on some prescribed activity or on some belief adhered to. If they did not do so, their uniqueness could neither be recognized nor their group kept strong. We need not deny that the Spirit is present to any particular group, large or small. Yet we do know that, if the group tends to violence, to persecution, to exclusion on doctrinal grounds, then its activity cannot be inspired by the Holy Spirit but by some parochial concern. The Spirit can appear in groups who stress rigorous practice and ascetic discipline. It encourages such commitment. But the Spirit does not limit itself to such and it rejects none.

Of course, to say that the Spirit cannot reject anything also indicates its commitment to healing. It must take in everything, reject nothing, if it is to take the tragedies which haunt the world, accept that destruction, and then move to restore it. We must reject many things if we are to preserve our sanity and to conserve our modest powers. But the Spirit's difference from us marks out its 'holiness'. Like God whom it represents, alone of the many spirits who seek to influence us, it is capable of rejecting nothing and accepting all. The Spirit, then, reflects the reverse side of God's ability to create galaxies. That for whom worlds begin to spring into being at its evolutionary command must be able to restore all who bear the brunt of that world's destructive consequences and be able move to heal all broken spirits -- in time, just as our world's creation has taken time. Due to our freedom and our responsibility, there is no automatic guarantee that God will do this in every instance or at any given moment. The Spirit can and has prescribed conditions. But its presence is still felt by us as that which initially rejects nothing and will move at its appointed time.

The Spirit's rejection of nothing had its origin in God's creative act, no matter how long that evolution took or how damaged the resulting order has become. We can see this role in Jesus' presence to us, since it is Jesus' most characteristic Act. He rejected none; he invited all to come to have their suffering relieved and to have their labor supported. For this non-discriminatory policy, Jesus was crucified. It appeared to some of his disciples at the time that God could not be present in him because Jesus had overstepped the limits of religious orthodoxy. But his resurrection is the symbol of God's power to accept all non-exclusively and to be confined to no single religious prescription, although divinity may be accessed -- as well as offended -- by some religious practices. Still, the Spirit that rejects nothing and remains open offers us a sign of its divinity. Its power needs no imposed restrictions in order to be effective.

3. THE SPIRIT CANNOT CONTROL THOSE WHO CLAIM ITS INSPIRATION

In spite of the Spirit's openness to all and its rejection of nothing, it is paradoxical that not all who claim its inspiration can be believed. There are tests: is it non-destructive; Jesus' test of love and relief of suffering; the Buddha's compassion for all sentient beings; the Jew's faithfulness to Yahweh's commands. But even its most venturesome representatives claim that the Spirit's inspiration cannot be controlled, because that would counter the Spirit's freedom and openness, if in any literal fashion it gave the Good Housekeeping Seal of Approval to some and denied it to others. That is our job: To test the validity of the Spirit's inspiration in its presence to us and in the various solicitations which come to us. The outlines of our religious belief and practice define what we accept as the Spirit's inspiration and what we reject as misleading, at least for us or our group. But since all religions do not agree about this, the Holy Spirit cannot be limited to any one existing orthodoxy.

God wishes that the Spirit would control those distortings, even destructive representatives, who can most often be detected as false prophets because the concerns they urge on us are primarily their own. A Holy Spirit represents God's healing presence to all who suffer, and so the benefit of its presence should not be used to reward any individual or organization but for all people who are in need of it. Thus, God is sometimes maligned because the Spirit's representatives too often appear unholy in their motives, in their self-focus. God, then, does not totally reject tests for the purity of the Spirit, for orthodoxy of practice. Quality control is crucial in all religions. But in line with the policy of unlimited openness, the Spirit itself does not move overtly to control those who make claims to its inspiration.

Anyone who follows the words of any religious leader knows his or her advice on how the "true" religious Spirit is to be discerned, e.g., Mary Baker Eddy, Joseph Smith, Mohammed. But unfortunately, religious rigor too easily turns into cold exclusion, and so we must not let any religion's prescriptions be taken as final in its characterization of the Spirit. Moreover, the central aspect of the Holy Spirit is its refusal to be limited to any past inspirational movement or person. It stays receptive to new forms of inspiration opening up in the future; and so must we do so too, if we do not want to miss its presence in our day. Thus, we cannot know in advance whose claims to the Spirit's inspiration we must doubt or at least suspect. If the Spirit stays continually open and authorizes no single form for its presence, if it does not openly control those who claim to speak in its name, we need to develop and sustain a similar constant openness if we want to encounter its presence.

Although not all who claim the inspiration of the Spirit can be accepted, and some are even positively destructive, we must make the attempt to stay open to all. That is the immense task which is imposed on us very limited human beings by the Spirit's failure to set up controls on those who claim its inspiration. Of course, we can follow some established religious guidelines, something as safe as the Gospels or as structured as the Roman Church or Mohammed's prescriptions. But in doing so it is possibly to miss the Spirit's presence, even if it does inspire authors and church builders. Yet the Spirit refuses limitations put on the words written by its inspiration or on the rituals devised in response to its presence. Words and rituals go dry. The Holy Spirit is a constantly novel source of inspiration, one whom many can claim as their source.

4. THE SPIRIT CANNOT AVOID ANGER

Wherever we think of a Spirit which we call 'holy', an Alice-in-Wonderland mood takes hold. We think of it as "Jesus meek and mild", or in the devoted affection of a Mary or a Martha for Jesus. True, Jesus did get angry but only seldom, the Buddha almost never. But if the Holy Spirit represents God for us, Jesus may not have come "after the flood" so much to represent God's anger again as to evidence God's love. But as our "Jesus substitute", the Spirit may actually represent "more" of God than Jesus' passion/compassion ever can, since we have the Hebrew prophets to thank for our image of the "angry God". Jeremiah announces God's anger to a wayward, prostituting people. The Spirit, in spite of its role as comforter in a difficult age, cannot hold back from anger at all times, that is if it is to represent God fully.

By giving us "the sign of the dove" God has promised not to destroy the earth again. That Jesus announces God's love and offer of restoration, all this does not cover up the fact that much of the action in our world, just as in Noah's time, must shock God into anger through its lack of human care and in its avoidance of ethical/religious duty. Thus, God cannot be present to us in a blatantly secular world, a corrupt, cynical, and political venture, without risking the Spirit's uncontrollable anger. When heaven witnesses what human beings do to one another, often calling on God's name to support their ungodly activities, God supports the Spirit's move to protest and to display anger. If God has a place and a day in mind when the Spirit's divine anger will be overcome, we are not there yet.

Our outbursts often represent a petty, selfish disposition, a frustration over our failed projects. On the other hand, God is angered because we frustrate divinity's projects, those for the brother/sisterhood of mankind and the love of neighbor, the healing of suffering in the world. Thus, we call God's anger 'righteous' anger, where so much of ours is jealous and motivated by envy. Furthermore, much of the destruction in our lives comes from uncontrolled anger or rage. God does not 'rage', though his prophets do. But a Holy Spirit is never represented by an uncontrolled rage. It's anger is expressed over human self-destruction, over our failure to listen to any of the valuable spiritual guides we have been sent. The Spirit's anger is intended to provoke us, to call us back to constructive, rather than to take always selfish, paths. The Spirit's anger is a goad, never a destroyer.

Yet of course, since the Spirit's movements are discreet and unseen, the anger it inspires is indirect. In this case, even deserved anger cannot help but be mixed with human motives and projects which in fact are tangential to the Spirit's aim for the restoration of humanity. But whenever we feel anger that we can label 'righteous', when we feel it as an outrage over human failure and self-centered concentration, in these outbursts we can feel the Spirit's presence and learn God's intended aim. This is never simple or clear or identical to any of our highly touted projects, but it is an evidence of God's concern. The Spirit must be unable to control anger if God is to be made manifest properly. No God can long stay silent toward the world as we observe it.

5. THE SPIRIT CANNOT LOSE ITSELF

"Lost, lost" is a theme which haunts many novels. Camus' 'stranger' is lost. Even Jesus at times appears lost in the gospel accounts, and indeed for his disciples the crucifixion seemed to seal both his lostness and theirs. If God restored Jesus from his lost condition, and so restored the disciples faith, the Spirit offers, not God's willingness to experience loss but divinity's inability, in the last analysis, to set anything aside. Existentialists have told us that there is much to be learned that is edifying if we recognize our 'lost' or 'alienated' position. There is much to be learned about our religious dreams in accepting Jesus loss in his crucifixion, just as in Jesus resurrection we can recognize God's power to work against loss. When the Spirit comes, it represents God's ability to protect all against ultimate loss, whether now or in the future.

We know that we say the world must continually be held in existence by God's power but that nevertheless its continuance is sure, not quixotic, because once committed divinity does not fail continually to sustain. Extending this, in spite of our human undependability and rapid shift of moods which Jesus life also illustrated, the Spirit is recognized in a steady display of power and commitment against loss.

This may be one reason why some who speak in tongues claim to do so under its inspiration. A flow of power like that, when it enters any one of us, causes the disruption of normal modes and a heightening of all experience. Such assurance of safety against loss demands a far more vocal response than any normal language can express.

Although God cannot become lost, the Spirit brings itself and us closer to that experience, just because lostness is central to our human problem and the Spirit is God's messenger to us. Thus, God's presence to us in that form, when it is experienced, comes as overwhelming security and return from a lost condition. Loss is involved here, in the sense that the descent of the Spirit, the "healing in its wings", often demands a surrendering of everything which blocks God's entrance. This may be sin in any of its forms, self-centeredness, destruction of others, inability to convey love, intoxication with our own powers in any form, whether creative or destructive. If so, we remember Jesus' remark that he who would save his life must lose it for his sake. Since that is also for God's sake, this giving over of the self's demands actually allows the Spirit to enter, and with it comes security against ultimate loss.

In this way the Spirit can demand loss of self. And in the experience of self-emptying, of voiding whatever blocks God's kingdom or opposes Jesus' message, that loss alone allows the Holy Spirit entrance. What begins as loss of self ends in a guarantee against final loss, but this will only come to a self that emerges from a purging loss, one that replaces its self-centered concerns with God's. We can sense the Spirit's presence, then, when we see or feel the loss of some aim that comes close to causing a destruction of love. But then we next find it replaced, not at our bidding but by a Spirit's support which is experienced as God's. In this way the Hebrew prophets, and Jesus too, sustained themselves against final loss. Jesus surrendered his work, his own spirit, his protection, into God's hands, which opened him to ultimate loss of life; but then he was protected against final loss by the Spirit's descent, his rescuer from death.

6. THE SPIRIT CANNOT WITHHOLD DESIRE

Much of our experience of God involves paradox. Thus, we should not expect to find the Spirit's descent into our lives to be smooth or even all-resolving. We have noted that the emptying of self-desire is the condition for the Spirit's entrance; experienced loss becomes security. But the Spirit itself cannot lose or even withhold all desire on its part. It is not, as we are, forced into a loss of desire in order to inaugurate it's self-projects. Of course, this is partly because it is a 'Holy' Spirit and partly because it represents desires which are other than selfish. That is, the Spirit never comes to us saying "follow me". It has no 'me' to follow, whereas Jesus did assume human personhood, and so many are confused into thinking that it is an individual who he calls them to follow. Thus, the Spirit's inspiration can guide us to follow God from the start.

There is no need for the Spirit to withhold desire, since its central desire is for us to be filled with God's spirit. Thus, it can overwhelm us with emotion, cause desires to rise in us which we had not known before and still we do not feel that these desires must be controlled. In other instances, if desire cannot be controlled, we face damage or loss of self. The desires of the Spirit are non-destructive, non-individual, and so they direct us out to others where the need is so great that there is no reason to restrict desire. "The harvest is ripe but the workers are few". The range is unlimited, but one needs the inspiration of the uncontrolled desire of the Spirit in order to be able to tackle a project so immense, so beyond human capacity. The Spirit can bring us from petty projects to that limitless task.

Some theologians have placed God beyond desire, thinking that it would demean divinity to experience desire. But perhaps the Holy Spirit's role of immediate presence to us can make us realize our error in striping God of desire. If God is to be present to us, and if the Spirit expresses God's involvement in our lives, desire must characterize God too. One could not be present in the world scene and not feel desire. Too much needs to be loved; too much needs correction, and there is too little evidence that we have moved vary far in doing either. Our freedom is too wide ranging to predict or to guarantee progress. And if we go by the odds, human history works against non-retractable progress. Thus, in the divine freedom God knows that ultimate control lies in divinity's hands. But freedom brings with it a desire to accomplish, to prevent or to restore destruction, and thus God's Spirit as it descends to us exudes, never excludes, desire.

Evil, or destruction, is too strong, too prominent in our lives (and beauty too attractive) for any Spirit which comes to us to be able to restrain all desire. Every loss, every thwarted life, calls forth, from any spirit that represents God, a desire to heal. It is unfortunately true that this is not always immediately done. We hold God's commitment to human restoration in the form of a promissory note. Thus, the divine delay in the salvation offer, the continued prominence of the evil of destruction, all this fills any Spirit that comes to us with desire for a new future. And it sustains that desire as God's presence toward us till the promise of restoration can be accomplished. Thus, the Holy Spirit cannot withhold desire. Too much in our lives remains unfulfilled; the need in the age it ministers to is too great for it to rest.

7. THE SPIRIT CANNOT ACT TO BLOCK OUT EVIL

To say this may seem odd, since so many pray for the inspiration of the Spirit in order to avoid evil. Even Jesus taught us pray to be "kept from evil". So it would be ironic if the Holy Spirit, whose help we seek for our support, should be itself unable to block out all evil. But of course Jesus' recommended prayer means for us to try to do this for others, not to eliminate evil in itself. We have commented on the Spirit's passionate desire to turn us from self-centered ways, so it would be contradictory if it could not itself restrain, or if it was unable to offer spiritual sustenance against, evil tendencies. But: the Spirit cannot force this on any who do not seek its inspiration. So it is unable to block out all evil. Those who follow paths of destruction seek their own ends and do not stop, except in exhaustion when they witness supposed gains wiped out and would halt this if they could. But just as the Spirit is free to blow where it will, so are those who oppose it.

This is the battle of the Titans. For the Spirit is 'holy', and its powers are immense (we say, 'absolutely infinite', 'unlimited'). Yet our own daily experience testifies that those who seek to destroy for their own ends also wield immense power (even if it is not unlimited). We know that even the best and the most determined of us often cannot

prevent loss. Thus, the war is waged. But in addition to coming to our
defense and inspiring our power to resist, the Spirit is engaged in a
holding action for now. It is also present as a sign of God's future
intent, thus succeeding Jesus in that office. Evil rages; it uses every
subtlety of intellect and power and skill and attraction; it is opposed,
sometimes successfully, but never eliminated, only momentarily
contained. Its total reversal is not in the Spirit's program as it
represents God in the age-in-between. The Spirit's present power is
only a sign of God's future action.

What is hardest for us to understand is the fact that the forces which
rage all about us, attempting either to conquer or to destroy if
necessary, flow originally from God's own nature and were not locked
out of the plan of creation. 'Being' means 'power', as Plato pointed
out, and its gift is not restricted to the 'good'. God could have allowed
only "The Pastoral Symphony" to be written, but even our music
testifies eloquently that conflicting powers swirl all about in the world.
Thus, the Spirit's task is in a way harder than Jesus'. He could
represent God's love and compassion and forgiveness to a world which
would not have suspected that about God, given their observations of
those around them. Jesus could succumb to the forces of evil and still
represent "God's kind side". The Spirit has the thankless task of
simultaneously opposing evil and offering us inspiration to do this too,
all the while representing God's harsh, judgmental side, which placed
destruction in the world and allows it still to rage. Except as God has
set limitation, for instance, the one he gave to Satan concerning Job,
evil does not destroy the world's frame and all life within it, only fairly
large quantities.

Thus, the comfort, the inspiration which the Spirit brings to us in
our battle is solely provisional. But after all, its role is 'provisional'. It
represents God's projected intervention to stop, to control, to repair
all, and it is also our access to divinity in the age before our world's
ultimate reordering. In that role, it would not represent God fully
unless the Spirit also represented the still rampant forces of evil, even
their often fascinating attractiveness. Yet at the same time it also
conveys the message that this age is not-for-always. Not all are
repelled by the powers capable of destroying us, else not so many
would fall into addiction, drugs, or under the spell cast by money,
power, sex. So the attractive qualities in evil represent God's allowing

hand, hard as that is for us – or for Job – to accept. But the Spirit also represents to us God's claim against the future.

8. THE SPIRIT CANNOT PREDICT THE FUTURE

Since God lives in self-restrained freedom, the Spirit that represents such a divinity dwells in controlled freedom too. Yet we cannot determine or predict the Spirit's inspiring descent. Often there are times when we must try to live in divinely inspired silence. Thus, as much as the Spirit was given to be our potential guide ("potential", since not all will accept it) for God in the intervening age, it cannot predict the future for us in exact detail. We can remain close to traditional Trinitarianism and claim that this is because God's picture of the future does not come in clearly at the celestial "space center" TV monitoring room either, and that would be correct. Many do feel that they predict the future under the inspiration of the Holy Spirit, and they may not be wholly wrong in thinking so. But God's powers of perception are greater than ours, even if not fully subject to the Spirit's total divine control or to exact prediction.

Were the future known fully to God, the Spirit's presence and its role would be superfluous. God would have no reason to "be with us", having once sent his son with the message of the amazing divine intent or having given Mohammed his definitive revelation to clear up uncertainties for diverging Christians. After that, there would be nothing for us to do but to act out our parts. God would have no further need for involvement in the world, once having experienced rejection. But just because the world's stage is still open to the decisions made by the players who strut about on it, God needs to maintain a minimum presence, else divinity's message in Jesus would soon be forgotten. That drama did not end in obvious victory. If the powers of the world continue their subtle hidden or even open warfare as if Jesus had never come, then that "kingdom within" which he inaugurated needs undergirding by a Holy Spirit. That is, it does if it is to be sustained amidst ever-gathering darkness.

God enjoys freedom, else divinity would have adopted the role of Aristotle's Unmoved Mover. Likewise, the Spirit evidences that joy which comes in the freedom of contingency and in the uncertainty of facing the continued outbreak of chaos. True, the Spirit has God's unlimited power at its disposal, whereas our weakness often causes us to trade freedom for security, or even for a momentary addictive release from the anxieties of the uncertainties which freedom introduces. So the Spirit represents a divine joy that descends like fire. It conveys joy to us when it inspires, because it is based on the invulnerability of God's power. However, in the-age-in-between, God's power has actually been made vulnerable, as Jesus crucifixion testifies. The Zen master who achieves satori is able to lose that gift too. Just as no virtue or accomplishment is beyond corrosion, so even in heaven joy must be tempered by sorrow over present loss.

The Spirit's inability to predict the future precisely, or to unleash God's power to bring destruction under full control, thus mutes all celebration, just as all Christian rejoicing should be muted in the knowledge that they are celebrating in advance of a still unknown deadline. There is the thrill in the uncertainty of challenge to all who take up any inspiration-induced project, but there is also a risk and an awareness of possible loss, such as every mountain climbing team feels in its ascent to the highest peak. In that sense, the Spirit does not wish to predict the future as it presents challenges to us. But for the not-strong, and for the religious ones who are sensitive to human frailty, we can also appeal to the Spirit for inspiration in order to face our unknown future.

9. THE SPIRIT CANNOT LIVE OR ACT BEYOND THOUGHT

In both Western and Eastern mysticism, thought exists on a lower level than the fully divine which transcends thought. In the Zen tradition, thought can be a block to our desired enlightenment. 'Nothingness' is more important than thought, as it is for Meister Eckhart too in his meditation on emptiness as the supreme experience of God -- the 'wasteland', as T.S. Eliot expressed it. Although Christian mystics have at times seemed to join their Eastern counterparts in refusing thought as central, using such concepts as the 'wasteland' for a creator-God (which Buddhists do not tend to feature), thought must be an instrument of creation; in no other way can "the word be made flesh". One can argue that any direct experience of God is "beyond thought" ultimately, in the sense that all agree that words are not adequate to express this fully.

However, where Jesus is concerned we can never place our understanding of his nature beyond all thought, even though we probably do want to say that his recorded words, or even his disciples' words about him, can never exhaust his nature or fully express our understanding of "who he was". However, if Jesus was a human figure, if he was "fully man" and so could never be conceived as living beyond thought, even if Jesus did not expect his own words to convey his gospel or his disclosure of God fully, the Holy Spirit is not so easily tied to the natural world. As God's direct relationship to the world in our time, it could inspire us to move beyond thought, and its inspiring Spirit can lift us beyond our imagination. Yet oddly, the Holy Spirit cannot ultimately live beyond thought any more than Jesus could or did. Why?

Because the Spirit is God's representation to us in our time. So if it existed beyond thought itself, it would be unable to bring God to us in comprehensible form. This is not to say that any words about God uttered on the inspiration of a Holy Spirit are thus full of literal truth. The Spirit probably operates symbolically in its communication, not by a strict verbal inspiration, just as Jesus did. Thus, words attributed to the Spirit's inspiration can be misleading if taken too literally, rather than as designed to inspire us, to lift us individually to new heights of insight. Yet if words can mislead by being taken literally, the Holy Spirit is nevertheless still tied to thought, to its and our use of words to express what the Spirit has granted to us as insight. Like the Spirit itself, suspended between earth and heaven as a mediator, the words it inspires are at the same time parochial, earthy, and yet capable of causing the attentive mind to touch God.

Freedom demands our constant use of thought, if it is not to get out of control and run amok, which it so often tragically does. God must stay with thought too in order to control the outcome of that super-freedom. This power is a divine quality and is given to us, when it comes, as a divine gift. Jesus was free, and even in his agony he did not reject God's demands. On the other hand, we know that the Holy Spirit to be free because it is the instrument of divine grace, and we know that is never given to us automatically or in every situation.

True, if this happened more often, the world would be less tragic. The Spirit itself does not always descend on us in our need, even when we want it desperately, e.g., the Jewish holocaust, Jesus crucifixion. Thus, we implore the Spirit's inspiration; we know it is not irrational or even beyond thought. But we recognize that its very commitment to thought is an indication of its freedom and its right to self-determination.

10. THE SPIRIT CANNOT DENY ITS WILL

We must accept the Spirit's freedom of determination to action (descent) or non-action(withdrawal) as beyond our control. But it is not beyond our solicitation. Due to its tie to thought that it will not break, it follows that neither can it deny its own will. Some have argued that divinity lies beyond volition, and traditional piety has called for the denial of our will as a sign of submission to God, not unlike the Zen seeker's necessity to abandon intense desire as a condition for enlightenment. Yet what is demanded of us, by the Zen master or by Jesus in the surrender of our will, is oddly enough not applicable to the Holy Spirit. It's will is God's will, and it cannot be set aside.

God's will never ceases to sustain the world. As Elijah proved to doubters, Yahweh neither slumbers nor sleeps. Similarly, as the representative of God to us in our time, the Spirit does not deny or fail to support the results of an inspired divine descent, once given. This does not, somewhat unfortunately, mean that every claimed inspiration can be believed. That would lead to contradiction and to intellectual chaos. We can feel authenticated by the power of the Spirit. But when anyone speaks or acts to represent this, the responsibility for believing or denying that must be our own. Divinity only inspires by the Spirit's presence; it does not confirm our response. That is our decisions, and we can be wrong or distort a presentation of God's spirit, even without intending to do so. We grasp for adequate words or symbols to express what we have felt, but our phrasing can be misleading. In our natural enthusiasm, we may overstate our case and even God's.

Still, the Spirit cannot deny its will, that is, denounce even a distorted message that its descent has inspired. It never withdraws. It allows every expression of its inspiration, all of our various artistic renderings, even if they do not do justice to the divine Spirit behind them. And the Spirit's consistency of will is important to us, because this means that, wherever inspiration has once moved, the coals of its remaining husks can be fanned and inspiration perhaps renewed. We know this does not happen automatically simply on reading or hearing or even seeing works that result from inspiration. But our knowledge of the consistency of the will of the Spirit, like God's guarantee not to destroy the world, tells us that in our searching and probing for the results of the Spirit's descent, which lie all around us enshrined in word and form, the Spirit is ever present and can reinspire.

But just as its inspiration was free and not restrained for the one who first inaugurated the production of the creations we study or observe, the knowledge of the Spirit's continued presence in its products in no way guarantees that the one who approaches them later will receive an inspiration too, not even the devout seeker. The Spirit's guarantee not to deny what it has willed, that its inspiration remains codified and enshrined in many places, is still coupled with its original freedom. It can no more be controlled by those who seek inspiration in its products than by the one who was first moved by its descent upon his or her life. Like God, the Spirit adjusts to novelty and to changed contexts. It does not desert the traditions which claim its inspiration, but neither is it tied to any previous form in the choice for its mode of descent in God's later days.

11. THE SPIRIT CANNOT BE COERCED

We are well aware that God cannot be coerced, although people never cease to try. We have slightly more feeling that Jesus might be coerced, due to his expression of love and compassion for all who suffer. Because we deem him as God's presence in our human form, we feel Jesus to be "with us" and so able to share our lot. Still, as portrayed, we know Jesus was not coerced to take either an easier course for his mission or to abandon it when it led him toward death. With the Holy Spirit, we feel slightly more at its mercy. It does not move in visible form among us as Jesus did, and as his disciples tell us he still can do today. We pray for the Spirit's inspiration; we know only that our work prospers when it comes under its inspiration. But we also know that, despite the desperate needs produced by sex and alcoholism and the drug culture, its appearance to us cannot be coerced.

This is just as well, in spite of how anxious we are at times for its re-inspiration, particularly when we enter dry periods after having just felt the power of its creative flow. But our inability to coerce the Spirit to fit our "production schedule", tells us something important about the Spirit's free nature and the contingence involved in any creative process. We prepare; we solicit; we train our skills; we prepare our spirits, humble or powerful. But the Spirit's non-coercion policy is a lesson in humility, in our ultimate dependence, in our freedom, and in the uncontrollable nature of any creative enterprise. Magnificence can not be programmed. It is recognized only after the fact, sometimes long after.

Brute force is all around us, but this is not God's elected means. And so the Spirit represents the divine by standing totally outside force, although the world thrives (or tries to) on little else. The Spirit does not force us; God does not. Force is the instrument of non-infinite powers who fear they can be overpowered. Thus, our inability to coerce the Spirit is an indirect indication, if we study it, of our own freedom. The Spirit can descend upon us, or it can try to; we can be unprepared (like the foolish virgins), and it will no more coerce us than it will accept our coercion. Of course, tragically, this can lead to loss, even to destruction, and to our inner life becoming a spiritual desert. Thus, we have the very common religious feeling of being deserted by God, as Jesus expressed it from the cross.

The Spirit's presence can be overlooked, or at least go unresponded to. It's failure to use force, just as it will not be coerced, makes it (to us) a strange representative of a God who leaves us our freedom even at the expense of denying us the presence of any Holy Spirit, or who leaves us alone in our inability to accept its guiding inspiration. The Spirit works in non-obvious ways, and it cannot even be counted as the source of the inspiration for even monumental acts or worthy products. It does not create physical universes, despite John's gospel opening. Not all spirits are holy, as we know. So we have no infallible test for its presence, neither in papal elections nor in an evangelist's sermon. We sometimes wish the Spirit would overwhelm us and evidence its inspiration beyond denial. But it does not coerce, just as it will not be coerced by our pleas, not even when they are genuine.

12. THE SPIRIT CANNOT BE CAPTURED IN ONE FORM

Religiously inclined people have always wished that their particular encounter with God's would prove unitary and uniform for all peoples. Non-theistic religions offer an initial challenge to this goal, although there still is a difference between monotheism and polytheism. The irony is that, even within strong monotheistic religions ("Thou shalt have no other gods before me"), the reports are far from uniform. So that in spite of the desire for agreement, the various experiences, and therefore the various descriptions, of the "one God" neither agree nor are reconcilable. Similarly, when one looks for the inspiring Spirit of God, one hopes its behavior will be consistent and uniform for all. Such is not the case; it varies just as our conceptions of God do. However, for Christians at least all unite in Jesus, except that Mohammed's revelation proves to us that all disagreement about God did not end, even with God's own incarnation.

Still, if one contrasts the behavior of the Holy Spirit with the disagreements about Jesus or with our constant arguments about God, one does find greater similarities between the impact of the Spirit's descent on those who experience it than one does among direct seekers after God. Thus, the Holy Spirit is a fitting representative of God's presence, since its work often unites those caught up in its inspiration. Unfortunately, it does not cause them all to become one absolutely, neither in thought nor in action. But all testify to a Spirit beyond themselves which lifts them to heights of insight and creativity, or at least to a quiet reconciliation which they cannot attribute to their own powers or talents. As it settles on one, he or she is aware of a connection to powers beyond the self and feels like an instrument. We call such a Spirit 'divine', because it lifts us beyond ourselves and does so independent of our powers, natural or artificial.

Thus, no formula can be given to one who seeks such inspiration. The Spirit's paths are not defined in advance. God eludes us, due to divinity's failure to fit within our words and descriptions. The Spirit eludes our control, because it will not be routinized, although ironically many (not all) ceremonies celebrating its presence are elaborately ritualized. Still, the Spirit does inspire our use of words and other symbolic forms. Its effects are easily discerned in its novel results, in its impressive style. But the Spirit behind those gifts can neither be characterized in a single way nor be programmed invariably to yield satisfaction for us. The Spirit descends, but where and when it wills. But since God cannot be captured, the Spirit reflects the same transcendence, even when coupled with its immediately felt effects. We must stay open to novelty of forms while rejecting no classical one.

This is one reason why the religious seeker is called a 'pilgrim'. He or she must be prepared to wander, to glimpse what it looks for as spirit's source, to feel its presence, but to know that the task of following what is recommended is just beginning and is subject to constant revision. We can tell a Holy Spirit by its fruits, as Jesus reports, but this does not give us a lock on its future. To seek inspiration only in some of its past forms is undeniably possible, but you are also warned not to stay only to established formulae. The Spirit is contextual in its descent. You have to ask how being a seeker now makes any one of the classical paths become important for you, or whether you need to focus on a new time and place.

13. THE SPIRIT CANNOT DENY THE HOLOCAUST

In spite of its inspirational, i.e., divine qualities, life under the spirit's guidance is not all a bed of roses. Why? Because it does not directly oppose evil, and because holocausts are still possible. I say "directly", because those under its inspiration can be singled out by their healing presence and their restorative works. Under its guidance, divisions are healed, hatreds forgotten, love dispensed. It causes not only a creative flame but an outward flow in those under its inspiration. For this reason not all creative persons are divinely inspired. Many are vastly productive, but most are self-centered, following selfish reasons. This does not always effect the quality of their creative work. Thus, not all who become famous are under a 'holy' spirit's guidance. And yet many who are not publicly creative are under its care.

Partly because the Spirit's work is often private and secret and humble, it neither operates in power circles nor prevents all destruction, although many who once were destructive have been converted by its spirit, e.g. Malcolm X. Odd, too, that although God's power could control destruction and expose all self-centered persons no matter what their virtuous pose or cover-up words, the Spirit does not represent the divine power of full control, although its power can restore individuals. To say this is consistent, since the Holy Spirit represents God in the-in-between-age. In such an age God's controlling hand is often quiet. Holocausts are not denied, even if we accept the Spirit's present inspiration. Yet it does represent God's power as being available to all individuals, although as not yet operative to change the order of the world.

The Spirit can prevent individual holocausts, the destruction of the self by itself, when its inspiring spirit turns the individual to creative outer-directed acts rather than to public destruction or to inner anguish. God's failure not yet to act on the public scene to reconstitute the world order and human nature, all this delay does not deny the Spirit's individual activity. In that sense, in its healing, in its creative presence, it represents God again by telling us, as evidenced in inspired lives, that what God can do in the Spirit's descent, on an individual or on a small group, can be extended to the world as a whole. But not yet; the Spirit's continued presence testifies to that too. What it models now can be the basis for belief in God's ultimate plan. Just as the good suffer with the bad in any holocaust, so not all who are inspired are themselves saints.

This brings us to the mystery of the Holy Spirit's operation, as any encounter with the evil of destruction always does. The Spirit only inspires; it does not offer theodocies. It does not explain all of God's action toward men and women; it only testifies to God's power to inspire, to heal, to create, to turn individual self-destruction to positive ends. In the midst of a world torn by divisions and destructions that do not seem to end, the Spirit's ever surprising descent is a "sign of the dove", that is, that God will not let the whole earth be destroyed, either in divine anger or in human rage. When it is sensed, the Spirit's presence comes as a divine presence and undergirds the belief that God's love for the human race is real, even if only partially manifest at present. Jesus has gone; the Holy Spirit is the New Age connection to a constructive future.

14. THE SPIRIT CANNOT SPEAK TO US DIRECTLY

Although the Spirit represents God's presence to us since Jesus was withdrawn, it is an irony that the Spirit does not speak to us, cannot speak to us, directly. Jesus was for us in that sense a more immediate presence for God than the Spirit is today, although the irony is that almost all failed to see this at the time. Like Saul/Paul, later converts often claim to find God's presence in Jesus more clearly in a later day than did those who were present with him. Of course, here we see one work of the Holy Spirit: Those who are attracted to Jesus' present presence and feel God's power there are guided to that center by the Spirit's descent, since neither God nor Jesus are immediately open to us. All those who come into God's presence or who receive Jesus gospel do so under the Spirit's inspiration, since not all who hear respond.

So the effect of the Spirit's presence is like a speaking to us, but it is not direct. Not all who are moved to speak or to create or to act are aware of its instrumentality. It moves unseen; it inspires without itself taking direct action. Thus, we can easily tell when we or others are moved by a destructive spirit; but our creative, healing, transforming works are not always attributed to any outside spirit, let alone to one that is Holy. Thus, the Spirit often moves through secular means as much as by religious channels. Sometimes those channels are open to an inspiring movement. But many times a formal religion is closed in upon itself and becomes content to repeat routines. Where the Spirit's movement is not immediately religiously connected, its origins are often unrecognized and not inquired into.

Of course, God did seem to speak directly to the prophets. Jeremiah certainly thought he identified God's voice speaking to him. Christians have translated the prophetic speaking into Jesus presence, which involves a greater indirection. Thus, such an avenue to God is less direct, the divine word more liable to being mistaken, Jesus more capable of rejection. And all this is a less direct representation of God than is Jeremiah's. Thus, following Jesus' departure, the Holy Spirit sent to guide us represents God's less overt mode of approach. However, given the divine freedom, there is no reason to reject any claim for God's speaking. We need to search everywhere for God's meaning. And even when inspired, we can always be mistaken due to the divine self-imposed restrictions on overt presence. The Spirit's inspiration is unmistakably felt, although its mode is not always overpowering. We have to look back in time in order to discern its full effects.

Will there in time come a day of God's direct speaking, one when the Holy Spirit's indirection will be overcome? Yes, that is the Spirit's testimony, its line of inspiration, the sense of its divine presence, one that leads to a direct appearance, sometimes called the Day of Last Judgment. In this sense the Spirit often leads to repentance and to personal change, a foretaste of God's final judgment in miniature. When one is inspired to speak, or to work, or to perform under the Spirit's direction, one forecasts the day of God's direct encounter, often termed Jesus "second coming". The Spirit's movement now stirs us to attend to that future and to work for it. That is, it does so when we are open to the Spirit's guiding influence.

15. THE SPIRIT CANNOT BE VERY RELIGIOUS

To say this seems odd, since for every religion one can name the day and the place of the first movement of a divine Spirit is an anchoring rock, a founding action. To inspire is central in founding a belief, and many claim it as unique to their religion, even when what they mean is that the Spirit has moved them in special, perhaps novel, ways in its mode of individual operation. But we can name no religion that has not, in individuals or in periods, evidenced corruption so much so that we know that it does not contain a spirit that is Holy in that later day. Thus, as much effect as the movement of the Spirit had in the forming and in the sustaining of various religions, it will neither identify with any one, nor even with all religions. Past the day of revelation which caused their foundation, such as the day of Pentecost for Christians, or Mohammed's inspiration for Muslims, once their believe is established, too many religions cease to offer inspiration.

In rare cases, no Holy Spirit can any longer be found in once sacred precincts. In most cases, the discerning and persistent follower can find a spark buried in the coals that can ignite the founding power once again for him or her. But since this is usually an individual matter, either for a particular religious follower or for a newly reinspired leader, the Spirit never identifies with the hierarchy of formal religion as such, since there is much in any of their practices that it cannot take responsibility for. And more important, the Holy Spirit needs independence from institutions in order to guide reformers to restore a sense of the presence of the Holy Spirit's inspiration to a later group or to a religion that has lost its direction.

Thus, we know that in the post-inspirational period the Spirit withdraws and does not guide day to day operations. This, as we know all too well, is left to human devices. This puts us in the odd position of not being sure that the Spirit can be found in any existing temple, although the odd counterpart to this is that it may be found in every temple, church, or synagogue just as well, whether Zen or Hindu. Its presence is not necessarily in any but is simply available to all seekers in any location, 'holy places' not excluded. The Spirit will not obey every command. It is both in every temple, outside of every temple, and identical to none. Thus, since the Spirit is God's representative to us, just as Jesus was not identified with the orthodox religion of his day (but neither did he deny it), God is not formally present in any single religion and yet is available to all. Most individuals, however, will claim to find God in one place more than in another.

We know that most who are religious claim inspiration by a Spirit; and there is no reason to deny this. At the same time we know that a founding inspiration is not the same as the Spirit's continual identification with the resulting practices or structures. Thus, God can be celebrated by many, and he can be found by those who currently seek divinity. Yet such appearances are not subject to full priestly, institutional control. This is not to say that God rejects those who claim to represent divinity, or that the Spirit refuses to inspire or to bring God's presence within sanctuary walls. God does not exclude the divine Spirit from any location, but it is better for the Spirit to stay unidentified with and so uncontrolled by any religion. God's freedom is more faithfully represented.

EPILOGUE

Having thus outlined what the Holy Spirit can do and how the Spirit cannot act, God has been represented but not confined. One is free, following these or any other words, to stumble across the Spirit's presence, that is, to be found by the Spirit. But neither these words nor any others offer a secure map leading into God's presence. The divine nature is too free for such confinement and the Spirit too individual in its inspiration. Yet the Spirit moves across the face of the deep every day, so that the only question is whether we have developed a sensitivity both to its presence and to its current directions. There are of course periods of drought, dry spells, when God's silence seems deafening and the Spirit's absence acute. The activity is neither uniform nor wholly predictable, although we have clues left by those who have charted and cherished its presence.

How, then, should one seek for a Spirit that is Holy while attempting to escape destructive spirits? We look first to those who in our past and in the present seem to represent at least some spirit of God, as it has been known. We see the face of God in the kindness of another. We look for the descent of the Spirit in amazingly transformed lives and in an intense artistic creative spirit. This means not only where someone is simply productive -- the evil and the self-centered display active talent too -- but where the inspiration seems to heal, to construct, to unite, to re-form what is broken. As we argued that Jesus should be judged by his Acts, so we claim the Spirit is known by the Acts we designate as 'holy', in whatever religious or secular places these appear.

Some have argued that they find 'traces' of God in the world outside the world's dominant religions. It is of course the Holy Spirit's task to trace out God's action in the world which otherwise we might miss. Some have thought to see this in the beauty of the created order. It is there; but the trouble with these "traces" is that they are mixed with the destructive tendencies in the natural order, and so the world as a whole cannot testify to God without our using a selective guide. But in some special human behavior, the traces of God are more easily seen, and this is thanks to the work of the Holy Spirit. That is, the Spirit does not move mountains, although God could. But it does become visible when it appears in the transformed lives of certain people. Of themselves they are not "good spirits", but the Holy Spirit has inspired, even directed, their outlook and action, so that at least at times God seems nearer to us in such lives.

Of course, just as the spirit of any man or women is in itself interior and unseen, so we recognize the quality of a human spirit only by its Acts, as is true with Jesus and the Holy Spirit. Not always at the time, and often only in retrospect, we have to ask: What Spirit has lived and moved among us for a time? And such a person need not be in himself or herself thought by all to be all-good or even pious. There is a spirit discernible in human conduct and behavior that speaks to us of a greater Holy Spirit's movement and inspiration. The effect is such in its constructive, healing aspects so as not to be attributable to any individual simply-human power or virtue. Such persons are greater than themselves. Unfortunately, many others think that they are great by themselves. But they have known no Holy Spirit.

POSTSCRIPT

It is clear that God has "a secret life", since it is impossible that we will ever know "all about God". Even pious people do not claim to know God whole, and the various religion's mystics have claimed that such knowledge is impossible in theory. God transcends all final conceptualization, and of-course divinity is not found residing in concepts. That would be demeaning to true divinity. Christians claim God's revelation was given in Jesus, and Muslims feel God used Mohammed as a Prophet to complete the revelation and to cure uncertainties. Apart from the fact that all followers do not agree, just as all Jews do not feel that Moses declared all God had to say, no one can claim intimate knowledge of God's every action and thought, only certain perhaps crucial ones.

Jesus' claim to reveal God -- or that his followers claim that he did -- has never removed all uncertainly. In fact, paradoxically, if God offers new life and salvation to all, that makes God's operation as creator and sustainer of the world we find around us an even greater mystery. The taunt to Elijah: Is your God sleeping? --- rings true. What are God's actions now and what were they before Jesus; and more frustrating, what is the plan for the end of time? A great deal of detail is lacking, else 'faith' would not be required and simple human enlightenment would bring God into full focus, which it certainly has not been done, Descartes and Spinoza notwithstanding. Still, even the creator God or the Redeemer God are fairly easy to explain when compared to the Holy Spirit.

Jesus adds to this complexity by making the explanation of his relationship to God subject to doubt, whether or not we claim insight from his life and work. But if God not only creates and reveals the divine intention for the future, plus the possibility for a renewal of life in the present, if God also operates and is present in the world continually, this complicates a full 'scientific' explanation of the world and of our human nature. Moreover, the future is much less easy to see than the results of Jesus work or even the complexity of the world before us. Yet like Plato, we know that to reduce human life only to what we apprehend with the five senses not only limits our life but makes the height and depth of both human creativity and evil inexplicable.

Whatever Jesus' difference from other human beings may eventually be judged to be, it is not impossible for men and women from vastly different cultures to identify with him as fully human. His words and life story make that easy for many. As unsatisfactory as any divinity may be who is deduced on the basis of our understanding of the natural order, however majestic or even transcendent an evolutionary creator God may be, such a divinity is not incongruous with the world we know before us. In fact, many such Gods are constructed to provide "explanations" for the origin and nature of the world as we find it. But the Holy Spirit is quite different.

The Holy Spirit cannot, does not, operate as the world before us does, else it conveys no insight and serves no religious purpose. It must, then, tell us something about "the secret life of God". That is, it does so if we can learn to discern it or to feel moved by its presence. This bears some relationship to finding out what God has been doing since the creative burst that sent planets into orbit and sorted Nature out on a long agonizing trail leading in its time to the human species. If God conveyed important information to us in Moses, in Jesus, in Buddha, in Mohammed, etc., that is well and good. It can be gratefully received by some, even if others wish to use it as a basis for argument and for control over those around them. The mysterious presence and activity of a Holy Spirit may be the ultimate in difficulty for us to pin down. Yet artists and religious seers and creative persons of all types have felt its movement.

We have, of course, just outlined sketches of what the Holy Spirit can and cannot do. Given the elusiveness and individuality of the Spirit's mode of presence, even if every word of such an account were golden and testified to by witnesses, all this could open a reader to wider experience (perhaps). But it would still be a "learned ignorance", as Cusanus expressed it. In learning more about God, we learn ultimately how much we do not and cannot know and why our ignorance is increased by our divine encounter, as Nicholas said. This is due to the Holy Spirit's centrality in the life of God, and occasionally in ours, so that to learn about the Holy Spirit is perhaps to be brought nearer to the center of the locus of the divine mystery. We cannot say that we have not learned more about God, but it is yet reflected "in a glass darkly".

Central as the experience of the Spirit is for us, we are perhaps led back by it to the Acts of the Trinity. It may not be either in Jesus individually or in the Holy Spirit separately that God can be apprehended. This may not happen even in God as divinity's center itself. Unity is misleading in many ways, since the divine center is itself multiple, perhaps as a trinity of persons. At any, at every time we begin, we must begin with a particular approach. But if it should prove to be genuinely illuminating, this can spread out to at least three modes of the divine activity.

So long confined, for reasons of our human pursuit of security, God can paraphrase the Negro slave now and sing the lines from the spiritual: "Free at last. God Almighty's free at last!"

INDEX

About the Author

Frederick Sontag holds a B.A. degree from Stanford University in psychology and Philosophy, and MA and Ph.D. degrees in Philosophy and Theology from Yale University, as well as a LL.D. from the College of Idaho. He is presently the Robert Dennison Professor of Philosophy at Pomona College, Claremont, California, where he has taught since 1952.

His interests are in Philosophy of Religion, Metaphysics, and Existentialism. He is the author of numerous books (see list following) and articles in professional journals in these areas.

Other Books by Frederick Sontag

Divine Perfection: Possible Ideas of God, 1962

Approaches to Ethics (with Jones, Beckner, and Fogelin), 1962

The Existentialist Prolegomena: To a Future Metaphysics, 1969

The Future of Theology: A Philosophical Basis for Contemporary Protestant Theology, 1969

The Crisis of Faith: A Protestant Witness in Rome, 1969

The God of Evil: An Argument from the Existence of the Devil, 1970

God, Why Did You Do That?, 1970

The Problems of Metaphysics, 1970

How Philosophy Shapes Theology: Problems in the Philosophy of Religion, 1971

*The American Religious Experience: The Roots, Trends and the
Future of American Theology (with John K. Roth), 1972*

Love Beyond Pain: Mysticism Within Christianity, 1977

Sun Myung Moon and the Unification Church, 1977

*God and America's Future (with John K. Roth, 1977
What Can God Do?, 1979*

A Kierkegaard Handbook, 1979

The Elements of Philosophy, 1984

The Questions of Philosophy (with John K. Roth),1988

Emotion: Its Role in Understanding and Decision, 1989

*The Return of the Gods: A Philosophical/Theological
Reappraisal of the Works of Ernest Becker, 1989*

Uncertain Truth, 1995

*Wittgenstein and the Mystical: Philosophy as an Ascetic
Practice, 1995*

DATE DUE

MAY 5 2001			
			Printed in USA